Math
ADVANTAGE

HARCOURT
BRACE

Orlando • Atlanta • Austin • Boston • San Francisco • Chicago • Dallas • New York • Toronto • London

http://www.hbschool.com

ISBN 0-15-311435-5

17 18 19 20 030 2007 2006

Senior Authors

Grace M. Burton
Chair, Department of Curricular Studies
Professor, School of Education
University of North Carolina at Wilmington
Wilmington, North Carolina

Evan M. Maletsky
Professor of Mathematics
Montclair State University
Upper Montclair, New Jersey

Authors

George W. Bright
Professor of Mathematics Education
The University of North Carolina at
  Greensboro
Greensboro, North Carolina

Sonia M. Helton
Professor of Childhood Education
Coordinator, College of Education
University of South Florida
St. Petersburg, Florida

Loye Y. (Mickey) Hollis
Professor of Mathematics Education
Director of Teacher Education and Under-
  graduate Programs
University of Houston
Houston, Texas

Howard C. Johnson
Dean of the Graduate School
Associate Vice Chancellor for Academic Affairs
Professor, Mathematics and
  Mathematics Education
Syracuse University
Syracuse, New York

Joyce C. McLeod
Visiting Professor
Rollins College
Winter Park, Florida

Evelyn M. Neufeld
Professor, College of Education
San Jose State University
San Jose, California

Vicki Newman
Classroom Teacher
McGaugh Elementary School
Los Alamitos Unified School District
Seal Beach, California

Terence H. Perciante
Professor of Mathematics
Wheaton College
Wheaton, Illinois

Karen A. Schultz
Associate Dean and Director of Graduate
  Studies and Research
Research Professor, Mathematics Education
College of Education
Georgia State University
Atlanta, Georgia

Muriel Burger Thatcher
Independent Mathematics Consultant
Mathematical Encounters
Pine Knoll Shores, North Carolina

Advisors

Anne R. Biggins
Speech-Language Pathologist
Fairfax County Public Schools
Fairfax, Virginia

Carolyn Gambrel
Learning Disabilities Teacher
Fairfax County Public Schools
Fairfax, Virginia

Lois Harrison-Jones
Education Consultant
Dallas, Texas

Asa G. Hilliard, III
Fuller E. Callaway Professor
  of Urban Education
Georgia State University
Atlanta, Georgia

Marsha W. Lilly
Secondary Mathematics
  Coordinator
Alief Independent School District
Alief, Texas

Judith Mayne Wallis
Elementary Language Arts/
  Social Studies/Gifted Coordinator
Alief Independent School District
Houston, Texas

CONTENTS

▶ **Getting Ready for Grade 2** 1
Theme: All About Me

* Algebra Readiness

Harcourt Brace School Publishers

Chapters 1–2 ✓ Checkpoint

* Algebra Readiness

Harcourt Brace Schoo Publishers

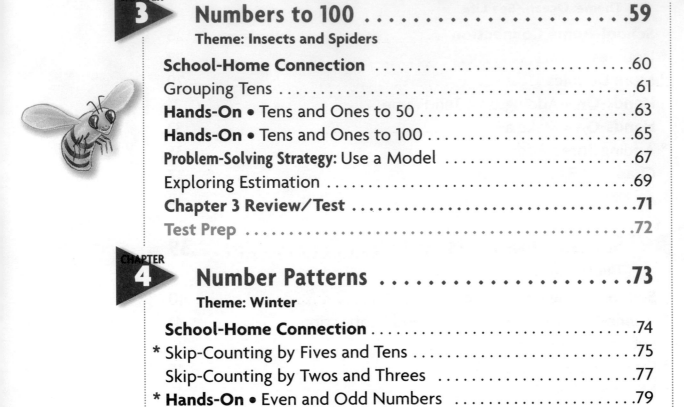

* **Algebra Readiness**

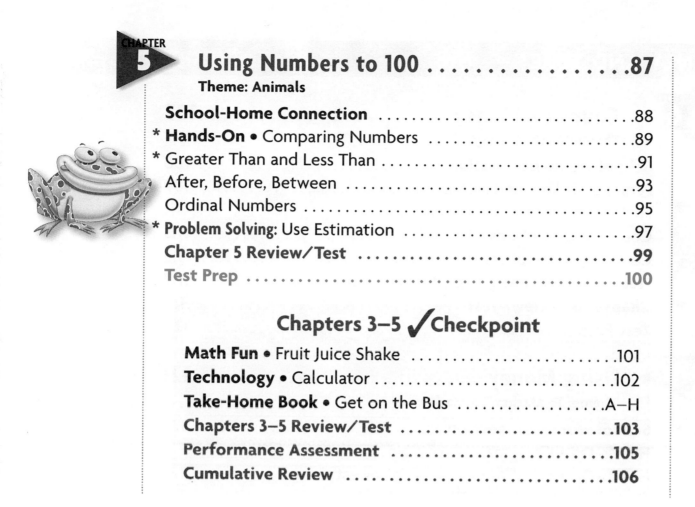

* **Algebra Readiness**

Harcourt Brace School Publishers

* Algebra Readiness

* Algebra Readiness

Harcourt Brace School Publishers

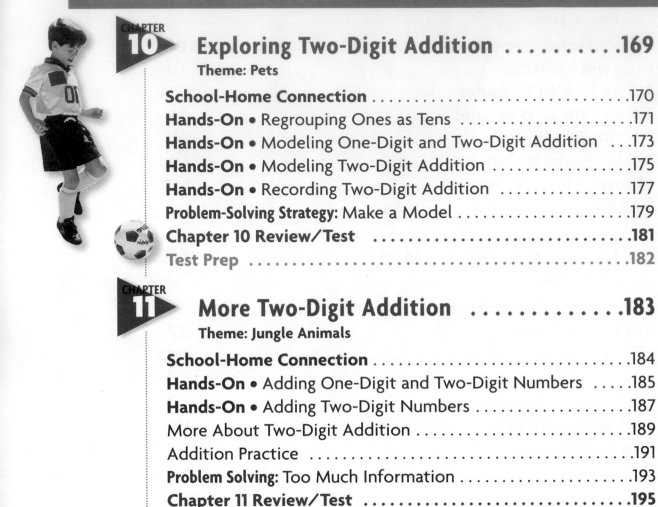

* Algebra Readiness

Harcourt Brace School Publishers

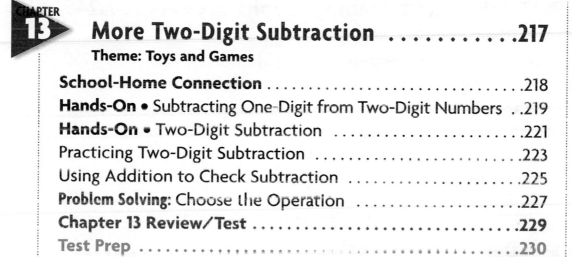

* Algebra Readiness

DATA, GRAPHING, AND PROBABILITY   CHAPTERS 14–16

* Algebra Readiness

Harcourt Brace School Publishers

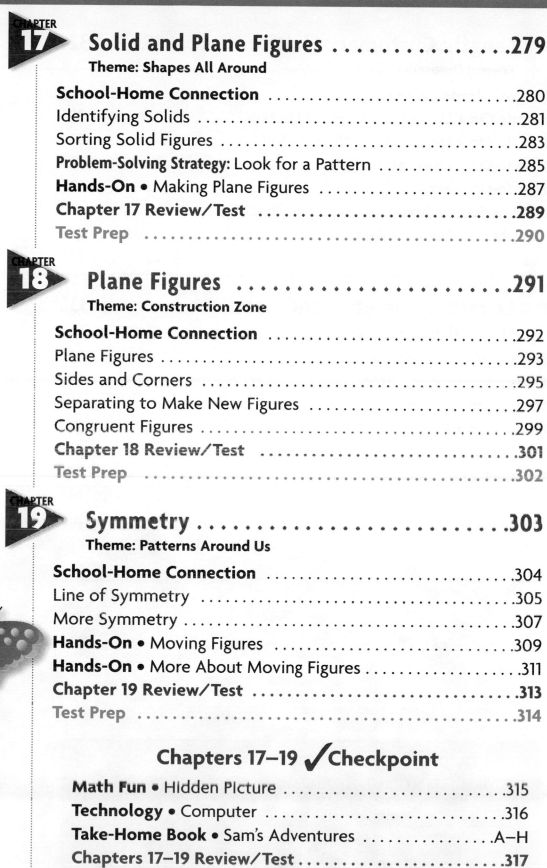

* **Algebra Readiness**

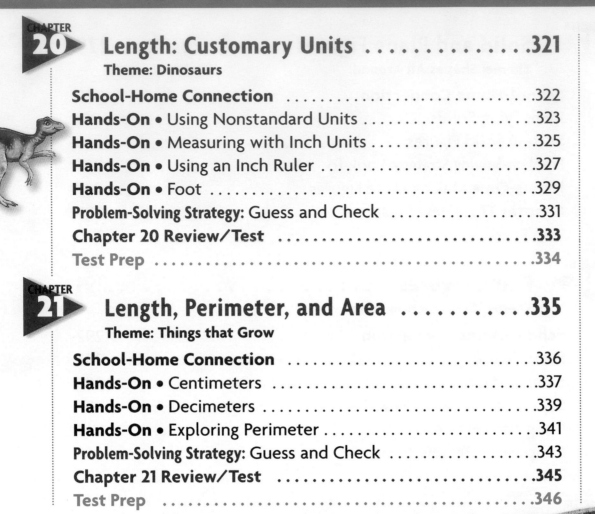

* **Algebra Readiness**

Harcourt Brace School Publishers

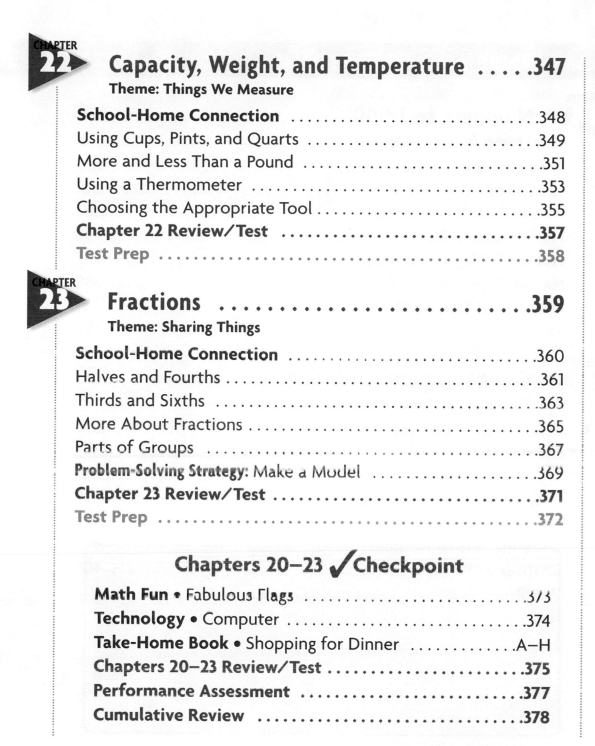

* **Algebra Readiness**

* Algebra Readiness

Harcourt Brace School Publishers

Harcourt Brace School Publishers

* **Algebra Readiness**

MULTIPLICATION AND DIVISION CONCEPTS

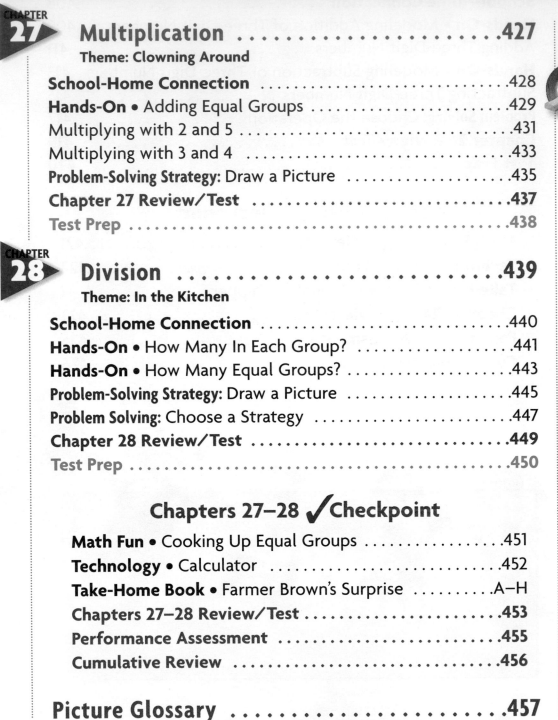

* **Algebra Readiness**

Getting Ready for Grade 2

Hi! My name is K.C. I will be your math friend. I am really excited about starting second grade.

This book belongs to

_____

How are these children using math?
How do you use math everyday?

Harcourt Brace School Publishers

**Circle the math tools.
What math tools do you use?**

2

Harcourt Brace School Publishers

SCHOOL-HOME CONNECTION

Dear Family,
   Today we started our math book.
In this chapter, we will review some
math ideas. Each lesson has a Home Note
with a way for me to show you what
I am learning.

   Love,
_____

4

Name _____

$$5 + 3 = 8$$

addend   addend   sum

Use the pictures.
Write the sum.

1

$$4 + 3 = \underline{}\ 7$$

2

$$2 + 4 = \underline{}$$

3

$$6 + 4 = \underline{}$$

4

$$7 + 2 = \underline{}$$

5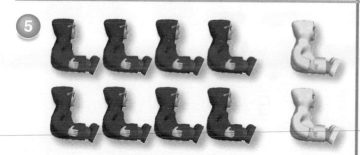

$$8 + 2 = \underline{}$$

6

$$5 + 4 = \underline{}$$

Practice

Use the pictures.
Write the sum.

1

6 + 3 = ___9___

2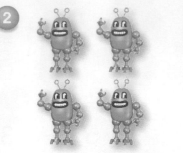

4 + 2 = _____

3

3 + 3 = _____

4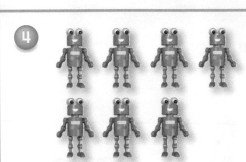

7 + 3 = _____

5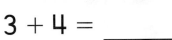

3 + 4 = _____

6

6 + 2 = _____

7

9 + 1 = _____

8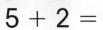

5 + 2 = _____

 Home Note Your child reviewed sums to ten.
ACTIVITY Have your child use small objects to show a number sentence.

$$6 \quad + \quad 3 \quad = \quad 9$$

> Changing the order of the addends does not change the sum.

$$3 \quad + \quad 6 \quad = \quad 9$$

Write the sum.

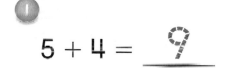

1	**2**	**3**
$5 + 4 =$ __9__	$2 + 6 =$ ___	$7 + 3 -$ ___
$4 + 5 =$ __9__	$6 + 2 =$ ___	$3 + 7 =$ ___
4	**5**	**6**
$6 + 4 =$ ___	$8 + 2 =$ ___	$1 + 8 =$ ___
$4 + 6 =$ ___	$2 + 8 =$ ___	$8 + 1 =$ ___
7	**8**	**9**
$7 + 2 =$ ___	$2 + 4 =$ ___	$4 + 3 =$ ___
$2 + 7 =$ ___	$4 + 2 =$ ___	$3 + 4 =$ ___

Talk About It ● Critical Thinking

What happens to the sum when you change the order of the addends?

REVIEW

$$\begin{array}{r} 5 \\ +2 \\ \hline 7 \end{array}$$

$$\begin{array}{r} 2 \\ +5 \\ \hline 7 \end{array}$$

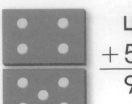

$$\begin{array}{r} 4 \\ +5 \\ \hline 9 \end{array}$$

$$\begin{array}{r} 5 \\ +4 \\ \hline 9 \end{array}$$

Write the sum.

1

$$\begin{array}{r} 3 \\ +2 \\ \hline 5 \end{array} \qquad \begin{array}{r} 2 \\ +3 \\ \hline 5 \end{array}$$

2

$$\begin{array}{r} 1 \\ +7 \\ \hline \end{array} \qquad \begin{array}{r} 7 \\ +1 \\ \hline \end{array}$$

3

$$\begin{array}{r} 4 \\ +5 \\ \hline \end{array} \qquad \begin{array}{r} 5 \\ +4 \\ \hline \end{array}$$

4

$$\begin{array}{r} 6 \\ +3 \\ \hline \end{array} \qquad \begin{array}{r} 3 \\ +6 \\ \hline \end{array}$$

5

$$\begin{array}{r} 8 \\ +2 \\ \hline \end{array} \qquad \begin{array}{r} 2 \\ +8 \\ \hline \end{array}$$

6

$$\begin{array}{r} 3 \\ +5 \\ \hline \end{array} \qquad \begin{array}{r} 5 \\ +3 \\ \hline \end{array}$$

7

$$\begin{array}{r} 5 \\ +1 \\ \hline \end{array} \qquad \begin{array}{r} 1 \\ +5 \\ \hline \end{array}$$

8

$$\begin{array}{r} 7 \\ +3 \\ \hline \end{array} \qquad \begin{array}{r} 3 \\ +7 \\ \hline \end{array}$$

REVIEW

Home Note Your child learned that changing the order of the addends does not change the sum.
ACTIVITY Have your child use small objects to show an addition sentence. Then change the order of the addends, and have your child show the new sentence.

6 six

Harcourt Brace School Publishers

Zero Property

Any number plus zero equals that same number.

$$4 + 0 = 4$$

$$0 + 5 = 5$$

Write the sum.

1

$$6 + 0 = \underline{6}$$

2

$$0 + 2 = \underline{\hspace{1cm}}$$

3

$$9 + 0 = \underline{\hspace{1cm}}$$

4

$$7 + 0 = \underline{\hspace{1cm}}$$

5

$$0 + 4 = \underline{\hspace{1cm}}$$

6

$$0 + 6 = \underline{\hspace{1cm}}$$

7
$$0 + 7 - \underline{\hspace{1cm}}$$

8
$$4 + 0 = \underline{\hspace{1cm}}$$

9
$$0 + 8 = \underline{\hspace{1cm}}$$

10
$$3 + 0 = \underline{\hspace{1cm}}$$

11
$$0 + 1 = \underline{\hspace{1cm}}$$

12
$$0 + 9 = \underline{\hspace{1cm}}$$

13
$$0 + 3 = \underline{\hspace{1cm}}$$

14
$$6 + 0 = \underline{\hspace{1cm}}$$

15
$$8 + 0 = \underline{\hspace{1cm}}$$

REVIEW

Practice

$$\begin{array}{r} 5 \\ +0 \\ \hline 5 \end{array}$$

$$\begin{array}{r} 0 \\ +6 \\ \hline 6 \end{array}$$

Write the sum.

1 $\begin{array}{r} 3 \\ +0 \\ \hline 3 \end{array}$	**2** $\begin{array}{r} 0 \\ +7 \\ \hline \end{array}$	**3** $\begin{array}{r} 6 \\ +0 \\ \hline \end{array}$	**4** $\begin{array}{r} 7 \\ +0 \\ \hline \end{array}$
5 $\begin{array}{r} 4 \\ +0 \\ \hline \end{array}$	**6** $\begin{array}{r} 0 \\ +9 \\ \hline \end{array}$	**7** $\begin{array}{r} 2 \\ +0 \\ \hline \end{array}$	**8** $\begin{array}{r} 0 \\ +5 \\ \hline \end{array}$
9 $\begin{array}{r} 8 \\ +0 \\ \hline \end{array}$	**10** $\begin{array}{r} 0 \\ +1 \\ \hline \end{array}$	**11** $\begin{array}{r} 0 \\ +3 \\ \hline \end{array}$	**12** $\begin{array}{r} 9 \\ +0 \\ \hline \end{array}$
13 $\begin{array}{r} 0 \\ +2 \\ \hline \end{array}$	**14** $\begin{array}{r} 0 \\ +4 \\ \hline \end{array}$	**15** $\begin{array}{r} 0 \\ +8 \\ \hline \end{array}$	**16** $\begin{array}{r} 1 \\ +0 \\ \hline \end{array}$

REVIEW

Home Note Your child learned that any number plus zero equals that number.
ACTIVITY Have your child use small objects to show 4 + 0 = 4 and then 0 + 4 = 4.

Find the sum.

Start at 5. Count on 1.
6
The sum is 6.

$5 + 1 = 6$

Start at 3. Count on 2.
4, 5
The sum is 5.

$3 + 2 = 5$

Count on to find the sum.

1 $3 + 1 = \underline{4}$	**2** $9 + 1 = \underline{}$	**3** $5 + 2 = \underline{}$
4 $7 + 1 = \underline{}$	**5** $7 + 2 = \underline{}$	**6** $6 + 1 = \underline{}$
7 $4 + 1 = \underline{}$	**8** $8 + 2 = \underline{}$	**9** $6 + 2 = \underline{}$
10 $5 + 1 = \underline{}$	**11** $8 + 1 = \underline{}$	**12** $4 + 2 = \underline{}$

Talk About It ● Critical Thinking

How do you use counting on to find a sum?

Find the sum.

Start at 5. Count on 3.
6, 7, 8
The sum is 8.

$5 + 3 = 8$

Count on to find the sum.

①	②	③
$6 + 2 = \underline{8}$	$4 + 3 = \underline{\quad}$	$8 + 2 = \underline{\quad}$

④	⑤	⑥
$6 + 1 = \underline{\quad}$	$9 + 1 = \underline{\quad}$	$4 + 1 = \underline{\quad}$

⑦
$$\begin{array}{cccccc} 3 & 5 & 5 & 4 & 4 & 3 \\ +1 & +3 & +1 & +1 & +5 & +2 \\ \hline \end{array}$$

⑧
$$\begin{array}{cccccc} 8 & 7 & 6 & 7 & 5 & 6 \\ +2 & +2 & +2 & +1 & +2 & +1 \\ \hline \end{array}$$

Problem Solving ● **Mental Math**

Find the sum.

⑨ Rob has 7 shirts.
He buys 2 more.
How many shirts
does Rob have?

_____ shirts

⑩ Susan has 5 pennies.
She finds 3 more.
How many pennies
does Susan have?

_____ pennies

Home Note Your child used counting on to find sums.
ACTIVITY Have your child tell you how to count on to add 7 + 3.

REVIEW

Harcourt Brace School Publishers

Name _____

Write the sum.

1 6 + 2 = __8__

2 3 + 4 = _____

3 7 + 0 = _____

4 9 + 1 = _____

5 7 + 3 = _____

6 2 + 5 = _____

7 6 + 3 = _____

8 3 + 5 = _____

9 8 + 2 = _____

10 8 + 1 = _____

11 4 + 6 = _____

12 7 + 2 = _____

13

$$\begin{array}{r} 5 \\ +0 \\ \hline \end{array} \qquad \begin{array}{r} 2 \\ +3 \\ \hline \end{array} \qquad \begin{array}{r} 8 \\ +2 \\ \hline \end{array} \qquad \begin{array}{r} 3 \\ +4 \\ \hline \end{array} \qquad \begin{array}{r} 5 \\ +2 \\ \hline \end{array} \qquad \begin{array}{r} 8 \\ +1 \\ \hline \end{array}$$

14

$$\begin{array}{r} 3 \\ +3 \\ \hline \end{array} \qquad \begin{array}{r} 3 \\ +0 \\ \hline \end{array} \qquad \begin{array}{r} 6 \\ +3 \\ \hline \end{array} \qquad \begin{array}{r} 6 \\ +4 \\ \hline \end{array}$$

15

$$\begin{array}{r} 7 \\ +1 \\ \hline \end{array} \qquad \begin{array}{r} 4 \\ +5 \\ \hline \end{array} \qquad \begin{array}{r} 0 \\ +9 \\ \hline \end{array} \qquad \begin{array}{r} 3 \\ +5 \\ \hline \end{array}$$

16

$$\begin{array}{r} 4 \\ +1 \\ \hline \end{array} \qquad \begin{array}{r} 3 \\ +7 \\ \hline \end{array} \qquad \begin{array}{r} 6 \\ +2 \\ \hline \end{array} \qquad \begin{array}{r} 2 \\ +2 \\ \hline \end{array}$$

REVIEW

Practice

Write the sum.

1

6¢

+ 2¢

8¢

2

7¢

+ 1¢

3

5¢

+ 4¢

4

6¢

+ 3¢

5

4¢

+ 3¢

6

3¢

+ 6¢

7

3¢

+ 7¢

8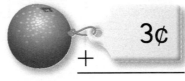

4¢

+ 5¢

9

6¢

+ 4¢

REVIEW

$$8 - 3 = 5$$

difference

Use the pictures.
Write the difference.

1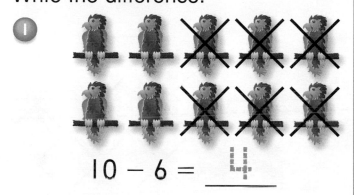

$$10 - 6 = \underline{\quad 4 \quad}$$

2

$$9 - 5 = \underline{\qquad}$$

3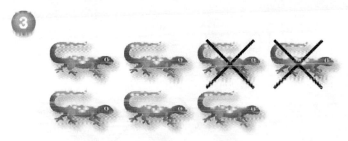

$$7 - 2 = \underline{\qquad}$$

4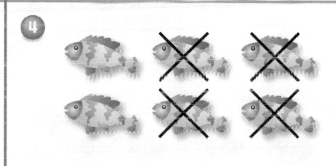

$$6 - 4 = \underline{\qquad}$$

5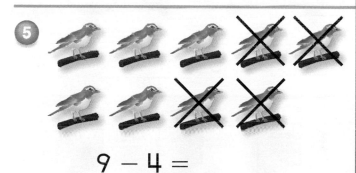

$$9 - 4 = \underline{\qquad}$$

6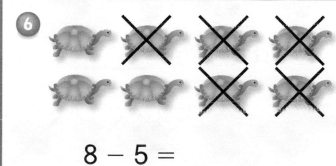

$$8 - 5 = \underline{\qquad}$$

7

$$8 - 6 = \underline{\qquad}$$

8

$$10 - 7 = \underline{\qquad}$$

Practice

Use the pictures.
Write the difference.

1

$10 - 3 = \underline{7}$

2

$8 - 6 = \underline{}$

3

$6 - 3 = \underline{}$

4

$10 - 6 = \underline{}$

5

$8 - 4 = \underline{}$

6

$8 - 5 = \underline{}$

7

$10 - 5 = \underline{}$

8

$6 - 1 = \underline{}$

 Home Note Your child used pictures to find differences through ten.
ACTIVITY Have your child draw pictures to show the subtraction problems on this page.

REVIEW

How many dogs are left?

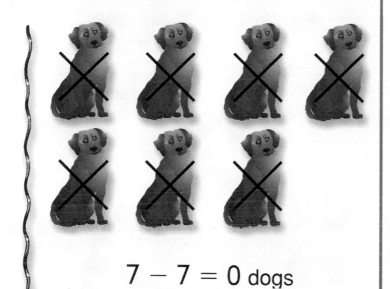

$7 - 7 = 0$ dogs

How many dogs are left?

$7 - 0 = 7$ dogs

Subtract.

1 $3 - 3 =$ _0_	**2** $9 - 0 =$ _9_	**3** $8 - 8 =$ ___
4 $8 - 0 =$ ___	**5** $4 - 0 =$ ___	**6** $6 - 6 =$ ___
7 $5 - 0 =$ ___	**8** $5 - 5 =$ ___	**9** $1 - 1 =$ ___
10 $2 - 0 =$ ___	**11** $4 - 4 =$ ___	**12** $9 - 9 =$ ___
13 $3 - 0 =$ ___	**14** $6 - 0 =$ ___	**15** $2 - 2 =$ ___

REVIEW

How many bears are left?

How many bears are left?

$$\begin{array}{r} 5 \\ -5 \\ \hline 0 \end{array}$$ bears

$$\begin{array}{r} 5 \\ -0 \\ \hline 5 \end{array}$$ bears

Subtract.

1.
$$\begin{array}{r} 8 \\ -0 \\ \hline 8 \end{array}$$
$$\begin{array}{r} 7 \\ -7 \\ \hline 0 \end{array}$$
$$\begin{array}{r} 8 \\ -8 \\ \hline \end{array}$$
$$\begin{array}{r} 9 \\ -0 \\ \hline \end{array}$$
$$\begin{array}{r} 2 \\ -2 \\ \hline \end{array}$$
$$\begin{array}{r} 4 \\ -4 \\ \hline \end{array}$$

2.
$$\begin{array}{r} 9 \\ -9 \\ \hline \end{array}$$
$$\begin{array}{r} 1 \\ -0 \\ \hline \end{array}$$
$$\begin{array}{r} 6 \\ -0 \\ \hline \end{array}$$
$$\begin{array}{r} 3 \\ -3 \\ \hline \end{array}$$
$$\begin{array}{r} 4 \\ -0 \\ \hline \end{array}$$
$$\begin{array}{r} 5 \\ -5 \\ \hline \end{array}$$

3.
$$\begin{array}{r} 2 \\ -0 \\ \hline \end{array}$$
$$\begin{array}{r} 7 \\ -0 \\ \hline \end{array}$$
$$\begin{array}{r} 3 \\ -0 \\ \hline \end{array}$$
$$\begin{array}{r} 6 \\ -6 \\ \hline \end{array}$$
$$\begin{array}{r} 1 \\ -1 \\ \hline \end{array}$$
$$\begin{array}{r} 5 \\ -0 \\ \hline \end{array}$$

Home Note Your child subtracted all or zero from a group.
ACTIVITY Show your child a group of up to 10 objects. Remove all of them or none of them. Have your child write the subtraction sentence.

REVIEW

How many more blue fish than green fish are there?

There are **2** more blue fish.

$6 - 4 = 2$

Compare the pictures. Then subtract.

1 How many more red fish than yellow fish are there?

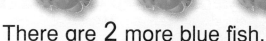

$10 - 7 = \underline{3}$ more red fish

2 How many more green fish than orange fish are there?

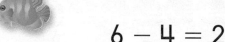

$8 - 5 = \underline{\hphantom{00}}$ more green fish

3 How many more blue fish than orange fish are there?

$6 - 3 = \underline{\hphantom{00}}$ more blue fish

4 How many more green fish than red fish are there?

$10 - 4 = \underline{\hphantom{00}}$ more green fish

5 How many more red fish than yellow fish are there?

$9 - 6 = \underline{\hphantom{00}}$ more red fish

6 How many more purple fish than yellow fish are there?

$8 - 7 = \underline{\hphantom{00}}$ more purple fish

Practice

Compare the pictures. Then subtract.

1 How many more red balloons than green balloons are there?

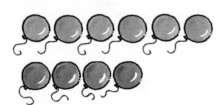

$8 - 5 =$ ____3____ more red balloons

2 How many more green balloons than red balloons are there?

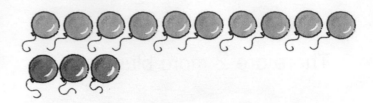

$10 - 3 =$ _____ more green balloons

3 How many more green balloons than red balloons are there?

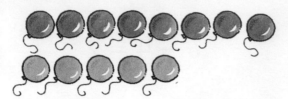

$6 - 4 =$ _____ more green balloons

4 How many more red balloons than green balloons are there?

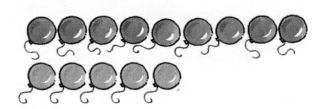

$9 - 5 =$ _____ more red balloons

5 How many more green balloons than red balloons are there?

$9 - 2 =$ _____ more green balloons

6 How many more red balloons than green balloons are there?

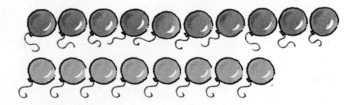

$10 - 8 =$ _____ more red balloons

REVIEW

Harcourt Brace School Publishers

 Home Note Your child subtracted by comparing numbers of objects.
ACTIVITY Have your child compare two groups of less than 10 objects and then subtract to find the difference.

18 eighteen

What is $9 - 1$?

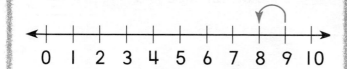

0 1 2 3 4 5 6 7 8 9 10

Start at 9. Count back 1.
8
The difference is 8.

$9 - 1 = 8$

What is $7 - 2$?

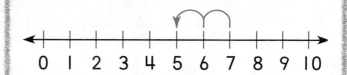

0 1 2 3 4 5 6 7 8 9 10

Start at 7. Count back 2
6, 5
The difference is 5.

$7 - 2 = 5$

Count back to find the difference.

1 $5 - 2 = \underline{3}$

2 $6 - 1 = \underline{\hphantom{0}}$

3 $4 \quad 1 = \underline{\hphantom{0}}$

4 $3 - 2 = \underline{\hphantom{0}}$

5 $7 - 1 = \underline{\hphantom{0}}$

6 $8 - 1 = \underline{\hphantom{0}}$

7 $9 - 2 = \underline{\hphantom{0}}$

8 $3 - 1 = \underline{\hphantom{0}}$

9 $8 - 2 = \underline{\hphantom{0}}$

10 $6 - 2 = \underline{\hphantom{0}}$

11 $4 - 2 = \underline{\hphantom{0}}$

12 $5 - 1 = \underline{\hphantom{0}}$

13 $9 - 1 = \underline{\hphantom{0}}$

14 $7 - 2 = \underline{\hphantom{0}}$

15 $2 - 1 = \underline{\hphantom{0}}$

Talk About It ● Critical Thinking

How do you use counting back to find a difference?

REVIEW

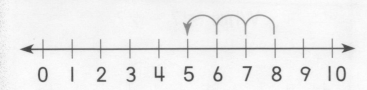

Practice

What is 8 − 3?

0 1 2 3 4 5 6 7 8 9 10

Start at 8. Count back 3.
7, 6, 5
The difference is 5.

$$\begin{array}{r} 8 \\ -3 \\ \hline 5 \end{array}$$

Count back to find the difference.

1
$$\begin{array}{r} 9 \\ -1 \\ \hline 8 \end{array}$$
$$\begin{array}{r} 5 \\ -2 \\ \hline \end{array}$$
$$\begin{array}{r} 6 \\ -2 \\ \hline \end{array}$$
$$\begin{array}{r} 5 \\ -1 \\ \hline \end{array}$$
$$\begin{array}{r} 7 \\ -2 \\ \hline \end{array}$$

2
$$\begin{array}{r} 10 \\ -2 \\ \hline \end{array}$$
$$\begin{array}{r} 3 \\ -2 \\ \hline \end{array}$$
$$\begin{array}{r} 6 \\ -3 \\ \hline \end{array}$$
$$\begin{array}{r} 7 \\ -1 \\ \hline \end{array}$$
$$\begin{array}{r} 8 \\ -1 \\ \hline \end{array}$$

3
$$\begin{array}{r} 8 \\ -2 \\ \hline \end{array}$$
$$\begin{array}{r} 9 \\ -3 \\ \hline \end{array}$$
$$\begin{array}{r} 4 \\ -1 \\ \hline \end{array}$$
$$\begin{array}{r} 4 \\ -3 \\ \hline \end{array}$$
$$\begin{array}{r} 10 \\ -1 \\ \hline \end{array}$$

4
$$\begin{array}{r} 2 \\ -1 \\ \hline \end{array}$$
$$\begin{array}{r} 7 \\ -3 \\ \hline \end{array}$$
$$\begin{array}{r} 3 \\ -1 \\ \hline \end{array}$$
$$\begin{array}{r} 6 \\ -3 \\ \hline \end{array}$$
$$\begin{array}{r} 5 \\ -1 \\ \hline \end{array}$$

5
$$\begin{array}{r} 5 \\ -3 \\ \hline \end{array}$$
$$\begin{array}{r} 10 \\ -3 \\ \hline \end{array}$$
$$\begin{array}{r} 9 \\ -2 \\ \hline \end{array}$$
$$\begin{array}{r} 6 \\ -1 \\ \hline \end{array}$$
$$\begin{array}{r} 4 \\ -2 \\ \hline \end{array}$$

REVIEW

Home Note Your child counted back to find the difference between two numbers.
ACTIVITY Have your child tell you how to count back to subtract 10 − 3.

Understand · Plan · Solve · Look Back

Solve.

Kim swam 4 laps on Monday.
Kim swam 3 laps on Tuesday.
How many laps did she swim in all?

Here are some steps to help you
solve the problem.

Step 1 Understand
Read the problem. Draw a line under
what you want to find out.
Circle the facts that are given.

Step 2 Plan
You can use ●○ to make a model to find
out how many laps Kim swam in all.

Step 3 Solve
Make a model.
Use ● to show how many laps
Kim swam on Monday.
Use ○ to show how many laps
Kim swam on Tuesday.
Write a number sentence to go with the model.

_____ ◯ _____ = _____ laps

Step 4 Look Back
Read the problem again.
Tell a classmate how your model shows the answer.

REVIEW

Practice

Use the four steps to solve the problem.

1 Sam collected 5 brown shells and 4 white shells. How many shells did he collect?

$$\underline{5} \enspace \bigoplus \enspace \underline{4} \enspace = \enspace \underline{9}$$

$\underline{9}$ shells

2 Nan saw 8 crabs. Then 4 crabs crawled into the ocean. How many crabs were left?

$$\underline{\hspace{1cm}} \bigcirc \underline{\hspace{1cm}} = \underline{\hspace{1cm}}$$

$\underline{\hspace{1cm}}$ crabs

3 Pat made 6 sand castles one day and 4 sand castles the next day. How many sand castles did she make?

$$\underline{\hspace{1cm}} \bigcirc \underline{\hspace{1cm}} = \underline{\hspace{1cm}}$$

$\underline{\hspace{1cm}}$ sand castles

4 Al saw 9 fish on Monday and 6 fish on Tuesday. How many more fish did he see on Monday?

$$\underline{\hspace{1cm}} \bigcirc \underline{\hspace{1cm}} = \underline{\hspace{1cm}}$$

$\underline{\hspace{1cm}}$ more fish

Home Note Your child made a model to solve problems.
ACTIVITY Have your child explain the four steps he or she would use to solve a problem.

Name _____

Concepts and Skills

Use the pictures.
Write the sum.

$$5 + 4 = \underline{\hspace{1cm}}$$

$$6 + 2 = \underline{\hspace{1cm}}$$

4	3	4	0	3	5
+3	+4	+0	+4	+5	+3

Count on to find the sum.

④ $4 + 1 = \underline{\hspace{1cm}}$

⑤ $7 + 2 = \underline{\hspace{1cm}}$

⑥ $6 + 3 = \underline{\hspace{1cm}}$

⑦

7	6	5	8	3	4
−1	+2	+3	+1	+2	+2

Use the pictures.
Write the difference.

⑧
$$9 - 4 = \underline{\hspace{1cm}}$$

⑨
$$10 - 3 = \underline{\hspace{1cm}}$$

Subtract.

⑩ $7 - 7 = \underline{\hspace{1cm}}$

⑪ $5 - 5 = \underline{\hspace{1cm}}$

⑫ $8 - 0 = \underline{\hspace{1cm}}$

9	6	7	4	5
−0	−6	−0	−4	−0

REVIEW

Compare the pictures. Then subtract.

14 How many more green fish than orange fish are there?

$9 - 7 =$ _____ more green fish

15 How many more yellow fish than purple fish are there?

$7 - 5 =$ _____ more yellow fish

Count back to find the difference.

16

$7 - 3 =$ _____

17

$8 - 2 =$ _____

18

$9 - 1 =$ _____

19
$$\begin{array}{r} 10 \\ -\ 3 \\ \hline \end{array}$$

20
$$\begin{array}{r} 5 \\ -2 \\ \hline \end{array}$$

21
$$\begin{array}{r} 8 \\ -3 \\ \hline \end{array}$$

22
$$\begin{array}{r} 6 \\ -1 \\ \hline \end{array}$$

Problem Solving

Use the four steps to solve the problem.

23 Bill fed 5 birds one day and 3 birds the next day. How many birds did he feed?

_____ ◯ _____ = _____ birds

24 Sue caught 8 fish on Saturday and 3 fish on Sunday. How many more fish did she catch on Saturday?

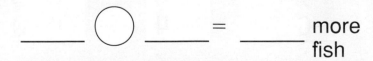

_____ ◯ _____ = _____ more fish

Review/Test

Addition Facts to 18

Write addition sentences about the picture.

Home Note In this chapter, your child will learn addition facts to 18.
ACTIVITY Have your child write addition sentences about the sea life in the picture.

SCHOOL-HOME CONNECTION

Dear Family,
   Today we started Chapter 1. We will practice adding numbers with sums of 18 or less. Here are the new vocabulary words and an activity for us to do together at home.

Love,

_____

 **Vocabulary**

doubles

$2 + 2 = 4$

doubles plus one

$2 + 3 = 5$ (one more)

doubles minus one

$2 + 1 = 3$ (one less)

Say one of the doubles. Have your child write the fact and the doubles-plus-one and doubles-minus-one facts that go with it. Then have him or her read all three number sentences.

ACTIVITY

Fold a piece of paper into four sections, and write one of these problems in each section.

$3 + 6 =$ _____

$5 + 2 =$ _____

$4 + 3 =$ _____

$7 + 3 =$ _____

Have your child draw pictures to find each sum.

 Visit our Web site for additional activities and ideas.
http://www.hbschool.com

Name _____

Doubles are two addends that are the same.

The sum is the answer when you add.

$$7 + 7 = 14$$

Use the pictures to find the sum.
Write the addition sentence.

1

_____ + _____ = _____

2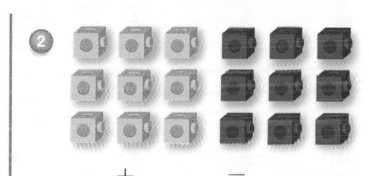

_____ + _____ = _____

3

_____ + _____ = _____

4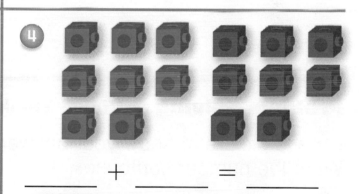

_____ + _____ = _____

5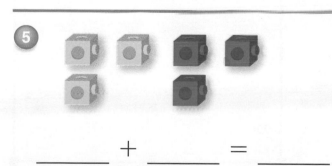

_____ + _____ = _____

6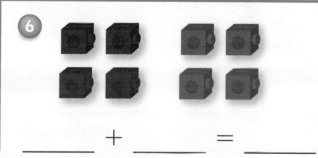

_____ + _____ = _____

Talk About It • Critical Thinking

Which doubles addition sentence has a sum greater
than 14 but less than 18?

Chapter 1 • Addition Facts to 18

Practice

Write the sum.

① 4 + 4 = __8__ | ② 9 + 9 = ____ | ③ 3 + 3 = ____

④ 6 + 6 = ____ | ⑤ 1 + 1 = ____ | ⑥ 5 + 5 = ____

⑦ 2 + 2 = ____ | ⑧ 8 + 8 = ____ | ⑨ 7 + 7 = ____

⑩
```
  5      6      9      1      4      8
 +5     +6     +9     +1     +4     +8
```

⑪
```
  7      8      3      2      0      6
 +7     +8     +3     +2     +0     +6
```

Problem Solving • Visual Thinking

Draw a picture to show your answer.
Write the number sentence.

⑫ Sam sees 9 birds.
2 birds fly away.
How many birds are left?

____ ⬭ ____ = ____
birds

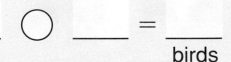
Home Note Your child added doubles.
ACTIVITY Have your child tell you the doubles facts from 1 + 1 to 9 + 9.

Chapter 1

Harcourt Brace School Publishers

Doubles	**Doubles plus one**	**Doubles minus one**

$4 + 4 = 8$	$4 + 5 = 9$	$4 + 3 = 7$
	$4 + 5$ is 1 more than $4 + 4$.	$4 + 3$ is 1 less than $4 + 4$.

Write the sum.
Write the doubles-plus-one fact.
Write the doubles-minus-one fact.

1. $5 + 5 = \underline{10}$

   $\underline{5} + \underline{6} = \underline{11}$

   $\underline{5} + \underline{4} = \underline{9}$

2. $7 + 7 = \underline{}$

   $\underline{} + \underline{} = \underline{}$

   $\underline{} \, 1 \, \underline{} = \underline{}$

3. $6 + 6 = \underline{}$

   $\underline{} + \underline{} = \underline{}$

   $\underline{} + \underline{} = \underline{}$

4. $3 + 3 - \underline{}$

   $\underline{} + \underline{} = \underline{}$

   $\underline{} + \underline{} = \underline{}$

5. $8 + 8 = \underline{}$

   $\underline{} + \underline{} = \underline{}$

   $\underline{} + \underline{} = \underline{}$

6. $9 + 9 = \underline{}$

   $\underline{} + \underline{} = \underline{}$

   $\underline{} + \underline{} = \underline{}$

Talk About It • Critical Thinking

How does knowing the sum of a double
help you know the sum of a double plus one?

Practice

Complete the addition table.
Color each doubles sum blue.
Color each doubles-plus-one sum green.
Color each doubles-minus-one sum red.

+	0	1	2	3	4	5	6	7	8	9
0	0									
1										
2										
3										
4										
5										
6										
7										
8										
9										

Home Note Your child added doubles, doubles plus one, and doubles minus one.
ACTIVITY Ask your child how knowing the sum of 3 + 3 helps him or her know the sum of 3 + 4.

Use a ten-frame and 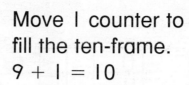 to add 9 + 3.

Put in 9 counters. Put 3 counters outside the ten-frame.	Move 1 counter to fill the ten-frame. 9 + 1 = 10	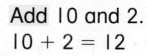 Add 10 and 2. 10 + 2 = 12

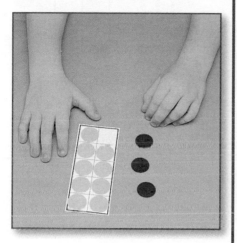

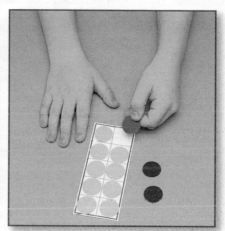

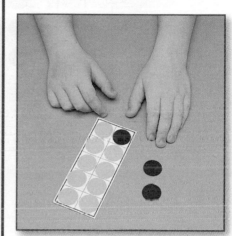

$$\begin{array}{r} 9 \\ +3 \\ \end{array}$$

$$\begin{array}{r} 10 \\ +\ 2 \\ \end{array}$$

$$\begin{array}{r} 10 \\ +\ 2 \\ \hline 12 \\ \end{array}$$

Use a ten-frame and .
Write the sum.

1

$$\begin{array}{r} 2 \\ +9 \\ \end{array} \qquad \begin{array}{r} 6 \\ +9 \\ \end{array} \qquad \begin{array}{r} 9 \\ +4 \\ \end{array} \qquad \begin{array}{r} 8 \\ +9 \\ \end{array} \qquad \begin{array}{r} 9 \\ +7 \\ \end{array} \qquad \begin{array}{r} 5 \\ +9 \\ \end{array}$$

2

$$\begin{array}{r} 9 \\ +8 \\ \end{array} \qquad \begin{array}{r} 3 \\ +9 \\ \end{array} \qquad \begin{array}{r} 9 \\ +1 \\ \end{array} \qquad \begin{array}{r} 9 \\ +6 \\ \end{array} \qquad \begin{array}{r} 9 \\ +5 \\ \end{array} \qquad \begin{array}{r} 4 \\ +9 \\ \end{array}$$

Talk About It ● **Critical Thinking**

How does using a ten-frame help you add on to 9?

Practice

Use a ten-frame and .
Write the sum.

$$
\begin{array}{r} 9 \\ +5 \\ \hline \end{array}
\qquad
\begin{array}{r} 10 \\ +\ 4 \\ \hline \end{array}
\qquad
\begin{array}{r} 10 \\ +\ 4 \\ \hline 14 \end{array}
$$

1

$$
\begin{array}{r} 3 \\ +9 \\ \hline \end{array}
\quad
\begin{array}{r} 6 \\ +9 \\ \hline \end{array}
\quad
\begin{array}{r} 9 \\ +3 \\ \hline \end{array}
\quad
\begin{array}{r} 9 \\ +6 \\ \hline \end{array}
\quad
\begin{array}{r} 4 \\ +9 \\ \hline \end{array}
\quad
\begin{array}{r} 2 \\ +9 \\ \hline \end{array}
$$

2

$$
\begin{array}{r} 9 \\ +2 \\ \hline \end{array}
\quad
\begin{array}{r} 5 \\ +9 \\ \hline \end{array}
\quad
\begin{array}{r} 9 \\ +8 \\ \hline \end{array}
\quad
\begin{array}{r} 9 \\ +1 \\ \hline \end{array}
\quad
\begin{array}{r} 1 \\ +9 \\ \hline \end{array}
\quad
\begin{array}{r} 9 \\ +2 \\ \hline \end{array}
$$

3

$$
\begin{array}{r} 8 \\ +9 \\ \hline \end{array}
\quad
\begin{array}{r} 9 \\ +4 \\ \hline \end{array}
\quad
\begin{array}{r} 7 \\ +9 \\ \hline \end{array}
\quad
\begin{array}{r} 2 \\ +9 \\ \hline \end{array}
\quad
\begin{array}{r} 9 \\ +7 \\ \hline \end{array}
\quad
\begin{array}{r} 9 \\ +5 \\ \hline \end{array}
$$

Mixed Review

Add.

4

$$
\begin{array}{r} 7 \\ +3 \\ \hline \end{array}
\quad
\begin{array}{r} 3 \\ +2 \\ \hline \end{array}
\quad
\begin{array}{r} 4 \\ +3 \\ \hline \end{array}
\quad
\begin{array}{r} 5 \\ +4 \\ \hline \end{array}
\quad
\begin{array}{r} 6 \\ +2 \\ \hline \end{array}
\quad
\begin{array}{r} 3 \\ +5 \\ \hline \end{array}
$$

5 $4 + 8 = \underline{}$ **6** $6 + 5 = \underline{}$ **7** $3 + 8 = \underline{}$

Home Note Your child used a ten-frame to add on to 9.
ACTIVITY Have your child explain how to use a ten-frame to add on to 9.

Harcourt Brace School Publishers

Use a ten-frame and to add 8 + 5.

Put in 8 counters. Put 5 counters outside the ten-frame.	Move 2 counters to fill the ten-frame. 8 + 2 = 10	Add 10 and 3. 10 + 3 = 13

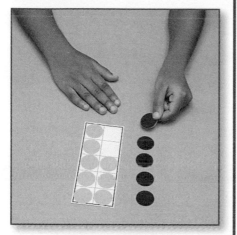

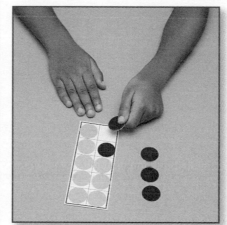

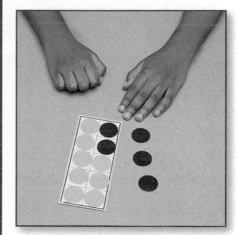

```
   5            10           10
 +8           + 3          + 3
 ___          ____         ____
                            13
```

Use a ten-frame and .
Start with the greater number. Find the sum.

1
```
   8         7         6         4         8         8
 +5        +6        +9        +6        +4        +6
 ___       ___       ___       ___       ___       ___
```

2
```
   3         9         7         4         5         9
 +7        +2        +8        +8        +7        +8
 ___       ___       ___       ___       ___       ___
```

3
```
   8         9         5         6         4         8
 +7        +4        +9        +5        +7        +3
 ___       ___       ___       ___       ___       ___
```

Practice

Use a ten-frame and ⬤ to find the sum.

1.

5 +8 **13**	8 +6	9 +6	5 +9	9 +8	8 +7

2.

9 +2	8 +4	9 +7	7 +7	3 +8	7 +6

3.

5 +7	4 +9	4 +7	9 +3	5 +6	8 +2

4.

6 +5	7 +9	9 +4	8 +8	5 +8	4 +6

Problem Solving

Solve.
Draw a picture to show how you got your answer.

5. Megan has 7 pink shells and 8 orange shells. How many shells does she have in all?

_____ shells

Home Note Your child used the strategy make a ten to find sums.
ACTIVITY Ask your child how he or she used a ten-frame to find the sums on this page.

Name _____

Make a ten.	Count on.	Use doubles.
3	2	8
7	7	3
+4	+5	+3
14	**14**	**14**
3 + 7 = 10	Say 7.	3 + 3 = 6
10 + 4 = 14	Count 8, 9.	6 + 8 = 14
	9 + 5 = 14	

Circle the addends you add first.
Write the sum.

1.
6
2
+4
Make a ten.

2.
2
2
+6
Use doubles.

3.
3
2
+5
Count on.

4.

6	6	1	9	9	5
7	3	3	2	1	8
+4	+6	+9	+3	+6	+5

5.

8	7	3	5	7	8
3	3	6	4	7	2
+2	+5	+3	+5	+2	+8

Talk About It ● Critical Thinking

How did you decide which two addends to add first?

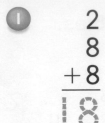

Practice

Write the sum.

1.
2	3	9	6	8	2
8	8	0	5	2	6
+8	+7	+9	+6	+3	+4
18					

2.
5	9	1	1	6	3
4	8	7	8	1	7
+5	+1	+7	+1	+7	+2

3.
2	4	2	5	5	9
7	5	8	2	3	1
+2	+4	+5	+5	+3	+7

4.
6	3	5	7	4	3
5	7	3	1	3	9
+4	+7	+2	+8	+4	+7

Write About It

5. Write a story about fish in the sea.
Add three numbers in your story.

Math Journal

Home Note Your child added three addends.
ACTIVITY Ask your child how he or she decided which two addends to add first.

Harcourt Brace School Publishers

Name _____

Concepts and Skills

Review/Test

Write the sum.

1   7 + 7 = _____

2   7 + 8 = _____

3   7 + 6 = _____

4

$$\begin{array}{r} 5 \\ +5 \\ \hline \end{array} \qquad \begin{array}{r} 5 \\ +6 \\ \hline \end{array} \qquad \begin{array}{r} 8 \\ +8 \\ \hline \end{array} \qquad \begin{array}{r} 8 \\ +7 \\ \hline \end{array} \qquad \begin{array}{r} 6 \\ +6 \\ \hline \end{array} \qquad \begin{array}{r} 6 \\ +7 \\ \hline \end{array}$$

5

$$\begin{array}{r} 3 \\ +9 \\ \hline \end{array} \qquad \begin{array}{r} 9 \\ +7 \\ \hline \end{array} \qquad \begin{array}{r} 4 \\ +9 \\ \hline \end{array} \qquad \begin{array}{r} 6 \\ +9 \\ \hline \end{array} \qquad \begin{array}{r} 9 \\ +8 \\ \hline \end{array} \qquad \begin{array}{r} 9 \\ +5 \\ \hline \end{array}$$

6

$$\begin{array}{r} 1 \\ 8 \\ +3 \\ \hline \end{array} \qquad \begin{array}{r} 2 \\ 8 \\ +5 \\ \hline \end{array} \qquad \begin{array}{r} 4 \\ 9 \\ +4 \\ \hline \end{array} \qquad \begin{array}{r} 6 \\ 3 \\ +4 \\ \hline \end{array} \qquad \begin{array}{r} 7 \\ 2 \\ +7 \\ \hline \end{array} \qquad \begin{array}{r} 9 \\ 1 \\ +8 \\ \hline \end{array}$$

Problem Solving

Solve.
Draw a picture to show how
you got your answer.

7 Cecil has 6 pink shells,
5 yellow shells, and 2 blue shells.
How many shells does he have?

_____ shells

Name _____

Test Prep

Mark the best answer.

1 Which number is the sum?

$$
\begin{array}{r}
6 \\
4 \\
+6 \\
\hline
\end{array}
$$

○ 13
○ 14
○ 15
○ 16

2 Rob has 7 blue boats, 4 red boats, and 7 green boats. How many boats does he have?

○ 15
○ 16
○ 17
○ 18

3 Which addition sentence matches the picture?

○ 7+7 = 14
○ 8+7 = 15
○ 8+8 = 16
○ 8+9 = 17

4 Which is the difference?

$$7 - 3 = \underline{}$$

○ 1
○ 2
○ 3
○ 4

5 Which subtraction sentence matches the picture?

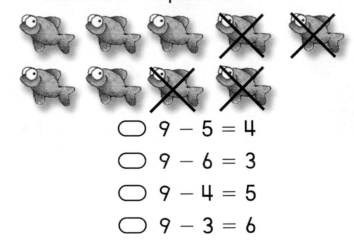

○ 9 − 5 = 4
○ 9 − 6 = 3
○ 9 − 4 = 5
○ 9 − 3 = 6

6 Look at the doubles fact. Which is the doubles-plus-one fact?

$$6 + 6 = 12$$

○ 6+5 = 11
○ 6+7 = 13
○ 7+7 = 14
○ 7+8 = 15

Subtraction Facts to 18

What subtraction stories can you tell about the bats and balls?

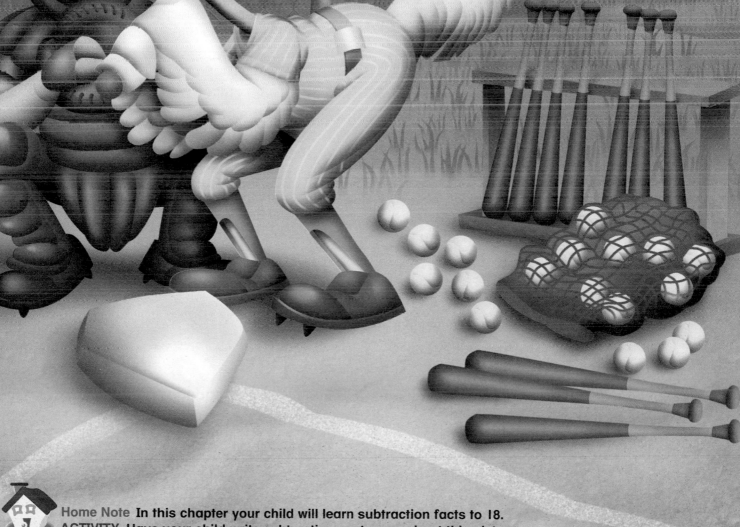

 Home Note In this chapter your child will learn subtraction facts to 18.
ACTIVITY Have your child write subtraction sentences about this picture.

Harcourt Brace School Publishers

SCHOOL-HOME CONNECTION

Dear Family,
   Today we started Chapter 2. We will subtract from numbers up to 18. Here are the new vocabulary words and an activity for us to do together at home.

Love,
_____

Vocabulary

A **fact family** is a group of addition and subtraction facts that use the same numbers.

Here is the fact family for 7, 8, and 15:

$7 + 8 = 15$ $8 + 7 = 15$

$15 - 7 = 8$ $15 - 8 = 7$

Ask your child to write fact families.

A **missing addend** is a number missing from the first part of an addition sentence.

For example, in $7 + \underline{\hspace{1cm}} = 15$, the missing addend is 8.
Give your child some problems like this to solve.

ACTIVITY

Place 18 small objects in a paper bag. Have your child remove some of the objects and say how many are left in the bag. Have your child look in the bag to count, and then have him or her say and write the subtraction sentence. Repeat with fewer than 18 objects.

Visit our Web site for additional activities and ideas.
http://www.hbschool.com

Harcourt Brace School P...

Relating Addition and Subtraction

$$\begin{array}{r} 7 \\ +5 \\ \hline 12 \end{array}$$

$$\begin{array}{r} 12 \\ -5 \\ \hline 7 \end{array}$$

Use ▬▬.
Add or subtract.

①	$\begin{array}{r}6\\+5\\\hline\end{array}$	$\begin{array}{r}11\\-5\\\hline\end{array}$	② $\begin{array}{r}4\\+3\\\hline\end{array}$	$\begin{array}{r}7\\-3\\\hline\end{array}$	③ $\begin{array}{r}3\\+7\\\hline\end{array}$	$\begin{array}{r}10\\-7\\\hline\end{array}$

① $\begin{array}{r}6\\+5\\\hline\end{array}$ $\begin{array}{r}11\\-5\\\hline\end{array}$ ② $\begin{array}{r}4\\+3\\\hline\end{array}$ $\begin{array}{r}7\\-3\\\hline\end{array}$ ③ $\begin{array}{r}3\\+7\\\hline\end{array}$ $\begin{array}{r}10\\-7\\\hline\end{array}$

④ $\begin{array}{r}9\\+7\\\hline\end{array}$ $\begin{array}{r}16\\-7\\\hline\end{array}$ ⑤ $\begin{array}{r}8\\+3\\\hline\end{array}$ $\begin{array}{r}11\\-3\\\hline\end{array}$ ⑥ $\begin{array}{r}5\\+8\\\hline\end{array}$ $\begin{array}{r}13\\-8\\\hline\end{array}$

⑦ $\begin{array}{r}9\\+8\\\hline\end{array}$ $\begin{array}{r}17\\-8\\\hline\end{array}$ ⑧ $\begin{array}{r}6\\+8\\\hline\end{array}$ $\begin{array}{r}14\\-8\\\hline\end{array}$ ⑨ $\begin{array}{r}8\\+7\\\hline\end{array}$ $\begin{array}{r}15\\-7\\\hline\end{array}$

Talk About It ● Critical Thinking

How does knowing $7 + 5 = 12$ help you solve $12 - 5$?

Add or subtract.

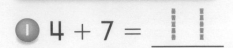

① 4 + 7 = **11**

② 11 − 7 = **4**

③ 7 + 5 = _____

④ 12 − 5 = _____

⑤ 9 + 6 = _____

⑥ 15 − 6 = _____

⑦ 6 + 4 = _____

⑧ 10 − 4 = _____

⑨ 9 + 5 = _____

⑩ 14 − 5 = _____

⑪ 8 + 7 = _____

⑫ 15 − 7 = _____

Problem Solving

Solve.

⑬ Mary got a toy baseball for 9¢ and a toy bat for 8¢. How much money did she spend? _____ ¢

⑭ Nathan had 17¢. He spent 8¢. How much money did he have left? _____ ¢

 Home Note Your child related addition and subtraction.
ACTIVITY Have your child explain how knowing that 5 + 6 = 11 helps him or her solve 11 − 5 = ___.

Name _____

A number line can help you subtract.

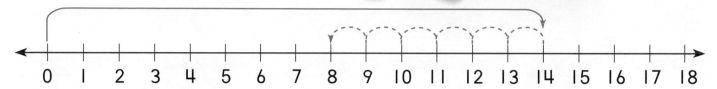

0 1 2 3 4 5 6 7 8 9 10 11 12 13 14 15 16 17 18

To subtract 14 − 6, start at 14.
Count back 6 spaces.

14 − 6 = 8

Subtract.
Use the number line.

 1

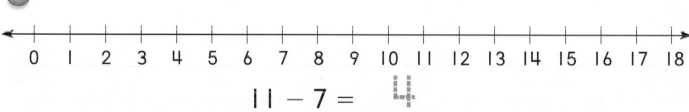

0 1 2 3 4 5 6 7 8 9 10 11 12 13 14 15 16 17 18

11 − 7 = ___4___

 2

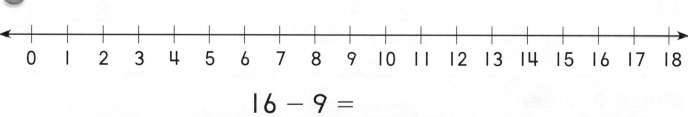

0 1 2 3 4 5 6 7 8 9 10 11 12 13 14 15 16 17 18

16 − 9 = _____

 3

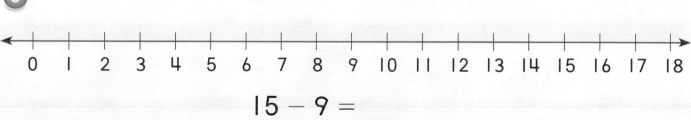

0 1 2 3 4 5 6 7 8 9 10 11 12 13 14 15 16 17 18

15 − 9 = _____

Talk About It • Critical Thinking

How can a number line help you subtract?

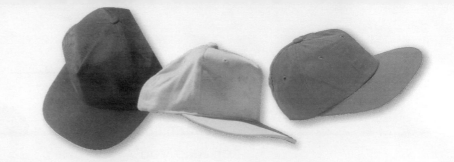

Subtract.
Use the number line.

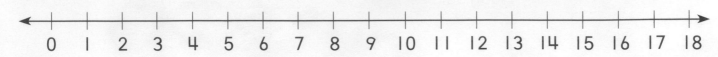

0 1 2 3 4 5 6 7 8 9 10 11 12 13 14 15 16 17 18

① $16 - 7 = \underline{9}$

② $12 - 5 = \underline{}$

③ $12 - 4 = \underline{}$

④ $16 - 8 = \underline{}$

⑤ $15 - 8 = \underline{}$

⑥ $10 - 1 = \underline{}$

⑦ $11 - 3 = \underline{}$

⑧ $18 - 9 = \underline{}$

⑨ $13 - 6 = \underline{}$

⑩ $11 - 2 = \underline{}$

⑪ $15 - 7 = \underline{}$

⑫ $17 - 9 = \underline{}$

⑬ $13 - 7 = \underline{}$

⑭ $12 - 9 = \underline{}$

⑮ $14 - 8 = \underline{}$

Mixed Review

Add or subtract.

⑯

8	0	6	4	5	0
-0	$+7$	-6	-0	-5	$+9$

 Home Note Your child used a number line to subtract.
ACTIVITY Have your child use a number line to subtract from 18 or less.

Harcourt Brace School Publishers

Name _____

Write the fact family for the set of numbers.

6 blue   **7 red**

13 in all

> 6, 7, and 13 are the numbers in this fact family.

1

6 + 7 = 13	7 + 6 = 13
13 – 6 = 7	13 – 7 = 6

2

8   **9**

17

___ + ___ = ___   ___ + ___ = ___

___ – ___ = ___   ___ – ___ = ___

3

6   **8**

14

___ + ___ = ___   ___ + ___ = ___

___ – ___ = ___   ___ – ___ = ___

Write the fact family for the set of numbers.

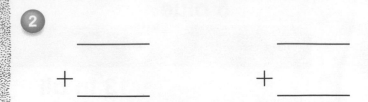

1

$$\begin{array}{r} 4 \\ + 8 \\ \hline 12 \end{array}$$

$$\begin{array}{r} 8 \\ + 4 \\ \hline 12 \end{array}$$

12
8 4

$$\begin{array}{r} 12 \\ - 8 \\ \hline 4 \end{array}$$

$$\begin{array}{r} 12 \\ - 4 \\ \hline 8 \end{array}$$

2

$$\begin{array}{r} \underline{} \\ + \underline{} \\ \hline \end{array}$$

$$\begin{array}{r} \underline{} \\ + \underline{} \\ \hline \end{array}$$

16
9 7

$$\begin{array}{r} \underline{} \\ - \underline{} \\ \hline \end{array}$$

$$\begin{array}{r} \underline{} \\ - \underline{} \\ \hline \end{array}$$

3

$$\begin{array}{r} \underline{} \\ + \underline{} \\ \hline \end{array}$$

$$\begin{array}{r} \underline{} \\ + \underline{} \\ \hline \end{array}$$

15
7 8

$$\begin{array}{r} \underline{} \\ - \underline{} \\ \hline \end{array}$$

$$\begin{array}{r} \underline{} \\ - \underline{} \\ \hline \end{array}$$

4

$$\begin{array}{r} \underline{} \\ + \underline{} \\ \hline \end{array}$$

$$\begin{array}{r} \underline{} \\ + \underline{} \\ \hline \end{array}$$

11
4 7

$$\begin{array}{r} \underline{} \\ - \underline{} \\ \hline \end{array}$$

$$\begin{array}{r} \underline{} \\ - \underline{} \\ \hline \end{array}$$

Home Note Your child learned about fact families.
ACTIVITY Give your child the numbers 5, 7, and 12, and have him or her write the fact family.

Name _____

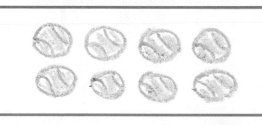
The missing number is called a missing addend.

7 + _____ = 15

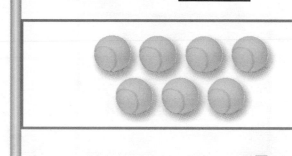

7 + __8__ = 15

Draw tennis balls.
Write the missing addend to
complete the number sentence.

 1

6 + _____ = 11

 2

9 + _____ = 16

 3

7 + _____ = 13

Talk About It ● Critical Thinking

How can you find the missing addend when you know
the sum?

Draw baseballs.
Write the missing addend.

1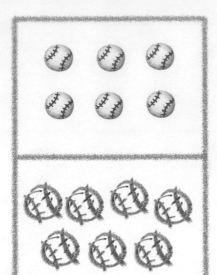

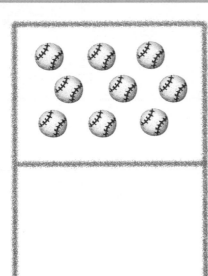

$$\begin{array}{r} 6 \\ +\ 7 \\ \hline 13 \end{array}$$

2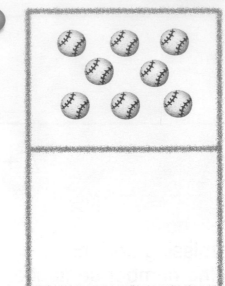

$$\begin{array}{r} 8 \\ +\ \square \\ \hline 17 \end{array}$$

3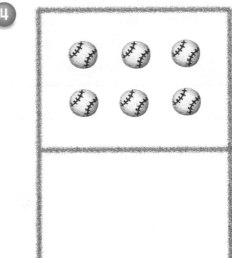

$$\begin{array}{r} 9 \\ +\ \square \\ \hline 16 \end{array}$$

4

$$\begin{array}{r} 6 \\ +\ \square \\ \hline 14 \end{array}$$

Write About It

5 Write the missing addend. Write a sentence that tells how you know it is the missing addend.

$$8 + \underline{\hspace{1cm}} = 13$$

Math Journal

Home Note Your child found missing addends.
ACTIVITY Have your child use groups of small objects to show how to find missing addends.

Harcourt Brace School Publishers

Name _____

Understand • Plan • Solve • Look Back

Draw a picture or make a model.
Write a number sentence to solve.

1. There were 15 boys at the game.
Then 6 boys went home. How
many boys were still at the game?

$$15 \bigcirc - 6 = 9$$

_____ 9 boys

2. After the game, 9 girls and 7
boys had a picnic. How many
children were at the picnic?

_____ $\bigcirc$ _____ = _____

_____ children

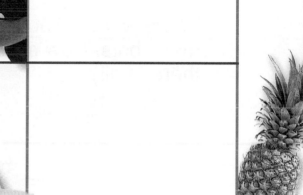

3. In the yard, 7 girls played catch.
Then 6 more girls joined them.
How many girls played catch?

_____ $\bigcirc$ _____ = _____

_____ girls

4. There were 18 boys on the field.
Then 9 boys left. How many boys
were still on the field?

_____ $\bigcirc$ _____ = _____

_____ boys

Chapter 2 • Subtraction Facts to 18

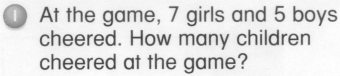

Draw a picture or make a model.
Write a number sentence to solve.

1 At the game, 7 girls and 5 boys
cheered. How many children
cheered at the game?

$$7 \oplus 5 = 12$$

_____12_____ children

2 There were 5 wooden bats and 8
metal bats. How many bats were
there in all?

____ ◯ ____ = ____

_____ bats

3 There were 16 girls and 8 boys
playing ball. How many more girls
than boys were playing ball?

____ ◯ ____ = ____

_____ more girls

4 At the game, 4 girls sat together.
Then 9 more girls joined them. How
many girls were sitting together?

____ ◯ ____ = ____

_____ girls

Home Note Your child wrote number sentences to solve story problems.
ACTIVITY Make up a story problem for your child to solve.

Harcourt Brace School Publishers

Name _____

Concepts and Skills

Subtract. Use the number line.

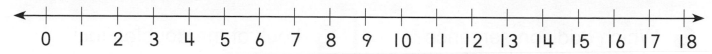

$\begin{array}{ccccccccccccccccccc} 0 & 1 & 2 & 3 & 4 & 5 & 6 & 7 & 8 & 9 & 10 & 11 & 12 & 13 & 14 & 15 & 16 & 17 & 18 \end{array}$

1 $15 - 7 = $ _____   **2** $11 - 5 = $ _____   **3** $12 - 9 = $ _____

Write the fact family for the set of numbers.

4   **5**

8

_____ $+$ _____ $=$ _____   **13**   _____ $+$ _____ $=$ _____

_____ $-$ _____ $=$ _____   _____ $-$ _____ $=$ _____

Draw baseballs. Write the missing addend
to complete the number sentence.

5

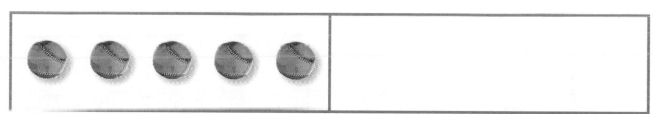

$5 + $ _____ $= 14$

Problem Solving

Draw a picture or make a model.
Write a number sentence to solve.

6 There were 16 red balls and 7 orange
balls in the box. How many more red
balls than orange balls were in the box?

_____ ◯ _____ $=$ _____

_____ more red balls

Name _____

Test Prep

Mark the best answer.

1 Which addition sentence matches the picture?

○ 6 + 8 = 14
○ 6 + 7 = 13
○ 6 + 6 = 12
○ 6 + 5 = 11

2 The vet helps 9 black cats and 6 white cats. How many cats does the vet help?

○ 15
○ 16
○ 17
○ 18

3 Which number sentence solves the problem?

There were 15 dogs playing. Then 7 dogs took a nap. How many dogs were still playing?

○ 8 + 7 = 15
○ 7 + 8 = 15
○ 15 − 8 = 7
○ 15 − 7 = 8

4 Look at the doubles fact.

8 + 8 = 16

Which is the doubles-minus-one fact?

○ 8 + 9 = 17
○ 8 + 7 = 15
○ 8 + 6 = 14
○ 8 + 5 = 13

5 Which belongs in the fact family for this set of numbers?

5	7	12

○ 5 + 2 = 7
○ 12 + 5 = 17
○ 12 − 5 = 7
○ 7 − 5 = 2

6 Which number is the missing addend?

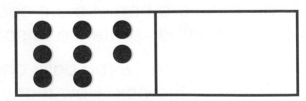

8 + ____ = 14

○ 5
○ 6
○ 7
○ 8

Harcourt Brace School Publishers

Name _____

You will need:

1. Roll the number cube.

2. Move your counter the number of spaces the number cube shows.

3. Find the sum or difference.

4. If your answer is not correct, move back one space.

5. The first one to reach END wins.

Fact Baseball

START

6 + 9

16 − 7

8 + 2

9 − 5

7 + 7

15 − 6

9 + 2

15 − 7

11 − 0

8 + 5

12 − 3

9 + 9

14 − 6

7 + 6

17 − 8

15 − 9

4 + 7

END

Home Note Your child has learned addition and subtraction facts to 18.
ACTIVITY Play this game to help your child practice addition and subtraction facts.

Harcourt Brace School Publishers

Math Fun

Technology

Name _____

 54 fifty-four

Use a .
Write the keys you press.
Write the sum or difference.

1 6 + 7 + 6 = ___19___

ON/C | 6 | + | 7 | + | 6 | = | 19

2 4 + 8 + 2 = _____

ON/C | | | | | |

3 17 − 8 = _____

ON/C |  | | | |

4 Write an addition sentence.
Write the keys you press.
Write the sum.

____ + ____ + ____ = ____

ON/C | | | | | | |

At the Reef

written by Linda Cave

illustrated by
Russel Benfanti

Harcourt Brace School Publishers

 This book will help me review addition facts to 18.

This book belongs to _____ .

A

Many fish swim near the rocks.

_____ have stripes.

_____ have spots.

_____ fish at the reef.

Harcourt Brace School Publishers

The octopus likes to hide.

It has _____ arms to get inside.

D

Here is a squid hunting a snack.

It has _____ arms with eyes in back.

The octopus and the squid together

have_____ arms.

E

F

Pretty fish live here too.

_____ are orange.

_____ are blue.

_____ pretty fish.

But just one shark!

H

Name _____

Concepts and Skills

Write the sum.

1 $7 + 7 =$ _____

2 $4 + 4 =$ _____

3 $8 + 8 =$ _____

4 $6 + 6 =$ _____

5 $5 + 5 =$ _____

6 $9 + 9 =$ _____

7

$$\begin{array}{r} 5 \\ +6 \\ \hline \end{array} \qquad \begin{array}{r} 5 \\ +4 \\ \hline \end{array} \qquad \begin{array}{r} 6 \\ +7 \\ \hline \end{array} \qquad \begin{array}{r} 6 \\ +5 \\ \hline \end{array} \qquad \begin{array}{r} 8 \\ +9 \\ \hline \end{array} \qquad \begin{array}{r} 8 \\ +7 \\ \hline \end{array}$$

8

$$\begin{array}{r} 9 \\ +2 \\ \hline \end{array} \qquad \begin{array}{r} 4 \\ +9 \\ \hline \end{array} \qquad \begin{array}{r} 9 \\ +6 \\ \hline \end{array} \qquad \begin{array}{r} 7 \\ +4 \\ \hline \end{array} \qquad \begin{array}{r} 8 \\ +3 \\ \hline \end{array} \qquad \begin{array}{r} 5 \\ +7 \\ \hline \end{array}$$

9

$$\begin{array}{r} 7 \\ 3 \\ +5 \\ \hline \end{array} \qquad \begin{array}{r} 2 \\ 2 \\ +8 \\ \hline \end{array} \qquad \begin{array}{r} 4 \\ 3 \\ +4 \\ \hline \end{array} \qquad \begin{array}{r} 6 \\ 9 \\ +1 \\ \hline \end{array} \qquad \begin{array}{r} 6 \\ 5 \\ +4 \\ \hline \end{array} \qquad \begin{array}{r} 5 \\ 5 \\ +2 \\ \hline \end{array}$$

Add or subtract.

10 $\begin{array}{r} 7 \\ +4 \\ \hline \end{array} \qquad \begin{array}{r} 11 \\ -4 \\ \hline \end{array}$ **11** $\begin{array}{r} 5 \\ +8 \\ \hline \end{array} \qquad \begin{array}{r} 13 \\ -8 \\ \hline \end{array}$ **12** $\begin{array}{r} 9 \\ +3 \\ \hline \end{array} \qquad \begin{array}{r} 12 \\ -3 \\ \hline \end{array}$

13 $\begin{array}{r} 6 \\ +9 \\ \hline \end{array} \qquad \begin{array}{r} 15 \\ -9 \\ \hline \end{array}$ **14** $\begin{array}{r} 8 \\ +4 \\ \hline \end{array} \qquad \begin{array}{r} 12 \\ -4 \\ \hline \end{array}$ **15** $\begin{array}{r} 6 \\ +7 \\ \hline \end{array} \qquad \begin{array}{r} 13 \\ -7 \\ \hline \end{array}$

Subtract. Use the number line.

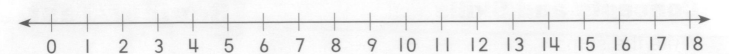

16. $13 - 6 = $ _____

17. $11 - 5 = $ _____

18. $15 - 7 = $ _____

19. $14 - 5 = $ _____

20. $16 - 9 = $ _____

21. $17 - 8 = $ _____

Write the fact family for the set of numbers.

| 4 | 7 | 11 |

22. _____ $+$ _____ $=$ _____   _____ $+$ _____ $=$ _____

_____ $-$ _____ $=$ _____   _____ $-$ _____ $=$ _____

Draw counters. Write the missing addend.

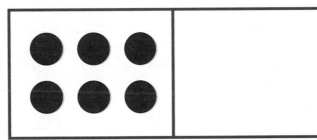

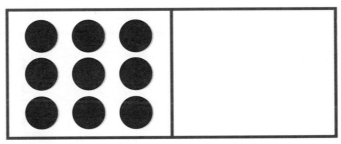

23. $6 + $ _____ $= 13$

24. $9 + $ _____ $= 14$

Problem Solving

Draw a picture or make a model. Write a number sentence to solve.

25. There were 8 girls and 6 boys playing ball. How many children were playing ball?

_____ ◯ _____ $=$ _____ children

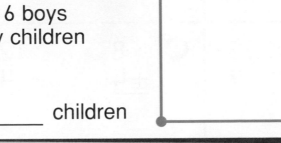

Harcourt Brace School Publishers

Name 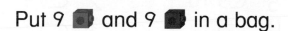 _____

Performance Assessment

Put 9 ◼ and 9 ◼ in a bag.

Take some cubes from the bag.
Make a red train and a blue train.

Draw the cubes.
Use the cubes to write a fact family.

1

___ + ___ = ___

___ + ___ = ___

___ − ___ = ___

___ − ___ = ___

2

___ + ___ = ___

___ + ___ = ___

___ − ___ = ___

___ − ___ = ___

Write About It

3 Write the missing addend.
Draw a picture to show how you
know it is the missing addend.

8 + ___ = 15

Name _____

Fill in the ◯ for the correct answer.

1	9 ◯11	2	8 ◯11	3	6 ◯10	4	2 ◯9
	+3 ◯12		+6 ◯12		4 ◯14		3 ◯11
	◯13		◯13		+6 ◯16		+6 ◯12
	◯14		◯14		◯18		◯13

5 Which belongs in the fact family for this set of numbers?

3	8	11

◯ 3 + 5 = 8   ◯ 11 − 8 = 3

◯ 11 + 3 = 14   ◯ 2 + 9 = 11

Subtract. Use the number line.

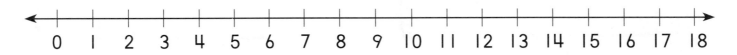

0 1 2 3 4 5 6 7 8 9 10 11 12 13 14 15 16 17 18

6	15 − 8 = ___	7	12 − 7 = ___	8	17 − 9 = ___
	◯6 ◯7		◯4 ◯5		◯6 ◯7
	◯8 ◯9		◯6 ◯7		◯8 ◯9

Which number sentence solves the problem?

9 There were 16 girls running. Then 8 girls stopped. How many girls were still running?

◯ 8 + 8 = 16

◯ 16 − 8 = 8

10 There were 6 black birds and 9 blue birds in the tree. How many birds were in the tree?

◯ 6 + 9 = 15

◯ 15 − 9 = 6

Harcourt Brace School Publishers

Numbers to 100

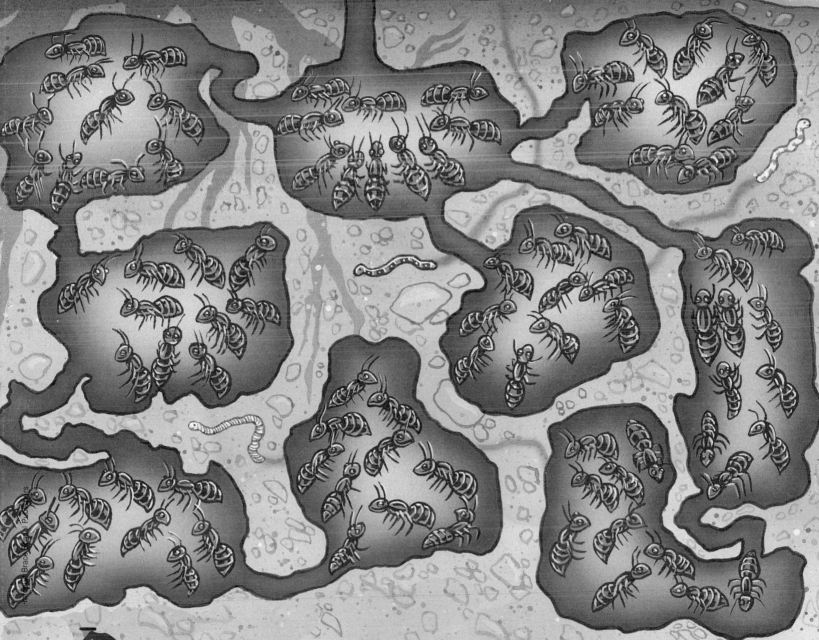

How does grouping the ants make them easier to count?

Home Note In this chapter your child will learn about tens and ones in numbers to 100. **ACTIVITY** Have your child circle each group of 10 ants in the picture.

SCHOOL-HOME CONNECTION

Dear Family,
Today we started Chapter 3. We will write numbers to 99 and learn how to estimate. Here are the new vocabulary words and an activity for us to do together at home.

Love,

_____

Vocabulary

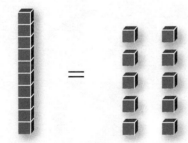

1 ten = 10 ones

ACTIVITY

Give your child between 11 and 99 small objects. Have him or her group the objects into tens and say and write how many groups of ten there are, how many ones are left over, and the total number of objects. Repeat with different numbers of objects.

Visit our Web site for additional activities and ideas.
http://www.hbschool.com

Harcourt Brace School Publishers

Grouping Tens

$$1 \text{ ten} = 10 \text{ ones}$$

Circle groups of tens.
Write how many tens and ones.

1
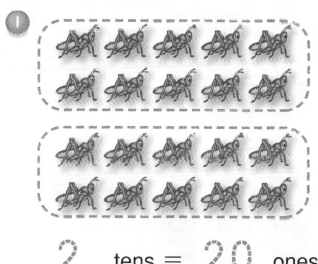

__2__ tens = __20__ ones

2
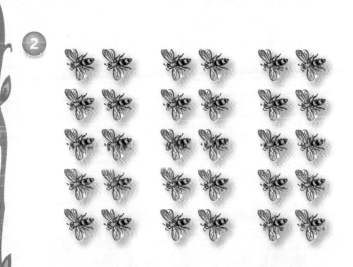

_____ tens = _____ ones

3
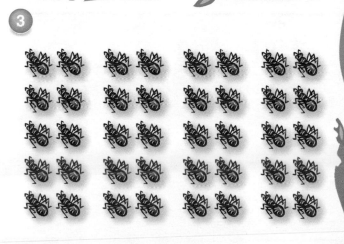

_____ tens = _____ ones

4
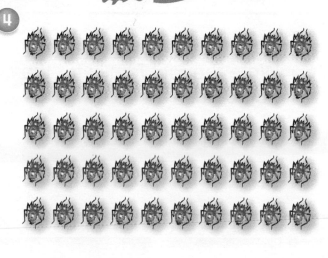

_____ tens = _____ ones

Count the spots. Write how many tens.
Then write how many ones.

①  _____5_____ tens = __50__ ones

②

_____ tens = _____ ones

③

_____ tens = _____ ones

④

_____ tens = _____ ones

⑤

_____ tens = _____ ones

Mixed Review

⑥ Write the fact family for the set of
numbers.

_____ + _____ = _____   _____ + _____ = _____

_____ − _____ = _____   _____ − _____ = _____

 Home Note Your child identified groups of ten.
ACTIVITY Ask your child to set out small objects in groups of ten and tell you how many tens and
ones there are.

Harcourt Brace School Publishers

Name _____

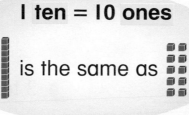

1 ten = 10 ones

is the same as

3 tens 4 ones = 34

Use Workmat 3 and .
Write how many tens and ones.
Then write the number.

1

__2__ tens __7__ ones = __27__

2

__ tens __ ones = __

3

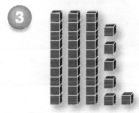

__ tens __ ones = __

4

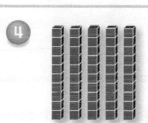

__ tens __ ones = __

5

__ tens __ ones = __

6

__ tens __ ones = __

Talk About It ● **Critical Thinking**

How many ones are there in a group of ten?
How can you tell?

Practice

Write the number.

1 2 tens 5 ones = _25_

2 3 tens 8 ones = _____

3 1 ten 6 ones = _____

4 0 tens 9 ones = _____

5 4 tens 7 ones = _____

6 2 tens 1 one = _____

7 1 ten 3 ones = _____

8 3 tens 0 ones = _____

9 2 tens 9 ones = _____

10 4 tens 6 ones = _____

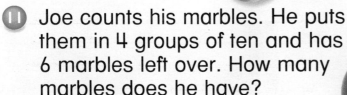

Problem Solving • **Visual Thinking**

Solve.
Then draw a model.

11 Joe counts his marbles. He puts
them in 4 groups of ten and has
6 marbles left over. How many
marbles does he have?

_____ marbles

Harcourt Brace School Publishers

Home Note Your child modeled and identified tens and ones to 50.
ACTIVITY Ask your child to set out 50 or fewer small objects in groups of tens
and ones and tell you the number.

Name _____

Use Workmat 3 and  .
Write how many tens and ones.
Then write the number.

7 tens 0 ones = 70

1

_9_ tens _3_ ones = _93_

2

___ tens ___ one = ___

3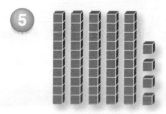

___ tens ___ ones = ___

4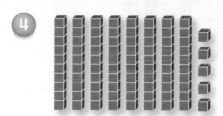

___ tens ___ ones = ___

5

___ tens ___ ones = ___

6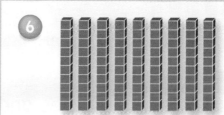

___ tens ___ ones = ___

Talk About It ● Critical Thinking

How do you know that a number has no ones?

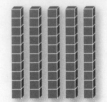

Practice

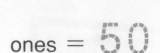

Write how many tens and ones.
Then write the number.

 1 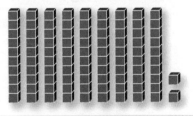 _____5_____ tens _____0_____ ones = _____50_____

 2 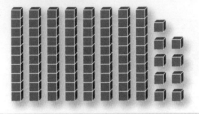 _____ tens _____ ones = _____

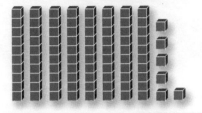 **3** _____ tens _____ ones = _____

 4  _____ tens _____ ones = _____

 5 _____ tens _____ ones = _____

 6 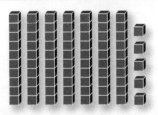 _____ tens _____ ones = _____

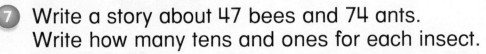

Write About It

7 Write a story about 47 bees and 74 ants.
Write how many tens and ones for each insect.

 Home Note Your child modeled tens and ones to 100.
ACTIVITY Say a number between 10 and 99, and have your child tell how many
tens and ones there are in that number.

Name _____

Understand · **Plan** · **Solve** · **Look Back**

Problem Solving
Use a Model

Use .
Make and draw a model.
Write how many tens and ones.
Then write the number.

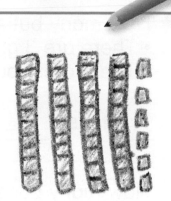

1 How many ants are on the log?
  • There are 4 groups of ten ants.
  • There are 6 ants alone.

___4___ tens ___6___ ones = ___46___ ants

2 How many crickets are in the grass?
  • There are 2 groups of ten crickets.
  • There are 7 crickets alone.

_____ tens _____ ones = _____ crickets

3 How many ladybugs are on the plant?
  • There are 5 groups of 10 ladybugs.
  • There are 4 ladybugs alone.

_____ tens _____ ones = _____ ladybugs

4 How many bees are in the hive?
  • There are 3 groups of 10 bees.
  • There are 5 bees alone.

_____ tens _____ ones = _____ bees

5 How many snails are in the woods?
  • There are 8 groups of 10 snails.
  • There are no snails alone.

_____ tens _____ ones = _____ snails

Harcourt Brace School Publishers

Chapter 3 • Numbers to 100

sixty-seven **67**

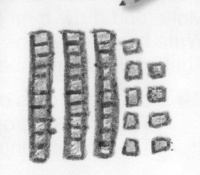

Use .
Make and draw a model.
Write how many tens and ones.
Then write the number.

1 How many butterflies are in the field?
- There are 3 groups of ten butterflies.
- There are 9 butterflies alone.

__3__ tens __9__ ones = __39__ butterflies

2 How many bugs are at the pond?
- There are 2 groups of ten bugs.
- There are 8 bugs alone.

_____ tens _____ ones = _____ bugs

3 How many beetles are in the garden?
- There are 7 groups of 10 beetles.
- There are no beetles alone.

_____ tens _____ ones = _____ beetles

4 How many crickets are in the grass?
- There are 6 groups of 10 crickets.
- There are 5 crickets alone.

_____ tens _____ ones = _____ crickets

5 How many ladybugs are on the log?
- There is 1 group of 10 ladybugs.
- There are 2 ladybugs alone.

_____ ten _____ ones = _____ ladybugs

 **Home Note** Your child modeled tens and ones to identify numbers.
ACTIVITY Ask your child to tell you how he or she knew how to model each number.

Exploring Estimation

Look at each group of ants.
Use these groups to help you choose the better estimate.

10 ants   25 ants   50 ants

1

about 25 ants

about 50 ants

2

about 10 ants

about 25 ants

3

about 10 ants

about 25 ants

4

about 25 ants

about 50 ants

Talk About It • Critical Thinking

How did the groups help you estimate each number of ants?

Look at each group of bees.
Use these groups to help you choose the better estimate.

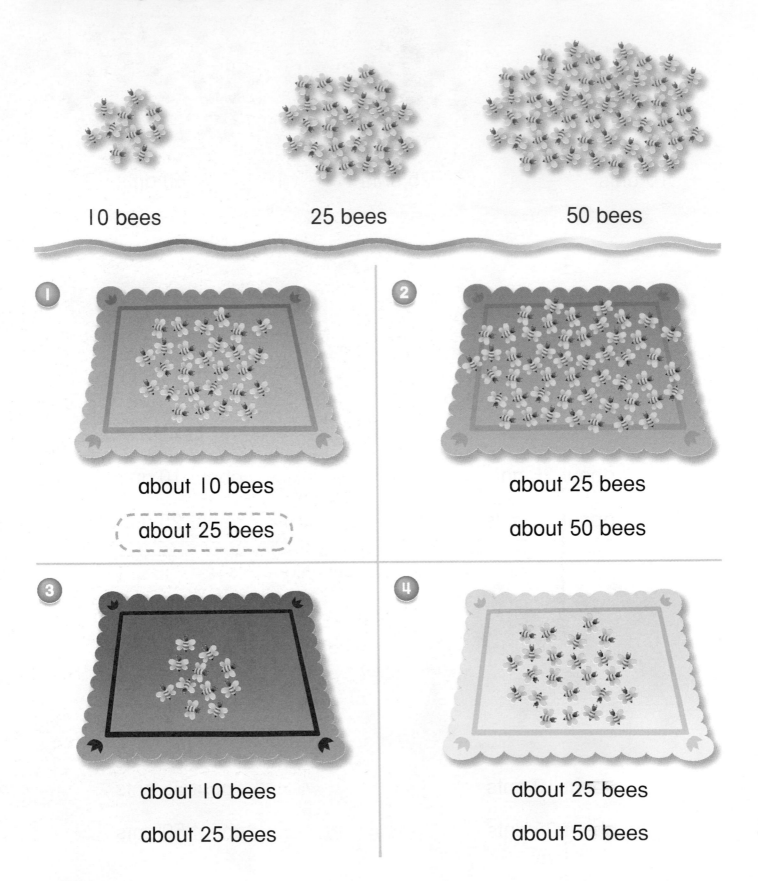

10 bees   25 bees   50 bees

1 about 10 bees

(about 25 bees)

2 about 25 bees

about 50 bees

3 about 10 bees

about 25 bees

4 about 25 bees

about 50 bees

Home Note Your child estimated using benchmarks of 10, 25, and 50.
ACTIVITY Ask your child to explain how he or she chose each estimate on the page.

Chapter 3

Name _____

Concepts and Skills

Count the spots. Write how many tens.
Then write how many ones.

_____ tens = _____ ones

Write how many tens and ones.
Then write the number.

2

____ tens ____ ones = ____

3

____ tens ____ ones = ____

Write the number.

4   8 tens 0 ones = _____

5   6 tens 9 ones = _____

6   I ten 6 ones = _____

7   0 tens 8 ones = _____

Problem Solving

Use ▭▭▭▭▭▭▭▭ ▪.
Write how many tens and ones.
Then write the number.

8 How many train cars does Greg have?
  • He has 5 groups of ten trains.
  • He has 7 train cars left over.

_____ tens _____ ones = _____ train cars

Name _____

Test Prep

Mark the best answer.

1 Which is the sum?

$$\begin{array}{r} 3 \\ 8 \\ +6 \\ \hline \end{array}$$

- ⭘ 15
- ⭘ 18
- ⭘ 17
- ⭘ 16

2 Jeanie has 5 blue beads, 8 pink beads, and 3 white beads. How many beads does she have?

- ⭘ 15
- ⭘ 16
- ⭘ 14
- ⭘ 18

3 Which is the difference?

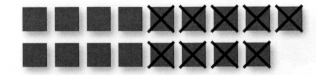

$$17 - 9 = \underline{}$$

- ⭘ 6
- ⭘ 8
- ⭘ 10
- ⭘ 7

4 Which subtraction sentence tells how many more yellow counters there are?

- ⭘ 8 − 2 = 6
- ⭘ 6 − 2 = 4
- ⭘ 6 − 4 = 4
- ⭘ 8 − 6 = 2

5 Which number has 7 tens and 2 ones?

- ⭘ 27
- ⭘ 71
- ⭘ 12
- ⭘ 72

6 Which number matches the picture?

- ⭘ 17
- ⭘ 73
- ⭘ 37
- ⭘ 23

Number Patterns

Harcourt Brace School Publishers

How can you count by fives to find the number of trees?

Home Note In this chapter your child will learn about skip-counting and number patterns. **ACTIVITY** Have your child explain how he or she counted the objects in the picture.

SCHOOL-HOME CONNECTION

Dear Family,
 Today we started Chapter 4. We will skip-count and find out about even and odd numbers. We will count on and count back, and look for number patterns. Here are the new vocabulary words and an activity for us to do at home.

Love,

_____

Vocabulary

Even numbers are the numbers you say when you count by twos. They can form pairs. 2, 4, 6, and 8 are even numbers.

Odd numbers are one more or one less than even numbers. They cannot form pairs. 1, 3, 5, and 7 are odd numbers.

A **pattern** is a list of numbers that follows a rule. In the series 3, 6, 9, 12, 15, the rule is count by three.

To **skip-count**, you start with any number and keep adding on the same number.

ACTIVITY

Give your child 13 single socks. Have him or her match each sock with its mate to make a pair. Have your child tell you whether he or she has an even number or an odd number of socks. Repeat the activity with a different number of socks.

Visit our Web site for additional activities and ideas.
http://www.hbschool.com

Harcourt Brace School Publishers

Name _____

Count by fives or by tens.
Write the numbers.

1

5, ___10___, ___15___, ___20___, ___25___, ___30___ pinecones

2

10, ___20___, ___30___, ___40___, ___50___, ___60___ leaves

3

5¢, _____¢, _____¢, _____¢, _____¢, _____¢, _____¢

4

10¢, _____¢, _____¢, _____¢, _____¢, _____¢, _____¢

5

25, 30, _____, _____, _____, _____, _____

6

30, 40, _____, _____, _____, _____, _____

7

60, 65, _____, _____, _____, _____, _____

Talk About It ● **Critical Thinking**

What patterns do you see?

Chapter 4 • Number Patterns

seventy-five **75**

Practice

Write the missing numbers.
Count by fives. Color those boxes 🖍.
Count by tens. Circle those numbers.

1.

1	2	3	4	5	6	7	8	9	10
11	12	13	14		16	17	18	19	
21	22	23	24		26	27	28	29	
31	32	33	34		36	37	38	39	
41	42	43	44		46	47	48	49	
51	52	53	54		56	57	58	59	
61	62	63	64		66	67	68	69	
71	72	73	74		76	77	78	79	
81	82	83	84		86	87	88	89	
91	92	93	94		96	97	98	99	

Problem Solving ● Mental Math

Solve.

2. Jen has 6 gloves.
Each glove has 5 fingers.
Count how many fingers there are.

_____ fingers

Home Note Your child counted by fives and tens.
ACTIVITY Ask your child to tell you what he or she notices about the number in the ones place when counting by tens.

Chapter 4

Name _____

Count by twos or by threes.
Write the numbers.

1

2, __4__, __6__, __8__, __10__, __12__ socks

2

3, __6__, __9__, __12__, __15__ pine trees

3

2, _____, _____, _____, _____, _____ mittens

4

3, _____, _____, _____, _____, _____ acorns

5

12, 14, _____, _____, _____, _____, _____, _____

6

9, 12, _____, _____, _____, _____, _____, _____

7

30, 33, _____, _____, _____, _____, _____, _____

Practice

Count by twos. Color those boxes 🖍.
Count by threes. Circle those numbers.

1.

1	2	3	4	5	6	7	8	9	10
11	12	13	14	15	16	17	18	19	20
21	22	23	24	25	26	27	28	29	30
31	32	33	34	35	36	37	38	39	40
41	42	43	44	45	46	47	48	49	50
51	52	53	54	55	56	57	58	59	60
61	62	63	64	65	66	67	68	69	70
71	72	73	74	75	76	77	78	79	80
81	82	83	84	85	86	87	88	89	90
91	92	93	94	95	96	97	98	99	100

Write About It

2. Write about some things that you
might count by twos.
Then write about some things that
you might count by threes.

Math Journal

Home Note **Your child counted by twos and threes.**
ACTIVITY **Ask your child to count by twos to 50.**

Even and Odd Numbers

Show the number of ■.
Snap the ■ together in pairs.
Write even or odd.

If each cube is in a pair, the number is even. If one cube is left over, the number is odd.

---

1 12   even

2 15 _____

3 9 _____

4 16 _____

5 14 _____

6 7 _____

7 10 _____

8 13 _____

Talk About It ● Critical Thinking

How do you know if a number is even or odd?

Show and draw the number of .
Write even or odd.

1

11 _odd_

2 8 _____

3 4 _____

4 13 _____

5 15 _____

6 6 _____

7 10 _____

8 5 _____

Mixed Review

Write the fact family for 5, 6, and 11.

9

	+		=				+		=	
	−		=				−		=	

 Home Note Your child learned about even and odd numbers.
ACTIVITY Give your child 20 small objects. Have him or her show you a number
between 1 and 20 and then tell you if the number is even or odd.

Harcourt Brace School Publishers

Name _____

To count on by tens,
keep adding 10 to
each number.

5   15   25   35   45

Count on by tens.
Write the number.

1

18, _28_ , _38_ , _48_ , 58, _68_ , _78_ , _88_

2

7, 17, _____ , _____ , _____ , _____ , _____ , _____ , _____

3

23, _____ , _____ , _____ , _____ , _____ , 83, _____

4

11, _____ , _____ , _____ , _____ , 61, _____ , _____ , _____

5

29, _____ , _____ , _____ , _____ , _____ , _____ , 99

Talk About It ● Critical Thinking

What do you notice about the tens place
when you count on by tens?

Harcourt Brace School Publishers

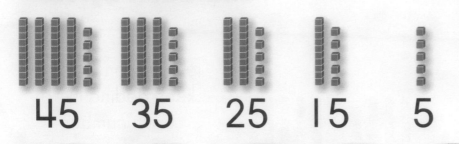

Practice

45 35 25 15 5

To count back by tens, keep subtracting 10 from each number.

Count back by tens.
Write the number.

 1

97, __87__, __77__, __67__, __57__, 47, __37__, __27__

 2

70, _____, _____, _____, _____, _____, _____, 0

 3

88, _____, _____, 58, _____, _____, _____, _____

 4

64, _____, _____, _____, _____, 14, _____

Problem Solving ● Mental Math

Solve.

5 Jake had 67 pinecones.
He found 10 more.
How many pinecones
does he have in all?

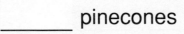

_____ pinecones

6 Leslie had 54 stickers.
She gave away 10.
How many stickers
does she have left?

_____ stickers

 Home Note Your child counted on and back by tens.
ACTIVITY Ask your child to tell you what he or she notices about the number in the tens place when counting back by tens.

82 eighty-two

Chapter 4

Harcourt Brace School Publishers

Understand · Plan · Solve · Look Back

Problem Solving
Look for a Pattern

Look for a pattern.
Write the missing numbers.
Write twos, threes, fives, or tens to name the rule.

1

Count by ___twos___.

2

Count by _____.

3

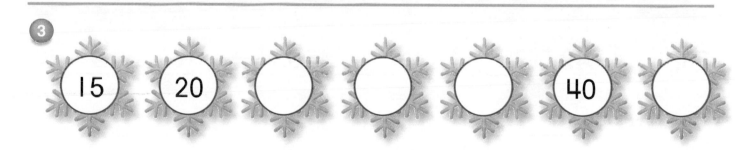

Count by _____.

4

Count by _____.

Look for a pattern.
Write the missing numbers.
Write twos, threes, fives,
or tens to name the rule.

1

45, _50_, _55_, 60, _65_, _70_, _75_, _80_, _85_, _90_

Count by _fives_.

2

18, _____, _____, 27, _____, _____, 36, _____, _____

Count by _____.

3

38, _____, 42, _____, _____, _____, 50, _____, _____, _____

Count by _____.

4

0, _____, _____, _____, 40, _____, _____, _____, 80, _____

Count by _____.

Home Note Your child looked for patterns and wrote the missing numbers.
ACTIVITY Ask your child how he or she decided which rule to write for each problem.

Name _____

Concepts and Skills

Count by fives.

1 25, 30, _____, _____, _____, _____, _____

Count by threes.

2 18, 21, _____, _____, _____, _____, _____

Draw the number of cubes.
Write even or odd.

3

5 _____

4

12 _____

Count on by tens.

5 23, _____, _____, 53, _____, 73, _____, _____

Count back by tens.

6 92, _____, _____, 62, _____, _____, 32, _____

Problem Solving

Look for a pattern.
Write the missing numbers.
Write twos, threes, fives, or tens to name the rule.

7 25, _____, 45, _____, _____, 75, _____, 95

Count by _____

Name _____

Test Prep

Mark the best answer.

1 Which is the missing addend?

$7 + \underline{\hspace{1cm}} = 15$

- ⚪ 7
- ⚪ 6
- ⚪ 8
- ⚪ 9

2 Mandy had 38 shells. She found 10 more. How many shells does she have?

- ⚪ 28
- ⚪ 30
- ⚪ 40
- ⚪ 48

3 Which number sentence solves the problem?

There were 17 boys swimming. Then 8 boys stopped. How many boys were still swimming?

- ⚪ $17 + 8 = 25$
- ⚪ $17 - 8 = 9$
- ⚪ $18 - 7 = 11$
- ⚪ $18 + 7 = 25$

4 There are 2 groups of 10 grapes. There are 7 grapes alone. How many grapes are there?

- ⚪ 20
- ⚪ 72
- ⚪ 13
- ⚪ 27

5 There are 3 rows of 10 cars. There are 8 cars alone. How many cars are there?

- ⚪ 23
- ⚪ 38
- ⚪ 11
- ⚪ 83

6 Sammy has 11 socks. He matches them to make pairs. Does he have an odd or even number of socks?

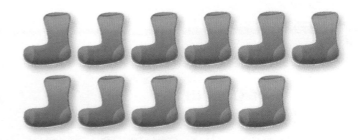

- ⚪ odd
- ⚪ even

Harcourt Brace School Publishers

Using Numbers to 100

Are there more flowers or vegetables in the garden? How do you know?

Home Note In this chapter, your child will use numbers to 100.
ACTIVITY Have your child compare the number of flowers and vegetables he or she sees in the picture.

SCHOOL-HOME CONNECTION

Dear Family,
 Today we started Chapter 5. We will compare and order numbers. Here are the new vocabulary words and an activity for us to do together at home.

Love,

_____

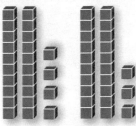

Vocabulary

The symbol for **greater than** is >.

24 > 23

The symbol for **less than** is <.

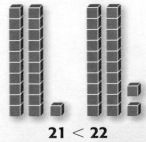

21 < 22

ACTIVITY

Give your child three grocery items with prices of less than 99¢. Have your child line up the three items in order by price from greatest to least, and then from least to greatest.

 Visit our Web site for additional ideas and activities.
http://www.hbschool.com

Name _____

Use Workmat 3 and .
Show each number.
Compare the tens and ones.
Circle the number that is greater.

I have more ones.
My number is greater.

We both have 2 tens.

Workmat 3

Tens	Ones

Workmat 3

Tens	Ones

1.   21   (24)

2. 43   39   3. 18   28   4. 8   80

5. 34   43   6. 33   31   7. 73   75

8. 19   15   9. 45   54   10. 50   49

11. 87   89   12. 70   7   13. 65   56

Talk About It • Critical Thinking

How do you know which number is greater?

Practice

Use Workmat 3 and ▭▭▭▭▭▭ ▭.
Show each number.
Compare the tens and ones.
Circle the number that is less.

35 is less than 36.

1. 36 (35)

2	59	49	3	67	76	4	20	30
5	19	11	6	45	43	7	48	51
8	85	89	9	21	12	10	40	39
11	16	6	12	69	61	13	96	99
14	30	29	15	23	32	16	55	65

Problem Solving ● Visual Thinking

Solve.
Draw a picture to show your answer.

17. Anne has 19 pennies.
She gave Jack 11 of her pennies.
Who has the greater number of
pennies now?

_____

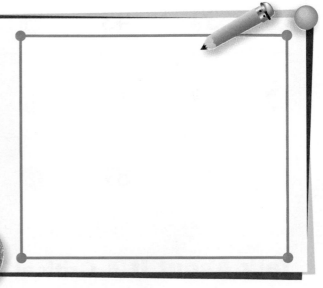

Harcourt Brace School Publishers

Home Note Your child compared 2 two-digit numbers to determine which is greater or which is less.
ACTIVITY Say two 2-digit numbers. Ask your child to tell how he or she knows which number is less.

Greater Than and Less Than

15 is greater than 12.

15 > 12

12 is less than 15.

12 < 15

Write greater or less.
Then write > or < in the circle.

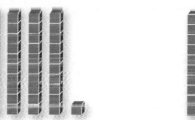

① 23 is ___less___ than 32.

23 ⬤< 32

② 41 is _____ than 40.

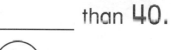

41 ◯ 40

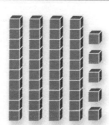

③ 54 is _____ than 45.

54 ◯ 45

④ 6 is _____ than 19.

6 ◯ 19

Talk About It ● Critical Thinking

How can you remember what the > and < signs mean?

Practice

Write greater or less.
Then write > or < in the circle.

1 98 is <u>greater</u> than 89.

98 ⟨ > ⟩ 89

2 5 is _____ than 15.

5 ◯ 15

3 35 is _____ than 38.

35 ◯ 38

4 60 is _____ than 59.

60 ◯ 59

5 45 is _____ than 54.

45 ◯ 54

6 76 is _____ than 67.

76 ◯ 67

7 56 is _____ than 36.

56 ◯ 36

8 9 is _____ than 11.

9 ◯ 11

Problem Solving • Reasoning

Solve.
Then draw a model to check your answer.

9 Carlos is thinking of a number.
It is 10 greater than 20.
It is 10 less than 40.
What number is it?

_____

Home Note Your child compared 2 two-digit numbers using the symbols > and <.
ACTIVITY Have your child compare the prices of two grocery items that cost less than $1.00 each and tell which price is greater.

Harcourt Brace School Publishers

Name _____

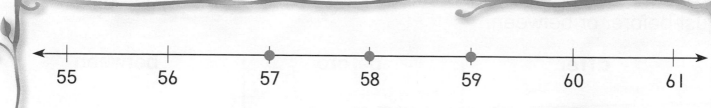

55   56   57   58   59   60   61

57 is just after 56.
59 is just before 60.
58 is between 57 and 59.

Write the number that is just after,
just before, or between.

1
26   **27**   28

2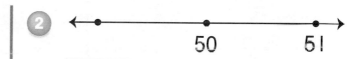
_____   50   51

3
35   _____   37

4
89   _____   91

5
14   _____   16

6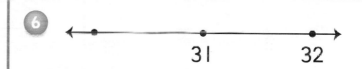
_____   31   32

7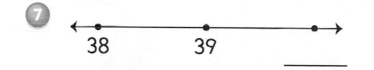
38   39   _____

8
83   _____   85

9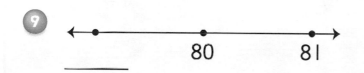
_____   80   81

10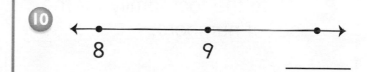
8   9   _____

11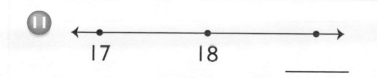
17   18   _____

12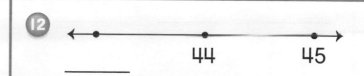
_____   44   45

13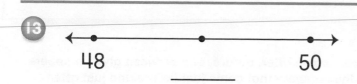
48   _____   50

14
_____   98   99

Chapter 5 • Using Numbers to 100

Practice

Write the number that is just after, just before, or between.

after	before	between
1. 34, _35_	_39_, 40	55, _56_, 57
2. 10, ____	____, 25	42, ____, 44
3. 98, ____	____, 8	75, ____, 77
4. 27, ____	____, 88	28, ____, 30
5. 50, ____	____, 61	9, ____, 11
6. 19, ____	____, 30	97, ____, 99
7. 79, ____	____, 33	26, ____, 28

Mixed Review

8. Write the fact family for the set of numbers.

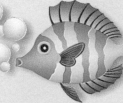

6   7   13

____ + ____ = ____   ____ + ____ = ____

____ − ____ = ____   ____ − ____ = ____

 Home Note Your child determined which numbers came after, before, and between given numbers. **ACTIVITY** Say a number. Have your child say the numbers that come just before and just after that number.

94 ninety-four

Harcourt Brace School Publishers

Name _____

Ordinal Numbers

| 1st | 2nd | 3rd | 4th | 5th | 6th | 7th | 8th | 9th | 10th |

Write the correct position of each child.

1. sixth
   6th

2. _____
   _____

3. _____
   _____

4. _____
   _____

5. _____
   _____

6. _____
   _____

Chapter 5 • Using Numbers to 100

ninety-five **95**

Practice

The first ten children are inside the school.

eleventh · twelfth · thirteenth · fourteenth · fifteenth · sixteenth · seventeenth · eighteenth · nineteenth · twentieth

11th 12th 13th 14th 15th 16th 17th 18th 19th 20th

Write the correct position of each child.

1. twelfth
   12th

2. _____
   _____

3. _____
   _____

4. _____
   _____

5. _____
   _____

6. _____
   _____

Write About It

7. Write a story about you and your friends. Use as many ordinal numbers as you can.

Math Journal

Harcourt Brace School Publishers

Home Note Your child used ordinal numbers from first (1st) through twentieth (20th).
ACTIVITY Ask your child to identify the position of an object between 1st and 20th in a series.

Chapter 5

Name _____

Understand • Plan • Solve • Look Back

10 11 12 13 14 15 16 17 18 19 20

Find 17 on the number line.
There are 7 spaces from 17 back to 10.
There are 3 spaces from 17 on to 20.
17 is closer to 20.

Tosha has 17 dog bones.
- Is 17 closer to 10 or 20?   20
- About how many dog
  bones does Tosha have?   about 20 dog bones

Use the number line to solve.

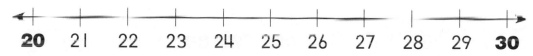

20 21 22 23 24 25 26 27 28 29 30

1 Farley has 29 dog bones.
- Is 29 closer to 20 or 30?   _____
- About how many dog bones
  does Farley have?   about _____ dog bones

2 Winnie has 22 dog bones.
- Is 22 closer to 20 or 30?   _____
- About how many dog bones
  does Winnie have?   about _____ dog bones

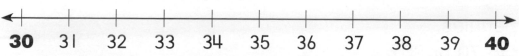

30 31 32 33 34 35 36 37 38 39 40

3 Sporto has 36 dog bones.
- Is 36 closer to 30 or 40?   _____
- About how many dog bones
  does Sporto have?   about _____ dog bones

Harcourt Brace School Publishers

Practice

Use the number line to solve.

←—+——+——+——+——+——+——+——+——+——+——+——→
50　51　52　53　54　55　56　57　58　59　**60**

1 Rob has 58 marbles.

- Is 58 closer to 50 or 60?　　_60_

- About how many marbles does Rob have?　　about _60_ marbles

2 Craig has 56 marbles.

- Is 56 closer to 50 or 60?　　_____

- About how many marbles does Craig have?　　about _____ marbles

3 Cameron has 54 marbles.

- Is 54 closer to 50 or 60?　　_____

- About how many marbles does Cameron have?　　about _____ marbles

←—+——+——+——+——+——+——+——+——+——+——+——→
70　71　72　73　74　75　76　77　78　79　**80**

4 Chris has 73 pennies.

- Is 73 closer to 70 or 80?　　_____

- About how many pennies does Chris have?　　about _____ pennies

5 Ian has 77 pennies.

- Is 77 closer to 70 or 80?　　_____

- About how many pennies does Ian have?　　about _____ pennies

6 Erika has 72 pennies.

- Is 72 closer to 70 or 80?　　_____

- About how many pennies does Erika have?　　about _____ pennies

Home Note Your child used a number line to estimate.
ACTIVITY Say a number between 40 and 50 (not 45). Ask your
child to use a number line to find the ten that number is closer to.

Harcourt Brace School Publishers

Name _____

Concepts And Skills

Review/Test

Compare the tens and ones.
Circle the number that is greater.

1   23   32   **2**   60   59

Write greater or less.
Then write > or < in the circle.

3 45 is _____ than 44.   **4** 29 is _____ than 30.

     45 ◯ 44   29 ◯ 30

Write the number that is just after, just before, or between.

5 69, _____   **6** _____, 20   **7** 86, _____, 88

8 Look at the crayons.
Color the balls.   **third**   **fifth**   **ninth**

first

Problem Solving

Use the number line to solve.

```
←——+——+——+——+——+——+——+——+——+——+——→
  80  81  82  83  84  85  86  87  88  89  90
```

9 Michele has 86 stickers.

    • Is 86 closer to 80 or 90?   _____

    • About how many
      stickers does Michele have?   about _____ stickers

Name _____

Test Prep

Mark the best answer.

1 Which statement is true?

- ⃝ 48 > 52
- ⃝ 48 < 52
- ⃝ 48 = 52
- ⃝ 52 = 48

2 Chad had 6 pennies. He gave one penny to each of 4 friends. How many pennies are left?

- ⃝ 3
- ⃝ 2
- ⃝ 10
- ⃝ 5

3 Margo saw 3 red birds. Then she saw 4 blue birds. How many birds did she see in all?

- ⃝ 1
- ⃝ 9
- ⃝ 7
- ⃝ 4

4 Which number comes between 63 and 65?

- ⃝ 61
- ⃝ 62
- ⃝ 64
- ⃝ 66

5 Which is the number?

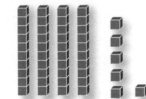

- ⃝ 36
- ⃝ 40
- ⃝ 44
- ⃝ 46

6 Leo has 2 groups of 10 buttons. He has 3 more buttons. How many buttons does Leo have?

- ⃝ 32
- ⃝ 23
- ⃝ 5
- ⃝ 15

Harcourt Brace School Publishers

Name _____

Fruit Juice Shake

You will need:
3 cups cold
   orange,
   pineapple, or
   grape juice
1 cup powdered
   milk
1 drop vanilla
1 cup ice cubes

Directions

1. Measure each ingredient. Put it into a blender.

2. Cover the blender. Blend until the ice is crushed.

3. Pour into cups and enjoy!

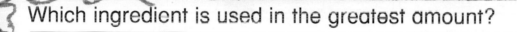

Which ingredient is used in the greatest amount?

_____
- -
_____

Which ingredient is listed second?

_____
- -
_____

Which ingredient is listed fourth?

_____
- -
_____

What do you do first to make a Fruit Juice Shake?

_____
- -

Home Note Your child has been learning about using numbers to 100.
ACTIVITY Have your child practice putting numbers in order when you use recipes together at home.

Harcourt Brace School Publishers

Name _____

| Calculator | Computer |

Use a 🖩.
Write the keys you press.
Write the mystery numbers.

1 What number is 10 greater than 25?

| ON/C | 2 | 5 | + | 1 | 0 | = | 35 |

2 What number is 25 less than 60?

| ON/C | | | | | | = | |

Mystery number

3 What number is 15 greater than 20?

| ON/C | | | | | | = | |

Mystery number

4 What number is 30 less than 65?

| ON/C | | | | | | = | |

Mystery number

What is the mystery number? _____

5 Monika's mystery number is 27. Draw the keys to show one way Monika could get 27.

Get on the Bus

written by Ann Lee
illustrated by Liisa Chauncy Guida

This book will help me review numbers to 100.

This book belongs to _____

Harcourt Brace School Publishers

Bear got into his big yellow bus to take some animals to their yearly picnic. "My bus holds only 100 animals," he said.

Bear came to the pond and saw some frogs. "Are there 100 of you?" he asked the frogs.

"No," said one frog. "There are _____ of us." The frogs got into Bear's big yellow bus.

The frogs were singing in the bus as Bear drove on down the road. A swarm of bees flew around Bear and his bus. "Are there 100 of you?" he asked the bees.

"No," said one bee. "There are _____ of us." The bees flew into the bus and sang with the frogs.

Around a turn in the road, Bear came to some
families of opossums hanging from a branch. Bear called,
"Are there 100 of you?"

"No," called down one opossum. "There are _____ of
us." The opossums got into the bus, but they did not sing.

Pretty soon a big bunch of grasshoppers jumped onto Bear's bus. "Are there 100 of you?" asked Bear. The animals in the bus stopped singing to listen to Bear and the grasshoppers.

"No," said one grasshopper. "There are _____ of us." The grasshoppers got on top of the bus.

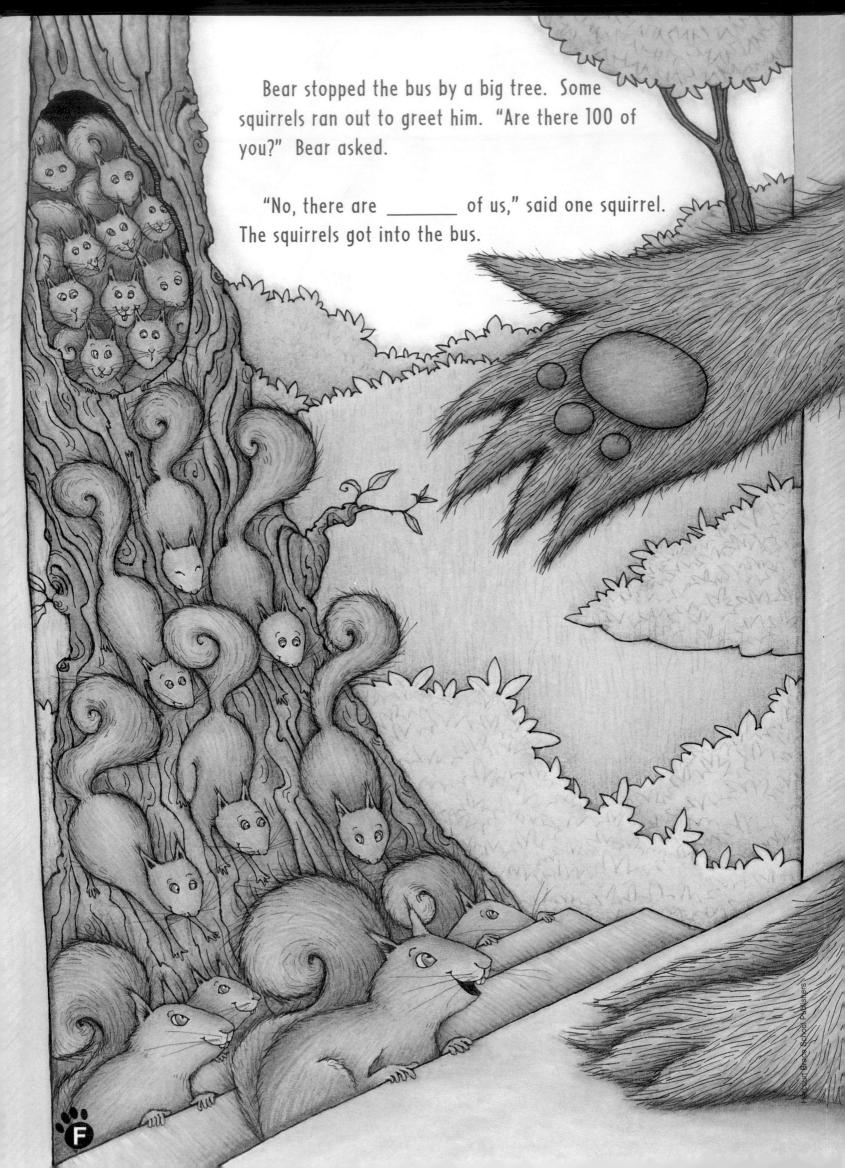

Bear stopped the bus by a big tree. Some squirrels ran out to greet him. "Are there 100 of you?" Bear asked.

"No, there are _____ of us," said one squirrel. The squirrels got into the bus.

F

Bear drove the bus until he came to some songbirds sitting on tree branches. "Hi!" said Bear. "Are there 100 of you?"

"No," said one bird. "There are _____ of us." The songbirds flew to the top of the bus and joined the grasshoppers.

Bear and the animals arrived at the picnic site. The frogs, the bees, the opossums, the grasshoppers, the squirrels, and the songbirds were excited to be together at the picnic. As Bear drove away, he heard one bee say, "Now there are 100 of us!"

Name _____

Concepts And Skills

Write how many tens and ones.
Then write the number.

 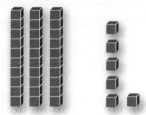

_____ tens _____ ones = _____

 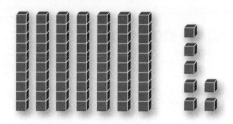

_____ tens _____ ones = _____

Look at the model. Circle the number that it shows.

37   47   57

38   73   83

5 Count by fives.

35,   40,   _____, _____, _____, _____, _____

6 Count by threes.

3,   6,   _____, _____, _____, _____, _____

Draw the number of cubes. Write even or odd.

6 _____   11 _____

9 Count on by tens.

27, _____, _____, _____, _____, 77, _____, _____

10 Count back by tens.

96, _____, _____, _____, 56, _____, _____, _____

Write greater or less. Then write > or < in the circle.

11 35 is _____ than 53.

35 ◯ 53

12 60 is _____ than 59.

60 ◯ 59

Write the number that is just after, just before, or between.

13 29, _____

14 _____, 50

15 63, _____, 65

Problem Solving

Draw a model. Write the number.

16 How many bees are in the hive?
• There are 4 groups of 10 bees.
• There are 2 bees alone.

_____ tens _____ ones = _____ bees

Use the number line to solve.

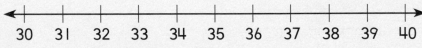
30 31 32 33 34 35 36 37 38 39 40

17 Joe has 34 marbles.
• Is 34 closer to 30 or 40? _____

• About how many marbles
  does Joe have?   about _____ marbles

Harcourt Brace School Publishers

Name _____

Performance Assessment

Use Workmat 3 and .

Build three numbers between 11 and 99.

Draw a picture to show each number.
Write how many tens and ones.
Then write the number.

1 _____ tens

_____ ones

_____ .

2 _____ tens

_____ ones

3 _____ tens

_____ ones

Write two of the numbers.
Circle the number that is greater.

4 _____   _____

Write About It

5 Write an even number.
Draw a picture to show how you
know the number is even.

_____

Name _____

Fill in the ⬭ for the correct answer.

1
7
+8
○ 13
○ 14
○ 15
○ 16

2
3
3
+6
○ 11
○ 12
○ 13
○ 14

3
14
−5
○ 7
○ 8
○ 9
○ 10

4
18
−9
○ 8
○ 9
○ 10
○ 11

5 How many tens and ones are there?

○ 1 ten 9 ones
○ 9 tens 1 one
○ 19 tens 0 ones
○ not here

6 Which is the number?

○ 8
○ 26
○ 46
○ 62

7 Count by threes. Which number comes after 15?

9, 12, 15, _____

○ 14   ○ 16
○ 17   ○ 18

8 Is 13 an even or odd number?

○ even   ○ odd

9 Which number is greater?

○ 36   ○ 26

10 Which number is less?

○ 47   ○ 74

11 Which number is just after 35?

35, _____
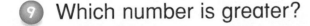

○ 34   ○ 37
○ 45   ○ not here

12 Which number is just before 81?

_____, 81
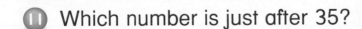

○ 71   ○ 79
○ 80   ○ not here

Cumulative Review • Chapters 1–5

Harcourt Brace School Publishers

Counting Money

25¢ 35¢ 45¢ 80¢

35¢ 50¢ 65¢ 40¢

75¢ 20¢ 50¢ 85¢ 25¢

80¢ What could you buy with these coins? 80¢ 20¢

40¢ 80¢ 90¢

Home Note In this chapter, your child will learn to count coins.
ACTIVITY Ask your child which item he or she would choose and
which coins he or she would use to buy it.

SCHOOL-HOME CONNECTION

Dear Family,
   Today we started Chapter 6. We will count with coins to 99¢, using combinations of pennies, nickels, dimes, quarters, and half-dollars. Here are the new vocabulary words and an activity for us to do together at home.

Love,

_____

Vocabulary

Set out the following coins: **penny**, **nickel**, **dime**, and **quarter**. Ask your child to name each coin and tell you its value. Then set out coins with a total of up to 99¢. Ask your child to tell you the total amount.

25¢,   35¢,   40¢,

45¢,   46¢

ACTIVITY

Ask your child to choose one grocery item that costs 99¢ or less. Have him or her use pennies, nickels, dimes, and quarters to show what coins could be used to buy the item.

Visit our Web site for additional activities and ideas.
http://www.hbschool.com

Pennies, Nickels, and Dimes

 or

I penny = 1¢

 or

I nickel = 5¢

 or

I dime = 10¢

Count on to find the total amount.

1

$\underline{1\,0}$ ¢, $\underline{2\,0}$ ¢, $\underline{2\,5}$ ¢, $\underline{3\,0}$ ¢, $\underline{3\,5}$ ¢, $\underline{3\,6}$ ¢ $\boxed{3\,6}$ ¢

2

_____ ¢, _____ ¢, _____ ¢, _____ ¢, _____ ¢, _____ ¢ ☐ ¢

3

_____ ¢, _____ ¢, _____ ¢, _____ ¢, _____ ¢, _____ ¢ ☐ ¢

4

_____ ¢, _____ ¢, _____ ¢, _____ ¢, _____ ¢, _____ ¢ ☐ ¢

5

_____ ¢, _____ ¢, _____ ¢, _____ ¢, _____ ¢, _____ ¢ ☐ ¢

Count on to find the total amount.

1

10¢, 20¢, 30¢, 40¢, 45¢, 50¢ 50¢

2

_____¢, _____¢, _____¢, _____¢, _____¢, _____¢ ☐ ¢

3

_____¢, _____¢, _____¢, _____¢, _____¢ _____¢ ☐ ¢

4

_____¢, _____¢, _____¢, _____¢, _____¢, _____¢ ☐ ¢

5

_____¢, _____¢, _____¢, _____¢, _____¢, _____¢ ☐ ¢

Mixed Review

Write > or < in the circle.

6 7 ◯ 70   **7** 25 ◯ 27   **8** 15 ◯ 13

 Home Note Your child counted pennies, nickels, and dimes to find the the total amount.
ACTIVITY Have your child practice finding total amounts of groups of coins to 50¢.

110 one hundred ten

Chapter 6

Harcourt Brace School Publishers

Nickels, Dimes, and Quarters

 or   or    or

I nickel = 5¢   I dime = 10¢   I quarter = 25¢

Count on to find the total amount.

1

2 5 ¢, 3 5 ¢, 4 0 ¢, 4 5 ¢, 4 6 ¢, 4 7 ¢ [4 7] ¢

2

_____ ¢, _____ ¢, _____ ¢, _____ ¢, _____ ¢, _____ ¢ [ ] ¢

3

_____ ¢, _____ ¢, _____ ¢, _____ ¢, _____ ¢, _____ ¢ [ ] ¢

4

_____ ¢, _____ ¢, _____ ¢, _____ ¢, _____ ¢, _____ ¢ [ ] ¢

Talk About It • Critical Thinking

What groups of nickels and dimes have the same value as I quarter?

Count on to find the total amount.

1.

25 ¢, 30 ¢, 31 ¢, 32 ¢, 33 ¢, 34 ¢ | 34 | ¢

2.

_____ ¢, _____ ¢, _____ ¢, _____ ¢, _____ ¢, _____ ¢ | | ¢

3.

_____ ¢, _____ ¢, _____ ¢, _____ ¢, _____ ¢, _____ ¢ | | ¢

4.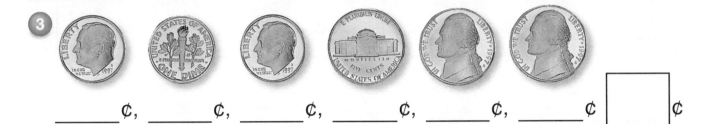

_____ ¢, _____ ¢, _____ ¢, _____ ¢, _____ ¢, _____ ¢ | | ¢

Problem Solving

Draw coins to solve.

5. Jill has 1 quarter, 1 dime, and 4 pennies. How much money does she have?

_____ ¢

🏠 **Home Note** Your child counted collections of coins to 50¢.
ACTIVITY Have your child practice counting mixed groups of coins to 50¢.

Harcourt Brace School Publishers

Draw and label the coins in order
from greatest to least value.
Write the total amount.

When you count with
coins, start with the
coin of greatest value.
Count on to the coins
of least value.

46 ¢

_____ ¢

_____ ¢

_____ ¢

Practice

Draw and label the coins in order from greatest to least value. Write the total amount.

1

(25¢) (10¢) (10¢) (5¢) (5¢)

55 ¢

2

_____ ¢

3

_____ ¢

4

_____ ¢

Write About It

5 Write about something you can buy. Draw the coins you would use to buy it.

Math Journal

Home Note Your child counted mixed collections of coins.
ACTIVITY Set out a group of coins with a total of up to 99¢. Have your child order them from greatest to least value and tell the total amount.

114 one hundred fourteen

Chapter 6

Harcourt Brace School Publishers

Name _____

 or

1 half-dollar = 2 quarters

1 half-dollar = 50¢

Write the total amount.

1

88 ¢

2

_____ ¢

3

_____ ¢

4

_____ ¢

Talk About It • Critical Thinking

What groups of nickels, dimes, and quarters have the same value as 1 half-dollar?

Write the total amount.

1

59 ¢

2

_____ ¢

3

_____ ¢

4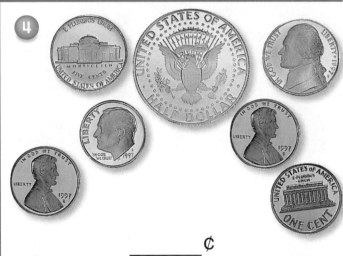

_____ ¢

Problem Solving

Draw a picture.
Solve.

5 Joe has 1 half-dollar, 2 dimes, and 5 pennies. How much money does he have?

_____ ¢

 Home Note Your child identified and counted half-dollars.
ACTIVITY Have your child practice counting mixed groups of coins to 99¢.

Understand • Plan • Solve • Look Back

Use coins to show the price.
Write how many of each coin you used.

1 Susan buys pizza for 76¢. What coins can she use? **76¢**	1	1	0	0	1
2 Dave buys a muffin for 91¢. What coins can he use? **91¢**					
3 Mary buys a cookie for 85¢. What coins can she use? **85¢**					
4 Bill buys a piece of pie for 57¢. What coins can he use? **57¢**					

Use coins to show the price.
Write how many of each coin you used.

	Half Dollar	Quarter	Dime	Nickel	Penny
① Lin buys a potato for 89¢. What coins can she use? **89¢**	1	1	1	0	4
② Jason buys a donut for 68¢. What coins can he use? **68¢**					
③ Carol buys a roll for 97¢. What coins can she use? **97¢**					
④ Tom buys a piece of cake for 75¢. What coins can he use? **75¢**					

Home Note Your child used the strategy Act It Out to solve problems.
ACTIVITY Set out an item that costs up to 99¢. Have your child show you the coins that could be used to buy it.

Harcourt Brace School Publishers

Name _____

Concepts and Skills

Count on to find the total amount.

_____ ¢, _____ ¢, _____ ¢, _____ ¢, _____ ¢, _____ ¢ [ ] ¢

Draw and label the coins in order from greatest to least value. Write the total amount.

_____ ¢

Write the total amount.

_____ ¢

_____ ¢

Problem Solving

Use coins to show the price. Write how many of each coin you used.

 Bill buys an ice cream cone for 49¢. What coins can he use?

 49¢

_____ _____ _____ _____

Name _____

Test Prep

Mark the best answer.

1 Kevin has 6 toy trucks, 2 toy cars, and 5 toy horses. How many toys does he have?

- ○ 10
- ○ 16
- ○ 14
- ○ 13

2 Joe saw 15 ducks. Then 7 swam away. How many ducks are left?

- ○ 6
- ○ 7
- ○ 8
- ○ 9

3 Sue has these coins. How much money does she have?

- ○ 58¢
- ○ 35¢
- ○ 48¢
- ○ 40¢

4 Melanie counts her marbles. She has 5 groups of ten with 8 left over. How many marbles does she have?

- ○ 85
- ○ 58
- ○ 55
- ○ 88

5 Which ball is third?

first

- ○ blue
- ○ yellow
- ○ red
- ○ green

6 Is 87 greater than or less than 38?

- ○ greater than
- ○ less than

Using Money

What are some different coins you could use to buy an apple?

Apples
25¢

Home Note In this chapter, your child is learning to use coins and count change.
ACTIVITY Have your child show you which coins he or she could use to buy an apple.

SCHOOL-HOME CONNECTION

Dear Family,
   Today we started Chapter 7. We will learn to show amounts of money. We will also learn to compare prices and to make change by using pennies. Here are the new vocabulary words and an activity for us to do together at home.

Love,

_____

Vocabulary

Give your child some pennies, nickels, and dimes. Have him or her group the coins in as many different ways as possible to make 25¢. Ask your child to tell about the different combinations, using the words **penny**, **nickel**, and **dime**.

penny   **nickel**   **dime**

ACTIVITY

As you and your child shop, let him or her pick out an item that costs 99¢ or less. Give your child more than enough coins to buy the item. Ask him or her to choose the coins needed to pay for the item.

 Visit our Web site for additional ideas and activities.
http://www.hbschool.com

Name _____

Use coins.
Show the amount of money in two ways.
Draw and label each coin.

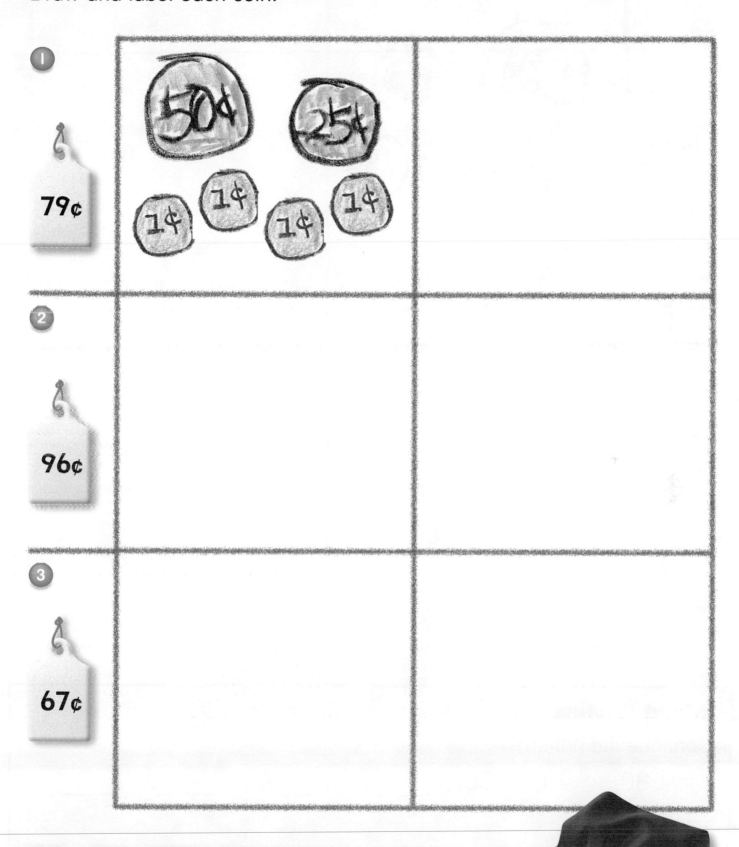

1. 79¢   50¢   25¢   1¢ 1¢ 1¢ 1¢

2. 96¢

3. 67¢

Talk About It • **Critical Thinking**

What is another way to show 67¢?

Harcourt Brace School Publishers

Use coins. Show the amount of money in two ways.
Draw and label each coin.

 1

 58¢

50¢   5¢
1¢   1¢   1¢

 2

 83¢

3

99¢

Mixed Review

Continue the pattern.

4   30,   40,   50, _____, _____, _____, _____

 Home Note Your child modeled the same amount of money in more than one way.
ACTIVITY Set out a group of pennies, nickels, dimes, and quarters. Work together to show 50¢ in
as many different ways as possible.

Name _____

Write the amount. Then use coins to show the same amount with fewer coins. Draw and label each coin.

1

75 ¢

2

_____ ¢

3

_____ ¢

Talk About It ● Critical Thinking

How can you show 62¢ with the fewest coins?

Practice

Write the amount. Then show the same amount with fewer coins. Draw and label each coin.

90¢

1

90 ¢

2

___ ¢

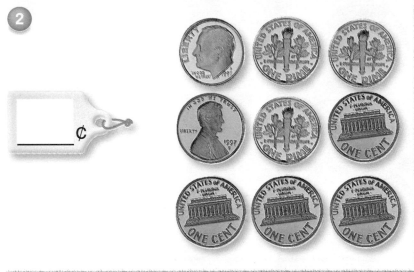

3

___ ¢

Harcourt Brace School Publishers

 Home Note Your child modeled amounts by using fewer coins.
ACTIVITY Set out a group of coins with a total of 99¢ or less. Have your child show the same amount with fewer coins.

Name _____

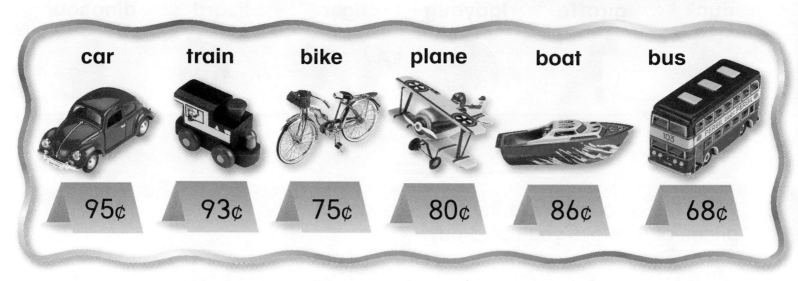

car	train	bike	plane	boat	bus
95¢	93¢	75¢	80¢	86¢	68¢

Write the amount. Write the names and prices of two toys you could buy.

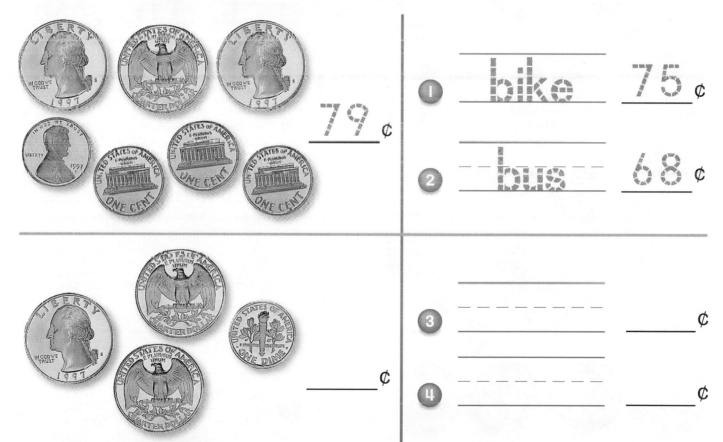

79 ¢

1 bike   75 ¢

2 bus   68 ¢

_____ ¢

3 _____   _____ ¢

4 _____   _____ ¢

_____ ¢

5 _____   _____ ¢

6 _____   _____ ¢

Practice

duck	giraffe	ladybug	tiger	lizard	dinosaur
65¢	70¢	90¢	79¢	85¢	99¢

Write the amount. Write the names and prices of two toys you could buy.

75 ¢

1. duck   65 ¢
2. giraffe 70 ¢

3. _____ _____ ¢

4. _____ _____ ¢

_____ ¢

5. _____ _____ ¢

6. _____ _____ ¢

_____ ¢

Write About It

7. You have 89¢. Which toy would you buy? Draw the fewest coins you need.

 Home Note Your child compared amounts to prices.
ACTIVITY Ask your child to count out loud each group of coins.

Harcourt Brace School Publishers

Chapter 7

Name _____

Count on from the price to find the change.

1 You have 20¢. You buy

16¢ 17¢, __18__¢, __19__¢, __20__¢

Your change is __4__ ¢

2 You have 40¢. You buy

37¢ 38¢, _____¢, _____¢

Your change is _____¢.

3 You have 35¢. You buy

33¢ 34¢, _____¢

Your change is _____¢.

4 You have 25¢. You buy

 21¢ 22¢, _____¢, _____¢, _____¢

Your change is _____¢.

Talk About It • Critical Thinking

How could you subtract to make change?

Count on from the price to find the change.

1 You have 50¢. You buy

48¢   49¢,   50 ¢

Your change is _____ 2 ¢

2 You have 65¢. You buy

62¢   63¢, _____ ¢, _____ ¢

Your change is _____ ¢.

3 You have 40¢. You buy

36¢   37¢, _____ ¢, _____ ¢, _____ ¢

Your change is _____ ¢.

Problem Solving • Visual Thinking

Use coins to solve.

4 Hans has 60¢. He buys a taco for 57¢. How much change does he get?

Hans gets _____ ¢ change.

Home Note Your child counted on from prices to determine change.
ACTIVITY When you buy items that cost less than 99¢, help your child count on from the price of the item to the amount given to the clerk to find the amount of change you get.

Name _____

Understand · Plan · Solve · Look Back

Use coins.
Solve. Then circle Yes or No.

1 Betty has 2 quarters, 1 dime,
   and 5 pennies. How much
   money does she have?

    65 ¢

   Does she have enough money
   to buy a loaf of bread?

   Yes   No

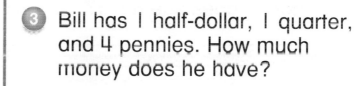

14¢   25¢   75¢   95¢   89¢

---

2 Lorna has 4 dimes, 2 nickels,
   and 3 pennies. How much
   money does she have?

   _____ ¢

   Does she have enough money
   to buy an apple?

   Yes   No

3 Bill has 1 half-dollar, 1 quarter,
   and 4 pennies. How much
   money does he have?

   _____ ¢

   Does he have enough money
   to buy milk?

   Yes   No

---

4 Peter has 1 quarter, 2 dimes,
   and 5 pennies. How much
   money does he have?

   _____ ¢

   Does he have enough money
   to buy eggs?

   Yes   No

5 Denise has 2 nickels and
   4 pennies. How much money
   does she have?

   _____ ¢

   Does she have enough money
   to buy a banana?

   Yes   No

Harcourt Brace School Publishers

Chapter 7 • Using Money

Practice

Use coins.
Solve. Then circle Yes or No.

1. Monika has 1 quarter, 2 dimes, and 3 pennies. How much money does she have?

    ¢

   Does she have enough money to buy a pencil?

   (Yes)   No

---

2. Kathy has 2 quarters, 1 nickel, and 2 pennies. How much money does she have?

   _____ ¢

   Does she have enough money to buy a ruler?

   Yes   No

3. José has 1 half-dollar, 4 dimes, and 9 pennies. How much money does he have?

   _____ ¢

   Does he have enough money to buy a box of crayons?

   Yes   No

4. Kim has 2 nickels and 5 pennies. How much money does she have?

   _____ ¢

   Does she have enough money to buy an eraser?

   Yes   No

5. Roberto has 3 dimes, 1 nickel, and 3 pennies. How much money does he have?

   _____ ¢

   Does he have enough money to buy paper?

   Yes   No

Home Note Your child used the strategy Act It Out to solve problems.
ACTIVITY Give your child some coins and an item priced less than 99¢. Ask him or her to tell if there is enough money to buy the item.

Harcourt Brace School Publishers

Chapter 7

Concepts and Skills

Write the amount. Then show
the same amount with fewer coins.
Draw and label each coin.

1

_____ ¢

Count on from the price to find the change.

2 You have 60¢. You buy

 57¢

58¢, _____ ¢, _____ ¢

Your change is _____ ¢.

Problem Solving

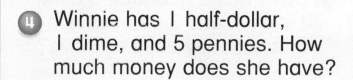

65¢

Use coins.
Solve. Then circle Yes or No.

3 Janie has 2 quarters,
1 nickel, and 2 pennies. How
much money does she have?

_____ ¢

Does she have enough
money to buy the car?

Yes   No

4 Winnie has 1 half-dollar,
1 dime, and 5 pennies. How
much money does she have?

_____ ¢

Does she have enough
money to buy the car?

Yes   No

Name _____

Test Prep

Mark the best answer.

1 Carla has 68 buttons. How many groups of ten can she make with them?

- ○ 6
- ○ 2
- ○ 14
- ○ 8

2 Dina picked 9 apples. Jake picked 7 apples. How many apples did they pick in all?

- ○ 2
- ○ 11
- ○ 17
- ○ 16

3 Dave has 2 quarters, 3 dimes, 1 nickel, and 3 pennies. How much money does he have?

- ○ 63¢
- ○ 78¢
- ○ 88¢
- ○ 83¢

4 Which number belongs below the point that is circled on the number line?

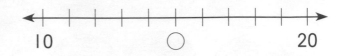

10   ○   20

- ○ 12
- ○ 15
- ○ 18
- ○ 22

5 Faye has 3 quarters. Does she have enough money to buy a muffin for 69¢?

- ○ yes
- ○ no

6 What are the next two numbers in the pattern?

3, 6, 9, 12, ____, ____

- ○ 11, 10
- ○ 13, 14
- ○ 15, 18
- ○ 18, 24

Harcourt Brace School Publishers

CHAPTER 8

Time on the Clock

What time do you go to school? What time do you go home?

Home Note In this chapter, your child will learn to tell time.
ACTIVITY Talk about what time your child leaves for school and arrives back home.

Dear Family,
    Today we started Chapter 8. We will learn how to tell time. Here are the new vocabulary words and an activity for us to do together at home.

Love,

_____

Vocabulary

As you talk with your child about his or her math work, use the words **hour hand** and **minute hand** to talk about the parts of a clock.

hour hand

minute hand

analog clock

digital clock

ACTIVITY

Ask your child to tell you what time a favorite TV show starts and what time the show ends. Have him or her tell you how long the show lasts.

Visit our Web site for additional ideas and activities.
http://www.hbschool.com

Harcourt Brace School Publishers

Name _____

minute hand
hour hand

 5:00

 There are 30 minutes in 1 half-hour.

hour hand
minute hand

5:30

Read the time. Write the time.

 ①

 ②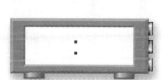

 ③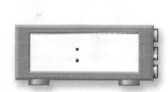

 ④

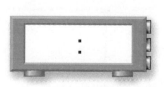 ⑤

 ⑥

  ⑦

 ⑧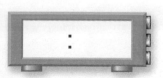

Talk About It ● Critical Thinking

Where is the minute hand when the clock shows the half-hour? Why?

Read the time. Write the time.

1. 4:30

2. :

3. :

4. :

5. :

6. :

7. :

8. :

9. :

10. :

11. :

12. :

Mixed Review

Write the amount. Then show the same amount with fewer coins. Draw and label each coin.

13.

_____ ¢

 Home Note Your child told the time to the hour and half-hour.
ACTIVITY On the hour and half-hour, ask your child to tell you the time.

Harcourt Brace School Publishers

Chapter 8

Name _____

Write the time.

1

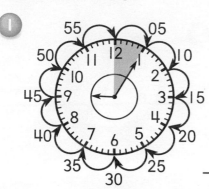

You can count by fives to find the minutes after the hour.

9:05

2

_____ : _____

3

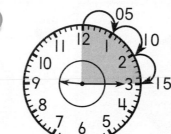

_____ : _____

4

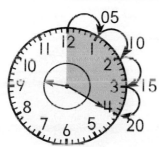

_____ : _____

5

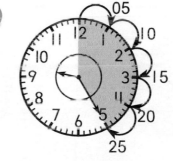

_____ : _____

6

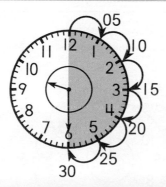

_____ : _____

7

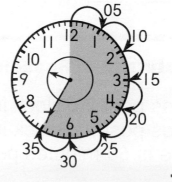

_____ : _____

Talk About It ● Critical Thinking

Why is it easier to count by fives than by ones to tell time?

Chapter 8 • Time on the Clock

one hundred thirty-nine **139**

Harcourt Brace School Publishers

Practice

Write the time.

1

5:15

2

___ : ___

3

___ : ___

4

___ : ___

5

___ : ___

6

___ : ___

7

___ : ___

8

___ : ___

9

___ : ___

Problem Solving ● Reasoning

10 50 minutes past 2 o'clock is 2:50.
55 minutes past 2 o'clock is 2:55.
What time is 60 minutes past 2 o'clock?

___ : ___

 Home Note Your child told the time to 5 minutes.
ACTIVITY Ask your child to tell you the time to 5 minutes.

140 one hundred forty

Harcourt Brace School Publishers

Chapter 8

Name _____

Write the time.

1 15 minutes 30 minutes

7:15

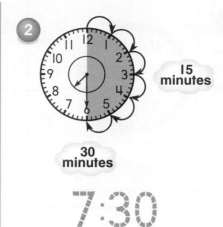

2 15 minutes 30 minutes

7:30

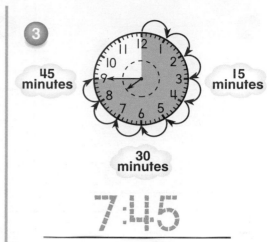

3 45 minutes 15 minutes 30 minutes

7:45

4 15 minutes

_____

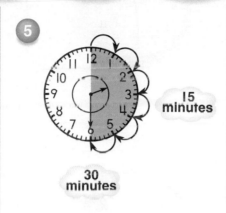

5 15 minutes 30 minutes

_____

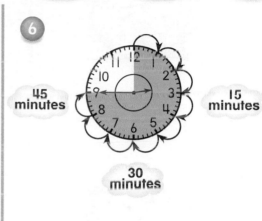

6 45 minutes 15 minutes 30 minutes

_____

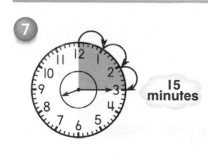

7 15 minutes

_____

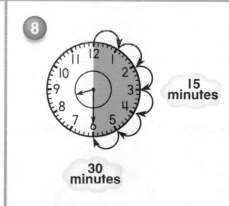

8 15 minutes 30 minutes

_____

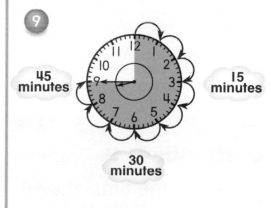

9 45 minutes 15 minutes 30 minutes

_____

Talk About It • Critical Thinking

What time will it be 15 minutes after 8:45?
How do you know?

Practice

Write the time.

1

1:45

2

_____

3

_____

4

_____

5

_____

6

_____

7

_____

8

_____

9

_____

Write About It

10 Write the time shown on the clock. Write about something you do at this time.

 Home Note Your child told the time to 15 minutes.
ACTIVITY Have your child tell you the time to 15 minutes.

Chapter 8

Name _____

Draw the minute hand to show the time.

1

4:15

2

9:35

3

10:05

4

6:15

5

8:25

6

11:10

7

7:45

8

3:40

9

2:00

10

12:30

11

5:20

Chapter 8 • Time on the Clock

one hundred forty-three **143**

Practice

Write the time.

 ①  ②

9:05
_____

③
_____

_____

④  ⑤

⑥

_____

_____

_____

⑦  ⑧

⑨

_____

_____

_____

Problem Solving ● Reasoning

Circle 1 second or 1 minute.

⑩ It takes about 1 second to sneeze. It takes about 1 minute to wash your hands. About how long does it take to tie your shoes?

1 second   1 minute

⑪ It takes about 1 second to blink your eyes. It takes about 1 minute to sharpen your pencil. About how long does it take to smile?

1 second   1 minute

 Home Note Your child practiced telling the time.
ACTIVITY Have your child tell you the time every 5 minutes from 5 minutes to 55 minutes after the hour.

144 one hundred forty-four

Chapter 8

Name _____

Understand • Plan • Solve • Look Back

Problem Solving
Act It Out

Read the clock. Use a  to solve the problem.
Write the new time.

① Ann gets up at 	Ann leaves for school 1 hour later. What time does she leave for school? 8:00 _____	
② Sue goes to soccer practice at 	Soccer practice lasts 30 minutes. What time does soccer practice end? _____	
③ Juan goes to his friend's house at 	Juan comes home 2 hours later. What time does he come home? _____	
④ School ends at 	Bill gets home 10 minutes later. What time does he get home? _____	

Harcourt Brace School Publishers

Read the clock. Use a  to solve the problem.
Write the new time.

1 Jack starts playing the piano at 	He plays for 30 minutes. What time does he finish playing the piano? **2:30**	
2 School starts at 	Lunch is 3 hours later. What time is lunch? _____	
3 Judy starts her homework at 	It takes her 35 minutes. What time does she finish her homework? _____	
4 Peter starts playing kickball at	He plays for 2 hours. What time does he finish playing kickball? _____	

 Home Note Your child found how long activities took.
ACTIVITY Ask your child how long some of his or her activities take. Choose activities that last 30 minutes or 1 hour.

Harcourt Brace School Publishers

Name _____

Concepts and Skills

Write the time.

_____

②

_____

③

_____

④

_____

⑤

_____

⑥

_____

⑦

_____

⑧

_____

⑨

_____

Problem Solving

Read the clock. Use a 🕐 to solve the problem. Write the new time.

⑩ Sarah goes shopping with her mom at  .

They shop for 2 hours.
What time do they
finish shopping?

_____

Name _____

Test Prep

Mark the best answer.

1 What time is it?

- ○ 10:15
- ○ 9:50
- ○ 10:45
- ○ 10:05

2 What time is it?

- ○ 4:15
- ○ 3:20
- ○ 9:20
- ○ 6:30

3 Which number does the model show?

- ○ 32
- ○ 23
- ○ 37
- ○ 42

4 Gus has I quarter, I dime, 3 nickels, and 2 pennies. How much money does he have?

- ○ 28¢
- ○ 77¢
- ○ 52¢
- ○ 47¢

5 Which number sentence matches the picture?

- ○ $5 + 6 = 11$
- ○ $5 + 5 = 10$
- ○ $6 + 6 = 12$
- ○ $6 + 7 = 13$

6 Which number sentence matches the picture?

- ○ $9 + 3 = 12$
- ○ $9 + 2 = 11$
- ○ $9 - 2 = 7$
- ○ $9 - 3 = 6$

Standardized Test Prep • Chapters 1–8

Harcourt Brace School Publishers

Time: Days, Weeks, Months

What season is this?
How do you know?

Home Note In this chapter, your child will learn about days, weeks, and months.
ACTIVITY Talk about the picture. Ask what clues your child used to tell the season.

SCHOOL-HOME CONNECTION

Dear Family,
   Today we started Chapter 9. We will use a calendar, put events in order, and read a schedule. Here are the new vocabulary words and an activity for us to do together at home.

Love,

_____

Vocabulary

Look at this month's calendar page together, and find the parts of it that go with these words: **month**, **week**, **day**, and **date**.

month	→	January						
day	→	Sunday	Monday	Tuesday	Wednesday	Thursday	Friday	Saturday
					1	2	3	4
date	→	5	6	7	8	9	10	11
		12	13	14	15	16	17	18
week	→	19	20	21	22	23	24	25
		26	27	28	29	30	31	

ACTIVITY

Help your child make a schedule of the activities that he or she does at home, such as homework, watching television, and helping with chores.

	6:00-6:30	6:30-7:00	7:00-7:30
Monday	wash dishes		
Tuesday		homework	watch TV
Wednesday	wash dishes		
Thursday			
Friday	wash dishes	homework	
Saturday			
Sunday		watch TV	

Visit our Web site for additional ideas and activities.
http://www.hbschool.com

Use the calendar to answer the questions.

NOVEMBER

Sunday	Monday	Tuesday	Wednesday	Thursday	Friday	Saturday
					1	2
3	4	5	6	7	8	9
10	11	12	13	14	15	16
17	18	19	20	21	22	23
24	25	26	27	28 Thanksgiving	29	30

1 What is the date of the third Tuesday?   November 19

2 How many days are in the month? _____

3 What is the day and date of Thanksgiving? _____ , _____

4 How many Wednesdays are in this month? _____

5 On which day does the month end? _____

6 How many Saturdays are in the month? _____

Practice

Fill in the calendar for this month. Then use the calendar to answer the questions.

	Sunday	Monday	Tuesday	Wednesday	Thursday	Friday	Saturday

1. How many days are in this month? _____

2. On which day does the month begin? _____

3. How many Fridays are in this month? _____

4. On which day will the next month start? _____

5. What is the date of the second Saturday in the month? _____

Home Note Your child learned to read a calendar.
ACTIVITY Have your child read a calendar and tell you the day, month, and date.

Name _____

Use the calendar to answer the questions.

There are 7 days in 1 week.
There are 12 months in 1 year.

January	February	March	April
Su M T W Th F Sa	Su M T W Th F Sa	Su M T W Th F Sa	Su M T W Th F Sa
1 2 3 4	1	1	1 2 3 4 5
5 6 7 8 9 10 11	2 3 4 5 6 7 8	2 3 4 5 6 7 8	6 7 8 9 10 11 12
12 13 14 15 16 17 18	9 10 11 12 13 14 15	9 10 11 12 13 14 15	13 14 15 16 17 18 19
19 20 21 22 23 24 25	16 17 18 19 20 21 22	16 17 18 19 20 21 22	20 21 22 23 24 25 26
26 27 28 29 30 31	23 24 25 26 27 28	23 24 25 26 27 28 29	27 28 29 30
		30 31	

May	June	July	August
Su M T W Th F Sa	Su M T W Th F Sa	Su M T W Th F Sa	Su M T W Th F Sa
1 2 3	1 2 3 4 5 6 7	1 2 3 4 5	1 2
4 5 6 7 8 9 10	8 9 10 11 12 13 14	6 7 8 9 10 11 12	3 4 5 6 7 8 9
11 12 13 14 15 16 17	15 16 17 18 19 20 21	13 14 15 16 17 18 19	10 11 12 13 14 15 16
18 19 20 21 22 23 24	22 23 24 25 26 27 28	20 21 22 23 24 25 26	17 18 19 20 21 22 23
25 26 27 28 29 30 31	29 30	27 28 29 30 31	24 25 26 27 28 29 30
			31

September	October	November	December
Su M T W Th F Sa	Su M T W Th F Sa	Su M T W Th F Sa	Su M T W Th F Sa
1 2 3 4 5 6	1 2 3 4	1	1 2 3 4 5 6
7 8 9 10 11 12 13	5 6 7 8 9 10 11	2 3 4 5 6 7 8	7 8 9 10 11 12 13
14 15 16 17 18 19 20	12 13 14 15 16 17 18	9 10 11 12 13 14 15	14 15 16 17 18 19 20
21 22 23 24 25 26 27	19 20 21 22 23 24 25	16 17 18 19 20 21 22	21 22 23 24 25 26 27
28 29 30	26 27 28 29 30 31	23 24 25 26 27 28 29	28 29 30 31
		30	

1 On which month does the year begin? _____ January

2 Which month follows October? _____

3 Which month has the fewest days? _____

4 Which is the fifth month in the year? _____

5 Name the month in which school starts. _____

6 Circle your birthday.
Write the month and the date. _____ _____

Use the calendar to answer the questions.

January						
Su	M	T	W	Th	F	Sa
		1	2	3	4	
5	6	7	8	9	10	11
12	13	14	15	16	17	18
19	20	21	22	23	24	25
26	27	28	29	30	31	

February						
Su	M	T	W	Th	F	Sa
						1
2	3	4	5	6	7	8
9	10	11	12	13	14	15
16	17	18	19	20	21	22
23	24	25	26	27	28	

March						
Su	M	T	W	Th	F	Sa
						1
2	3	4	5	6	7	8
9	10	11	12	13	14	15
16	17	18	19	20	21	22
23	24	25	26	27	28	29
30	31					

April						
Su	M	T	W	Th	F	Sa
		1	2	3	4	5
6	7	8	9	10	11	12
13	14	15	16	17	18	19
20	21	22	23	24	25	26
27	28	29	30			

May						
Su	M	T	W	Th	F	Sa
				1	2	3
4	5	6	7	8	9	10
11	12	13	14	15	16	17
18	19	20	21	22	23	24
25	26	27	28	29	30	31

June						
Su	M	T	W	Th	F	Sa
1	2	3	4	5	6	7
8	9	10	11	12	13	14
15	16	17	18	19	20	21
22	23	24	25	26	27	28
29	30					

July						
Su	M	T	W	Th	F	Sa
		1	2	3	4	5
6	7	8	9	10	11	12
13	14	15	16	17	18	19
20	21	22	23	24	25	26
27	28	29	30	31		

August						
Su	M	T	W	Th	F	Sa
					1	2
3	4	5	6	7	8	9
10	11	12	13	14	15	16
17	18	19	20	21	22	23
24	25	26	27	28	29	30
31						

September						
Su	M	T	W	Th	F	Sa
	1	2	3	4	5	6
7	8	9	10	11	12	13
14	15	16	17	18	19	20
21	22	23	24	25	26	27
28	29	30				

October						
Su	M	T	W	Th	F	Sa
			1	2	3	4
5	6	7	8	9	10	11
12	13	14	15	16	17	18
19	20	21	22	23	24	25
26	27	28	29	30	31	

November						
Su	M	T	W	Th	F	Sa
						1
2	3	4	5	6	7	8
9	10	11	12	13	14	15
16	17	18	19	20	21	22
23	24	25	26	27	28	29
30						

December						
Su	M	T	W	Th	F	Sa
	1	2	3	4	5	6
7	8	9	10	11	12	13
14	15	16	17	18	19	20
21	22	23	24	25	26	27
28	29	30	31			

1. What day is February 27?

Thursday

2. What is the date that follows November 30?

_____

3. What is the date one week before January 17?

_____

4. How many Mondays are in September?

_____

5. Name another month that has the same number of days as April.

_____

6. What is the date one week after May 11?

_____

Home Note Your child learned to use a calendar.
ACTIVITY Point out a date on a calendar. Ask your child to tell you the days and dates one week before and one week after that date.

Name _____

Write each time. Write early or late.

 Before the time is early. After the time is late.

① School starts at  .

9:00

Joe gets there at  .

9:15

Is Joe early or late?

late

---

② Sue is meeting Karen at the movie at

_____

Sue gets there at 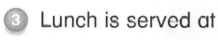 .

_____

Is Sue early or late?

_____

---

③ Lunch is served at  .

_____

Juan gets there at .

_____

Is Juan early or late?

_____

---

④ Matt needs to be home by .

_____

Matt gets there at  .

_____

Is Matt early or late?

_____

Harcourt Brace School Publishers

Write each time. Write early or late.

1 Soccer practice starts at .

Lin gets there at  .

Is Lin early or late?

3:30

3:20

early

---

2 Al is to meet Bobby at the game at .

Al gets there at .

Is Al early or late?

_____

_____

_____

---

3 The circus starts at  .

Monika gets there at  .

Is Monika early or late?

_____

_____

_____

Mixed Review

4 Count on to find the total amount.

_____¢, _____¢, _____¢, _____¢, _____¢, _____¢ _____¢

 Home Note Your child learned the concepts early and late.
ACTIVITY Discuss what time your child leaves for school. Say a time just before or just after that time. Have your child tell you whether the time is earlier or later than when he or she leaves for school.

Harcourt Brace School Publishers

Nathan and his dad made a cake.
Number the events in order.
Use the clocks to write the time of each event.

_____ _____   _____ _____

_____ _____   I   3:00

Talk About It ● **Critical Thinking**

How did you decide what time went with each picture?

1 Monika is getting ready for school.
Number the events in order.
Use the clocks to write the time of each event.

_____ _____

| : _____   7:00

_____ _____

_____ _____

Write About It

2 Write about getting ready to
go home after school.
Number the events in order.
Write the time of each event.

Math Journal

 Home Note Your child learned to sequence events.
ACTIVITY Ask your child to tell you in order the things he or she does to get ready for school and
the time he or she does each thing.

Chapter 9

Name _____

Use the schedule to answer the questions.

A schedule is a list showing when events happen.

My School Day

9:00–10:00 Math

10:00–10:30 Recess

10:30–11:30 Language Arts

11:30–12:00 Reading

12:00–1:00 Lunch

1:00–1:30 Science

1:30–2:00 Social Studies

2:00–2:30 Art

1. What time does reading class begin?

_11:30_

2. What time does science class end?

_____

3. How long is math class?

_____ hour

4. What time does school start?

_____

5. How long is recess?

_____ minutes

6. How much time passes from the end of lunch to the beginning of art class?

_____ hour

Harcourt Brace School Publishers

Practice

Make a schedule for your school day.
Use it to answer the questions.

My School Day

1. What time does the school day start?

   _____

2. What time does the school day end?

   _____

3. How long is math class?

   _____

4. What time is lunch?

   _____

5. What is your favorite time at school? Tell why this is your favorite time.

   _____

   _____

   _____

Harcourt Brace School Publishers

Home Note Your child learned to read a schedule.
ACTIVITY Help your child make a schedule of one weekend day's activities.

Name _____

Concepts and Skills

Use the calendar to answer the questions.

May						
Su	M	T	W	Th	F	Sa
				1	2	3
4	5	6	7	8	9	10
11	12	13	14	15	16	17
18	19	20	21	22	23	24
25	26	27	28	29	30	31

1 What is the date of the third Tuesday in May? _____

2 On which day does May end? _____

Write each time. Write early or late.

3 Ann's piano lesson is at . _____

Ann gets there at . _____

Is Ann early or late? _____

Number the events in order.
Use the clocks to write the time of each event.

4 | 2:25 | 2:20 | 2:30 |

_____ _____   _____ _____   _____ _____

Name _____

Test Prep

Mark the best answer.

1 What time is it?

- ◯ 6:15
- ◯ 6:35
- ◯ 7:30
- ◯ 7:45

2 Which is the total amount?

- ◯ 53¢
- ◯ 28¢
- ◯ 48¢
- ◯ 43¢

3 Ava had 4 hair bows. She made 7 more. How many does she have now?

- ◯ 8
- ◯ 3
- ◯ 11
- ◯ 14

4 Mike had 15 chips. He ate 7 chips. How many chips are left?

- ◯ 1
- ◯ 2
- ◯ 4
- ◯ 8

5 Look at the pattern.

60, 65, 70, 75, 80, ___, ___

Which numbers come next?

- ◯ 79, 78
- ◯ 81, 82
- ◯ 85, 86
- ◯ 85, 90

Name _____

My Story in Time

Write a story about the things you like to do during these 4 months.

December
Winter Fun

October
Fall Fun

September
School Starts

November
Thanksgiving

Harcourt Brace School Publishers

Home Note Your child has been learning about the calendar.
ACTIVITY Have your child write a story about the things he or she likes to do during the first 4 months of the year.

Technology

Name _____

| Calculator | Computer |

Use a 🖩.
Write the keys you press.
Write the answer.

1 Today is September 3. Sandy's birthday is in 2 weeks.
What is the date of her birthday?

ON/C | 3 | + | 7 | + | 7 | = | 17

September 17

2 Tina's uncle gave her 1 quarter, 1 dime, and 1 nickel.
How much did he give her?

ON/C | 2 | 5 | + | 1 | 0 | + | 5 | = | 40

40 ¢

3 Today is November 6. Thanksgiving is in 3 weeks.
What is the date of Thanksgiving?

ON/C | | | | | | | | = |

November _____

4 Barry found 1 quarter and 2 dimes in his pocket.
How much did he find?

ON/C | | | | | | | | | = |

_____ ¢

Harcourt Brace School Publishers

Grandma Rabbit's Birthday

written by Lucy Floyd

 This book will help me review time and money.

This book belongs to _____.

Rabbit woke up very excited for today was Grandma Rabbit's birthday. "Grandma's birthday party is at 3:00!" said Rabbit. "I must buy a gift for her! Let me see.

I have _____ ¢"

Rabbit met Toad on the way to the store. "Where are you going in such a hurry, Rabbit?" asked Toad.

"Today is Grandma Rabbit's birthday, and I must buy a gift for her!" said Rabbit.

"The party is at 3:00! My watch says _____."

"You have too many coins. You could lose some of those coins," Toad said. "Let me help you. You have 75¢. I can make the same amount with fewer coins. Trade with me."

Circle the coins that Toad can trade with Rabbit.

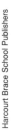
Harcourt Brace School Publishers

Then Rabbit met Turtle on the way to the store. "Where are you going in such a hurry, Rabbit?" asked Turtle.

"Today is Grandma Rabbit's birthday and I must buy a gift for her!" said Rabbit. "The party is at 3:00!

My watch says _____."

"You have too many coins. You could
lose some of those coins," Turtle said.
"Let me help you. You have 75¢. I can
make the same amount with fewer coins.
Trade with me."

Circle the coins that Turtle can trade
with Rabbit.

Harcourt Brace School Publishers

"Today is Grandma Rabbit's birthday and
now I can buy a gift for her," said Rabbit
as he looked at all the presents in the store.
What will Rabbit buy for Grandma?

"My watch says _____!"

How many minutes does Rabbit have to get

to the party? _____ minutes.

"Hurray!" said Rabbit. "I am the happiest rabbit because I got to the birthday party on time, and I have a gift for Grandma!"

Name _____

Concepts and Skills

1 Count on to find the total amount.

_____ ¢,   _____ ¢,   _____ ¢,   _____ ¢,   _____ ¢   ☐ ¢

2 Write the amount. Then show the same
amount with fewer coins. Draw and label each coin.

_____ ¢

3 Count on from the price to find the change.

You have 50¢. You buy

47¢

48¢,   _____ ¢,   _____ ¢

Your change is _____ ¢.

Write the time.

4

5

6

_____   _____   _____

7 Brad starts reading at  .

He reads for 30 minutes.
What time does he stop reading? _____

Use the calendar to
answer questions 8 and 9.

☀ **JULY** 🦋						
Sunday	Monday	Tuesday	Wednesday	Thursday	Friday	Saturday
		1	2	3	4	5
6	7	8	9	10	11	12
13	14	15	16	17	18	19
20	21	22	23	24	25	26
27	28	29	30	31		

8 On which day does the month begin? _____

9 What is the date of the third Sunday? _____

Problem Solving

10 Use coins to show the price.
Write how many of each coin you used.

67¢

_____   _____   _____   _____   _____

Chapters 6–9 • Review/Test

Name _____

Performance Assessment

Put 3 quarters, 3 dimes, 3 nickels and 3 pennies in a bag.

1 Take 5 coins. Draw and label the coins in order from greatest to least value.
Write the total amount.

	_____ ¢

2 Show the same amount with different coins.
Draw and label the coins.

_____ ¢	

_____ ¢	

Write About It

Solve.
Draw the hands on the
clock to show how you know.

3 Jo gets up to go to school at 7:30. She leaves for school 1 hour later. What time does she leave for school?

gets up

leaves for
school

_____

Harcourt Brace School Publishers

Name _____

Fill in the ◯ for the correct answer.

1
$$\begin{array}{r} 6 \\ +7 \\ \hline \end{array}$$
◯ 13
◯ 14
◯ 15
◯ 16

2
$$\begin{array}{r} 4 \\ +9 \\ \hline \end{array}$$
◯ 11
◯ 12
◯ 13
◯ 14

3
$$\begin{array}{r} 5 \\ 5 \\ +6 \\ \hline \end{array}$$
◯ 10
◯ 11
◯ 15
◯ 16

4
$$\begin{array}{r} 8 \\ 7 \\ +2 \\ \hline \end{array}$$
◯ 14
◯ 15
◯ 16
◯ 17

5 Which number sentence completes this fact family?

$$5 + 9 = 14$$
$$9 + 5 = 14$$
$$14 - 9 = 5$$

◯ $14 + 5 = 19$ ◯ $9 - 4 = 5$
◯ $14 - 5 = 9$ ◯ not here

6 Write + or −. Then solve.
There were 17 girls and 9 boys on the bus.
How many more girls than boys were there?

$$17 \bigcirc 9 = \underline{\qquad}$$

◯ 7 more girls   ◯ 8 more girls
◯ 17 more girls ◯ not here

7 Count by fives. Which number comes after 30?

$$20, 25, 30, \underline{\qquad}$$

◯ 31   ◯ 32
◯ 35   ◯ 40

8 Which is the pattern rule?

$$16, 18, 20, 22, 24$$

◯ Count by twos.
◯ Count by threes.
◯ Count by fives.
◯ Count by tens.

9 Count on.
Which is the total amount?

◯ 31¢   ◯ 35¢
◯ 45¢   ◯ not here

10 Beth has 1 quarter, 1 dime and 4 pennies.
How much money does she have?

◯ 34¢   ◯ 39¢
◯ 44¢   ◯ 93¢

CHAPTER 10 Exploring Two-Digit Addition

PET SHOW

ENTRIES
CATS 13
DOGS ... 20

What addition stories can you tell about the number of animals?

Home Note In this chapter your child is learning how to add two-digit numbers.
ACTIVITY Ask your child to tell you addition stories about the pet store.

SCHOOL-HOME CONNECTION

Dear Family,
  Today we started Chapter 10. We will begin to add two-digit numbers. Here are the new vocabulary words and an activity for us to do together at home.

  Love,

  _____

Vocabulary

When you add two numbers and the total of the two groups of ones is 10 or more, you need to **regroup**.

tens	ones
1	6
+	7
2	3

Add the **ones**.

$6 + 7 = 13$

Regroup the 13 **ones** to make 1 **ten** and 3 **ones**.

Add the **tens**.

ACTIVITY

Give your child some macaroni pieces and 6 strips of cardboard. Have your child glue 10 pieces of pasta on each strip. Give your child extra pieces.

Choose a number between 11 and 60. Ask your child to show you different ways to make 34. For example, 3 strips of 10 and 4 single pieces of pasta. Repeat with different numbers. Keep these macaroni tens and ones to use in Home Note activities.

Visit our Web site for additional ideas and activities.
http://www.hbschool.com

Name _____

Use Workmat 3 and 🟦🟦🟦🟦🟦🟦🟦🟦🟦🟦 🟦.
Add.

Join the ones. Write how many.	Can you make a ten?	If so, regroup 10 ones as 1 ten. Write how many tens and ones.

① 5 + 8 = __13__ ones	Yes No	__1__ ten __3__ ones
② 3 + 9 = _____ ones	Yes No	_____ ten _____ ones
③ 8 + 6 = _____ ones	Yes No	_____ ten _____ ones
④ 6 + 3 = _____ ones	Yes No	_____ tens _____ ones
⑤ 9 + 2 = _____ ones	Yes No	_____ ten _____ one

Talk About It ● Critical Thinking

Is 19 ones made up of 1 ten and 9 ones?
How do you know?

Practice

Use Workmat 3 and ▭▭▭▭▭▭▭▭ ▯.
Add.

	Join the ones. Write how many.	Can you make a ten?	If so, regroup 10 ones as 1 ten. Write how many tens and ones.
1	$8 + 7 =$ __15__ ones	(Yes) No	__1__ ten __5__ ones
2	$9 + 9 =$ ____ ones	Yes No	____ ten ____ ones
3	$5 + 4 =$ ____ ones	Yes No	____ tens ____ ones
4	$9 + 5 =$ ____ ones	Yes No	____ ten ____ ones

Mixed Review

Write the time.

5

     :

6

     :

7

     :

 Home Note Your child added two numbers and regrouped 10 ones as 1 ten.
ACTIVITY Ask your child to use macaroni to add two one-digit numbers. Have him or her tell you if regrouping is needed.

Chapter 10

Name _____

Show 15 + 6.	Join the ones. Can you make a ten?	Write how many in all.
	(Yes) No	21
	If so, regroup 10 ones as 1 ten.	

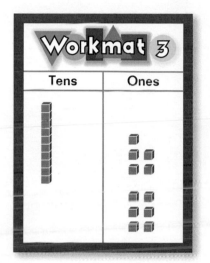

Use Workmat 3 and ▬▬▬▬▬ ▪.
Add.

Show.	Join the ones. Can you make a ten? If so, regroup 10 ones as 1 ten.	Write how many in all.
① 8 + 11	Yes No	_____
② 12 + 9	Yes No	_____
③ 17 + 7	Yes No	_____
④ 6 + 12	Yes No	_____

Talk About It ● Critical Thinking

How many ones make a ten?

Practice

Use Workmat 3 and ▭▭▭▭▭▭ ▫.
Add.

Show.	Join the ones. Can you make a ten? If so, regroup 10 ones as 1 ten.		Write how many in all.
1 6 + 17	(Yes)	No	23
2 15 + 9	Yes	No	____
3 13 + 6	Yes	No	____
4 8 + 12	Yes	No	____
5 16 + 5	Yes	No	____
6 9 + 14	Yes	No	____
7 12 + 7	Yes	No	____

Write About It

8 Write a story about adding two numbers.
One number is less than 10.
The other number is between 10 and 20.

 Home Note Your child learned to add a one-digit number and a two-digit number.
ACTIVITY Have your child use macaroni to add a one-digit number and a two-digit
number. Ask how he or she knows if regrouping is needed.

Harcourt Brace School Publishers

Modeling
Two-Digit Addition

Show 13 + 18.	Join the ones. Can you make a ten? (Yes) No If so, regroup 10 ones as 1 ten.	Write how many in all. 31

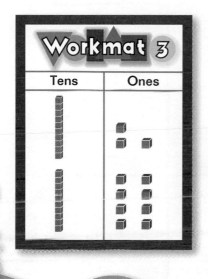

Use Workmat 3 and ▬▬▬▬▬ ▪.
Add.

Show.	Join the ones. Can you make a ten? If so, regroup 10 ones as 1 ten.	Write how many in all.
❶ 11 + 12	Yes No	_____
❷ 18 + 17	Yes No	_____
❸ 16 + 13	Yes No	_____
❹ 17 + 14	Yes No	_____

Practice

Work with a partner.
Use Workmat 3 and ▦▦▦▦▦▦ ▪.
Add.

Show.	Join the ones. Can you make a ten? If so, regroup 10 ones as 1 ten.	Write how many in all.
1 19 + 16	(Yes) No	35
2 14 + 13	Yes No	_____
3 12 + 18	Yes No	_____
4 17 + 16	Yes No	_____
5 13 + 15	Yes No	_____

Problem Solving

Use Workmat 3 and ▦▦▦▦▦▦ ▪.
Add.

6 Sam has 16 yellow fish
and 17 red fish.
How many fish does he have in all?

_____ fish

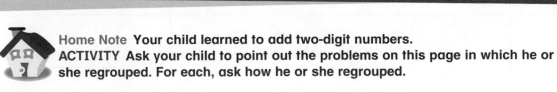

Home Note Your child learned to add two-digit numbers.
ACTIVITY Ask your child to point out the problems on this page in which he or
she regrouped. For each, ask how he or she regrouped.

Harcourt Brace School Publishers

Name _____

	tens	ones
	2	3
+	1	8
	4	1

Put tens and ones on the workmat to show both numbers.

Add the ones. Regroup if you need to.

Add the tens. Write how many.

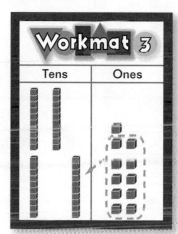

Use Workmat 3 and 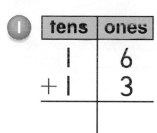.
Add.

1

tens	ones
1	6
+1	3

tens	ones

2

tens	ones
2	7
+1	5

tens	ones

3

tens	ones
2	0
+1	9

tens	ones

4

tens	ones
2	5
+2	9

tens	ones

Harcourt Brace School Publishers

Use Workmat 3 and ▭▭▭▭▭ ▪.
Add.

1

tens	ones
3	4
+1	8
5	2

tens	ones

2

tens	ones
2	3
+3	7

tens	ones

3

tens	ones
1	3
+2	4

tens	ones

4

tens	ones
3	6
+2	7

tens	ones

Problem Solving

Use Workmat 3 and ▭▭▭▭▭ ▪.
Add.

5 There are 15 Red team soccer fans and 13 Blue team soccer fans. How many soccer fans are there in all?

_____ soccer fans

Home Note Your child learned to record two-digit addition.
ACTIVITY Have your child use his or her macaroni tens and ones to show you how he or she found the sums of some of the problems on this page.

Harcourt Brace School Publishers

Name _____

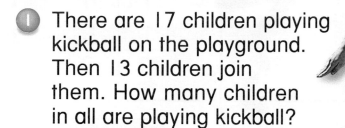

Understand • Plan • Solve • Look Back

Use Workmat 3 and ▭▭▭▭ ▯.
Add. Regroup if you need to.
Write the sum.

① There are 17 children playing
kickball on the playground.
Then 13 children join
them. How many children
in all are playing kickball?

_30_ children

tens	ones
1	7
+ 1	3
3	0

② The library has 15 books on baseball
and 11 books on soccer. How many
books does the library have about
soccer and baseball?

Soccer fun

_____ books

tens	ones
1	5
+ 1	1

③ At one table in the lunchroom, there
are 19 girls and 14 boys.
How many children are
sitting at the table?

_____ children

tens	ones
1	9
+ 1	4

④ In Ms. Dodge's class, 17 boys
and 15 girls bring their lunch to school.
How many children bring their lunch?

_____ children

tens	ones
1	7
+ 1	5

Harcourt Brace School Publishers

Practice

Use Workmat 3 and .
Add. Regroup if you need to.
Write the sum.

1. There are 12 boys and 15 girls playing soccer on the field. How many children are playing soccer?

_27_ children

tens	ones
1	2
+1	5
2	7

2. The Red Team scores 13 goals on Monday and 18 goals on Tuesday. How many goals do they score in all?

_____ goals

tens	ones
1	3
+1	8

3. The second grade has 14 cheese pizzas and 16 sausage pizzas at their soccer party. How many pizzas do they have?

_____ pizzas

tens	ones
1	4
+1	6

4. At the soccer party there are 19 blue balloons and 17 red balloons. How many balloons are there in all?

_____ balloons

tens	ones
1	9
+1	7

 Home Note Your child learned to make a model to solve a problem.
ACTIVITY Make up a problem like the ones on this page. Have your child use his or her macaroni tens and ones to solve the problem.

Harcourt Brace School Publishers

Concepts and Skills

Use Workmat 3 and ▬▬▬▬▬ ▪.
Add.

Show.	Join the ones. Can you make a ten? If so, regroup 10 ones as 1 ten.	Write how many in all.
1 $7 + 18$	Yes No	_____
2 $13 + 5$	Yes No	_____
3 $17 + 14$	Yes No	_____
4 $11 + 18$	Yes No	_____

5.

tens	ones
2	9
+2	8

tens	ones

6.

tens	ones
1	5
+2	4

tens	ones

Problem Solving

Use Workmat 3 and ▬▬▬▬▬ ▪. Add.
Regroup if you need to. Write the sum.

7 There are 12 soccer players on the Tigers team and 19 soccer players on the Lions team. How many soccer players are on both teams?

tens	ones
1	2
+1	9

_____ soccer players

Name _____

Test Prep

Mark the best answer.

1. The Green Team scored 15 goals. The Blue team scored 18 goals. How many goals did they score in all?

   ○ 23
   ○ 28
   ○ 38
   ○ 33

2. Is 37 greater than or less than 73?

   37 is _____ 73.

   ○ greater than
   ○ less than

3. Joey counts his peanuts. He puts them in 8 groups of ten and has 6 left over. How many peanuts does Joey have?

   ○ 66
   ○ 88
   ○ 68
   ○ 86

4. What time does the clock show?

   ○ 8:10
   ○ 8:15
   ○ 3:40
   ○ 3:35

5. Robert has 1 quarter, 3 dimes, and 4 pennies. How much money does he have?

   ○ 49¢
   ○ 59¢
   ○ 89¢
   ○ 95¢

6. Shelley read 36 books. Matt read 37 books. How many books did they read in all?

   ○ 74
   ○ 63
   ○ 73
   ○ 67

Harcourt Brace School Publishers

CHAPTER 11
More Two-Digit Addition

How far is it from the bears to the giraffes?

7 miles to giraffes

15 miles to alligators

18 miles to lions

10 miles to bears

Safari Rides

Home Note In this chapter, your child will learn more about two-digit addition.
ACTIVITY Have your child write an addition problem about the animals on this page. He or she should use 2 two-digit numbers.

SCHOOL-HOME CONNECTION

Dear Family,
   Today we started Chapter 11. We will add more two-digit numbers. Here are the new vocabulary words and an activity for us to do together at home.

Love,

_____

Vocabulary

ones
tens
regroup
sum

tens	ones
□	
3	8
+2	9

Add the **ones**. 8 + 9 = 17. There can be no more than 9 ones, so you **regroup 17** to make 1 ten and 7 ones. Write the 7 in the **ones** column, and write the 1 above the **tens** column. Add the tens. 1 + 3 + 2 = 6. The **sum** is 67.

ACTIVITY

Give your child a grocery receipt or ad from the newspaper. Have him or her find two items that each cost less than 50 cents and add their prices.

```
THANK YOU
FOR SHOPPING AT
OUR GROCERY STORE

LWFAT MILKGL    $2.79
SHRD WHT          4.85
  1 @ 3/99
ORANGES
SELTZER           .33
  1.71 LB         .47
@1.19/LB
WT ROMAINE
TOMATOES          2.03
                  1.79

TOTAL
           $12.26
```

Visit our Web site for additional ideas and activities.
http://www.hbschool.com

Adding One-Digit and Two-Digit Numbers

$24 + 8 =$ _____

Step 1
Add the ones.
$4 + 8 = 12.$

tens	ones
☐	
2	4
+	8

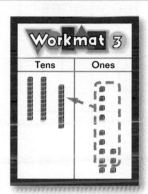

Step 2
Regroup 12 ones to make 1 ten and 2 ones. Write 1 to show the new ten.

tens	ones
1	
2	4
+	8
	2

Step 3
Add the tens.
Write how many.

tens	ones
1	
2	4
+	8
3	2

Use Workmat 3 and ▬▬▬▬ ▪.
Add. Regroup if you need to.

① tens	ones
☐	
2	7
+	9

② tens	ones
☐	
4	6
+	8

③ tens	ones
☐	
5	4
+	6

④ tens	ones
☐	
3	5
+	4

Talk About It ● Critical Thinking

How do you know if you need to regroup?

Practice

Use Workmat 3 and ▭▭▭▭▭▭ ▪.
Add. Regroup if you need to.

1

tens	ones
⬚	
5	7
+	5
6	2

2

tens	ones
⬚	
4	7
+	6

3

tens	ones
⬚	
2	3
+	8

4

tens	ones
⬚	
7	9
+	3

5

tens	ones
⬚	
4	1
+	9

6

tens	ones
⬚	
3	9
+	6

7

tens	ones
⬚	
1	3
+	5

8

tens	ones
⬚	
8	3
+	7

9

tens	ones
⬚	
3	6
+	5

10

tens	ones
⬚	
6	5
+	8

11

tens	ones
⬚	
5	2
+	6

12

tens	ones
⬚	
4	9
+	2

Problem Solving

Use Workmat 3 and ▭▭▭▭▭▭ ▪. Solve.

13 A toy tiger costs 18¢.
A toy elephant costs 9¢.
How much will both toys cost? _____ ¢

14 There are 9 pelicans at the zoo.
There are 6 more cranes than pelicans.
How many cranes and pelicans live at the zoo? _____ cranes and pelicans

Home Note Your child added two-digit and one-digit numbers.
ACTIVITY Have your child use small objects to add two-digit and one-digit numbers.

Harcourt Brace School Publishers

Chapter 11

Name _____

$12 + 18 =$ ___

Step 1

Add the ones.
$2 + 8 = 10.$

Do you need to regroup?

(Yes) No

tens	ones
1	2
+ 1	8

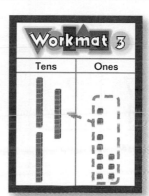

Step 2

Regroup if you need to.
Write how many.

tens	ones
1	2
+ 1	8
	0

Step 3

Add the tens.

tens	ones
1	2
+ 1	8
3	0

Use Workmat 3 and ▭▭▭▭▭▭▭ ▫ .
Add. Regroup if you need to.

① tens	ones		② tens	ones		③ tens	ones		④ tens	ones
2	3		2	1		4	2		6	7
+2	9		+1	9		+3	2		+2	5

Talk About It ○ **Critical Thinking**

How do you show that you regrouped?

Harcourt Brace School Publishers

Practice

Use Workmat 3 and ▭▭▭▭▭ ▮.
Add. Regroup if you need to.

1
tens	ones
3	7
+3	3
7	0

2
tens	ones
4	8
+3	5

3
tens	ones
5	4
+2	7

4
tens	ones
7	2
+1	7

5
tens	ones
7	2
+1	4

6
tens	ones
5	3
+1	9

7
tens	ones
3	7
+5	6

8
tens	ones
3	4
+3	6

9
tens	ones
2	8
+3	5

10
tens	ones
5	8
+2	4

11
tens	ones
2	3
+4	6

12
tens	ones
2	4
+3	9

Mixed Review

Write the number.

13 6 tens   4 ones = ☐

14 3 tens   9 ones = ☐

15 5 tens   0 ones = ☐

16 7 tens   2 ones = ☐

Home Note Your child added 2 two-digit numbers.
ACTIVITY Ask your child to tell you how he or she knows when regrouping is needed.

Name _____

There were 35 cranes and 29 pelicans drinking water at the pond. How many cranes and pelicans were at the pond in all?

Step 1 Add the ones. $5 + 9 = 14$.	**Step 2** Regroup if you need to.	**Step 3** Add the tens.
35 +29	1 35 +29 ___ 4	1 35 +29 ___ 64

There were __64__ cranes and pelicans.

Add.

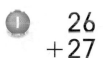

1

| 26 +27 | 53 +17 | 47 +21 | 39 +17 | 26 +19 | 73 +24 |

2

| 18 +45 | 32 +28 | 65 +15 | 46 +13 | 54 +19 | 49 +18 |

3

| 28 +49 | 11 +56 | 14 +26 | 47 +24 | 57 +17 | 39 +37 |

Talk About It ● Critical Thinking

Explain to a classmate how to add 2 two-digit numbers.

Practice

$13 + 21 + 27 = $ _____

Step 1 Add the ones. $3 + 1 + 7 = 11.$	**Step 2** Regroup if you need to.	**Step 3** Add the tens.
13 21 +27	13 21 +27 1	13 21 +27 61

Add.

1

13 23 +47	31 28 +32	42 19 +24	16 25 +28	23 56 +17	20 39 +31

2

33 47 +19	16 32 +12	56 28 +11	35 29 +25	58 19 +10	62 25 +12

3

25 22 +21	29 30 +31	13 38 +28	57 16 +15	19 34 +23	49 26 +11

Write About It

4 Write a story about animals in the jungle.
Add three numbers greater than 10 in your story.

Home Note Your child learned more about two-digit addition.
ACTIVITY On recycling day, have your child count the cans and then the bottles
you have used and add the two numbers.

Chapter 11

Name _____

Add.

 1

23	13	32	51	19	14
+17	+12	+29	+12	+24	+28

40

2

37	49	56	66	73	43
+44	+ 7	+27	+16	+19	+ 5

3

35	28	29	38	41	73
+24	+23	+36	+15	+25	+ 9

4

14	42	16	33	42	35
+17	+36	+39	+ 4	+39	+20

5

17	53	41	58
23	24	13	20
+ 9	+19	+25	+ 8

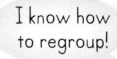

I know how to regroup!

6

27	32	25	57
25	37	23	19
+15	+29	+ 7	+21

Problem Solving

For a science project, three second grade classes decided to learn about jungle animals.

elephant	13 children
gorilla	15 children
flamingo	10 children
tiger	12 children
crocodile	17 children

1 Complete the graph to show how many children learned about each animal.

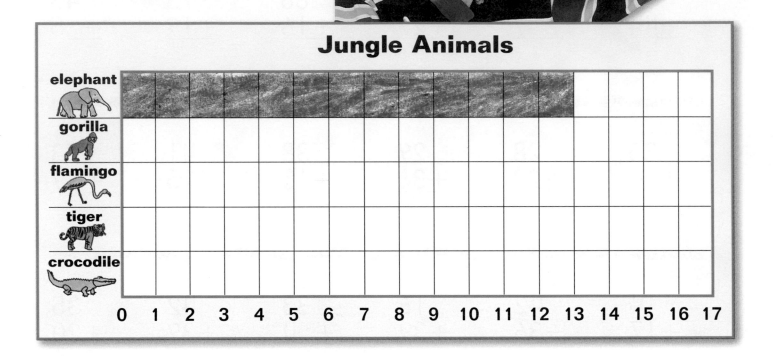

Jungle Animals

	0	1	2	3	4	5	6	7	8	9	10	11	12	13	14	15	16	17
elephant																		
gorilla																		
flamingo																		
tiger																		
crocodile																		

Use the graph to answer the questions.

2 How many children in all learned about gorillas and crocodiles? _____ children

3 How many children in all learned about elephants and tigers? _____ children

4 How many children in all learned about flamingos, tigers, and gorillas? _____ children

5 How many children in all learned about jungle animals? _____ children

Home Note Your child used data from a graph to practice two-digit addition.
ACTIVITY Have your child write his or her own addition questions, using data from the graph.

Name _____

Understand • Plan • Solve • Look Back

Draw a line through the sentence that is not needed. Then solve.

1. The Rodriguez family went on a trip. They saw 56 zebras and 38 lions. ~~Then they saw 16 children.~~ How many animals did they see?

$$\begin{array}{r} 1 \\ 56 \\ +38 \\ \hline 94 \end{array}$$

_94_ animals

2. They took 57 pictures on Monday. They took 34 pictures on Tuesday. ~~They took 18 pictures on Wednesday.~~ How many pictures did they take on Monday and Tuesday?

_____ pictures

3. Susie sent 29 postcards. Juan sent 32 postcards. The postcards cost 18¢ each. How many postcards did Susie and Juan send?

_____ postcards

4. Susie spent 23¢ for something to drink. Mrs. Rodriguez spent 12¢ for a drink. Juan spent 29¢ for a drink. How much did Susie and Juan spend in all for their drinks?

_____ ¢

Harcourt Brace School Publishers

Practice

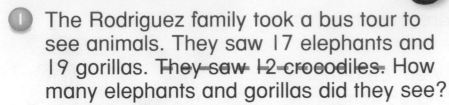

Draw a line through the sentence that
is not needed. Then solve.

1. The Rodriguez family took a bus tour to
see animals. They saw 17 elephants and
19 gorillas. ~~They saw 12 crocodiles.~~ How
many elephants and gorillas did they see?

   $\underline{36}$ elephants and gorillas

   $$\begin{array}{r} 17 \\ +19 \\ \hline 36 \end{array}$$

2. Juan saw 19 monkeys. Mrs. Rodriguez
saw 46 monkeys. Mr. Rodriguez saw 33
monkeys. How many monkeys did
Mrs. and Mr. Rodriguez see?

   _____ monkeys

3. Juan saw 29 blue birds and 34 red birds.
Susie saw 23 birds. How many birds did
Juan see?

   _____ birds

4. Susie saw 13 hippos. She saw 14 cheetahs.
Juan saw 24 hippos. How many hippos did
Juan and Susie see?

   _____ hippos

5. There were 37 giraffes at the lake. There
were 28 zebras at the lake. Susie and Juan
watched the animals at the lake for 20
minutes. How many animals were
at the lake?

   _____ animals

Home Note Your child solved problems with too much information.
ACTIVITY Have your child tell you why he or she didn't need the extra
information in each problem.

Harcourt Brace School Publishers

Name _____

Concepts and Skills

Add. Regroup if you need to.

1

tens	ones
☐	
2	6
+	7

2

tens	ones
☐	
4	9
+	9

3

tens	ones
☐	
2	4
+1	8

4

tens	ones
☐	
4	3
+3	8

5

```
  43      32      29      64      45      82
 +39     +61     +18     +27     +27     +17
```

6

```
  25      19      42      16      34      56
 +35     +78     +12     +29     +38     +27
```

7

```
  24      11      42      23      15      12
  18      21      31      25      25      29
 +32     +16     +19     +27     +35     +18
```

Problem Solving

Draw a line through the sentence that is not needed. Then solve.

8 The second grade planted 35 pine trees and 26 fir trees. They planted 15 flowers. How many trees did they plant? _____ trees

Name _____

Test Prep

Mark the best answer.

1 Jenny has 3 quarters and 2 dimes. How much money does she have?

- ⭕ 85¢
- ⭕ 70¢
- ⭕ 95¢
- ⭕ 77¢

2 Mrs. Lee has 23 books on one shelf and 18 books on another shelf. How many books does Mrs. Lee have?

- ⭕ 38
- ⭕ 42
- ⭕ 41
- ⭕ 44

3 Which number sentence solves the problem?

Margaret had 18 marbles. She gave 9 marbles to her friend. How many marbles does she have left?

- ⭕ $18 - 8 = 10$
- ⭕ $18 - 9 = 9$
- ⭕ $19 + 8 = 27$
- ⭕ $19 + 9 = 28$

4 George saw 28 elephants and 14 zebras. How many animals did he see in all?

- ⭕ 32
- ⭕ 42
- ⭕ 38
- ⭕ 40

5 The clock shows the time when Roger feeds his frog. What time does Roger feed his frog?

- ⭕ 4:15
- ⭕ 4:25
- ⭕ 5:20
- ⭕ 5:25

6 Is there an even or odd number of birds?

- ⭕ even
- ⭕ odd

Name _____

MATH FUN

You will need:

paper, pencil,

Going Camping

Who will get to the camp first?

1. Roll the number cube.

2. Move your counter the number of spaces the number cube shows.

3. Find the sum or follow the directions.

Start

45 +36

Ride hot air balloon. Go ahead 2 spaces.

18 +32   23 +14   63 +19   27 +36

44 +23

16 +45   36 +29   21 +28

Take boat across lake. Go ahead 2 spaces.

54 +17   62 +28

Forget camera. Go back 2 spaces.

Find short cut. Go ahead 1 space.

39 +12   45 +25   53 +27

Van breaks down. Lose a turn.

36 +19   42 +26

Camp

Harcourt Brace School Publishers

Home Note Your child has been learning to add two-digit numbers with and without regrouping. **ACTIVITY** As you play this game, ask your child how he or she knows whether to regroup and how he or she will do this.

Name _____

| Calculator | | Computer |

In a magic square, each row and each column has the same sum.
Find the sum for the first row. Press

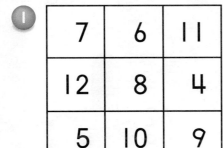

Write the sum.
Do this for each row and column.

11	10	15	_36_
16	12	8	___
9	14	13	___

___ ___ ___

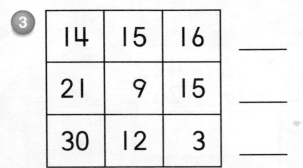

Use a 🖩. Write the sums.
Is the square a magic square?

1

7	6	11	___
12	8	4	___
5	10	9	___

___ ___ ___

Is this a magic square? ____

2

11	21	16	___
38	13	7	___
29	8	30	___

___ ___ ___

Is this a magic square? ____

3

14	15	16	___
21	9	15	___
30	12	3	___

___ ___ ___

Is this a magic square? ____

4

15	14	19	___
20	16	12	___
13	18	17	___

___ ___ ___

Is this a magic square? ____

Harcourt Brace School Publishers

The Lion's House

by David McPhail

 This book will help me review two-digit addition.

This book belongs to _____ .

A

A lion wanted to build a house. The lion had 14 pieces of wood and 21 nails.

But 14 pieces of wood and 21 nails was not enough to build a house.

Along came a bear. The bear wanted to build a house, too. The bear had 17 pieces of wood and 37 nails.

Harcourt Brace School Publishers

But even the bear's and lion's wood and nails together were not enough to build a house.

A rabbit came by pulling a wagon. "I have 26 pieces of wood and 52 nails," said the rabbit. "I want to build a house."

Harcourt Brace School Publishers

Together the lion, the bear and the rabbit had enough wood and nails to build a house.

They even had some wood and nails left over.

So they made a big bed and went to sleep.

The end

Harcourt Brace School Publishers

Concepts and Skills

Use Workmat 3 and ▭▭▭▭▭ ▫.
Add.

Show.	Join the ones. Can you make a ten? If so, regroup 10 ones as 1 ten.	Write how many in all.
① 5 + 17	Yes No	_____
② 13 + 6	Yes No	_____
③ 11 + 18	Yes No	_____
④ 14 + 19	Yes No	_____

Add. Regroup if you need to.

⑤
tens	ones
☐	
1	7
+1	6

⑥
tens	ones
☐	
2	3
+1	5

⑦
tens	ones
☐	
1	2
+1	8

⑧
tens	ones
☐	
2	4
+1	7

Add. Regroup if you need to.

9

tens	ones
2	1
+1	3

10

tens	ones
2	7
+2	6

11

tens	ones
4	2
+3	5

12

tens	ones
3	5
+1	5

13

tens	ones
4	2
+1	9

14

tens	ones
3	6
+1	2

15

tens	ones
1	7
+3	7

16

tens	ones
5	1
+3	2

17
```
  16
  54
+ 19
```

18
```
  11
  13
+ 22
```

19
```
  21
  12
+  7
```

20
```
  14
  19
+ 25
```

Problem Solving

Add. Regroup if you need to.

21 The bookstore has 14 books on trees and 18 books on flowers. How many books in all does the store have on trees and flowers?

_____ books

Draw a line through the sentence that is not needed. Then solve.

22 The second grade planted 26 red flowers and 15 yellow flowers on Monday. On Tuesday they planted 14 trees. How many flowers did they plant?

_____ flowers

Performance Assessment

Use Workmat 3 and 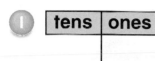 .
Build two numbers between 11 and 49.
Write an addition problem.
Add.
Draw a picture to show the sum.

① tens	ones

+

Workmat 3

Tens	Ones

② tens	ones

1

Workmat 3

Tens	Ones

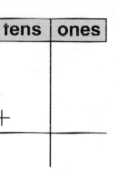

③ tens	ones

+

Workmat 3

Tens	Ones

④ tens	ones

+

Workmat 3

Tens	Ones

Write About It

⑤ Circle the problem in which you need to regroup to add. Explain how you know.

$$\begin{array}{r} 23 \\ +41 \\ \hline \end{array} \qquad \begin{array}{r} 23 \\ +38 \\ \hline \end{array}$$

Math Journal

Name _____

Fill in the ◯ for the correct answer.

1
$$\begin{array}{r} 9 \\ +3 \\ \hline \end{array}$$
◯ 11
◯ 12
◯ 13
◯ 14

2
$$\begin{array}{r} 15 \\ -\ 8 \\ \hline \end{array}$$
◯ 3
◯ 4
◯ 6
◯ 7

3 Compare.
Choose > or <.

53 ◯ 35

◯ >   ◯ <

4 Which coins show the price? 32¢

◯   ◯   ◯

5
$$\begin{array}{r} 43 \\ +25 \\ \hline \end{array}$$
◯ 22
◯ 52
◯ 68
◯ 78

6
$$\begin{array}{r} 60 \\ +19 \\ \hline \end{array}$$
◯ 69
◯ 79
◯ 80
◯ 89

7 Jenny goes shopping at .

It takes her 3 hours. What time does she finish shopping?

◯ 1:00   ◯ 3:00
◯ 4:00   ◯ 5:00

8 The library has 14 books on cats and 29 books on dogs. How many books in all does the library have on cats and dogs?

◯ 33 books   ◯ 35 books
◯ 43 books   ◯ not here

Exploring Two-Digit Subtraction

Wilderness Park

Animals Seen Today

Squirrels	3	6
Rabbits	1	5
Deer	1	2
Birds	9	4

Write subtraction stories to compare the numbers of animals.

Home Note In this chapter your child is learning to subtract two-digit numbers. **ACTIVITY** Ask your child to tell you subtraction stories about the picture.

two hundred three **203**

SCHOOL-HOME CONNECTION

Dear Family,
  Today we started Chapter 12. We will begin to subtract two-digit numbers. Here are the new vocabulary words and an activity for us to do together at home.

Love,

_____

Vocabulary

When you subtract two-digit numbers, you begin with the ones. In this example, since you cannot take 7 ones away from 3 ones, you need to **regroup**. This means you trade 1 ten for 10 ones, leaving 3 tens. You now have 13 ones, from which you can subtract 7 ones.

tens	ones
4	3
−1	7
2	6

ACTIVITY

Give your child 4 clear bags, each holding 10 pieces of popcorn, and 3 single pieces. Have him or her tell you how many pieces of popcorn there are. Then ask your child to subtract 7 pieces of popcorn. Show your child how to empty 1 bag of popcorn so that there are 13 pieces and 3 bags. Have him or her subtract the 7 pieces of popcorn and tell you how many pieces are left.

Visit our Web site for additional ideas and activities.
http://www.hbschool.com

Harcourt Brace School Publishers

Show 3 tens and 5 ones. Are there enough ones to subtract 7 ones?

Yes   (No)

If not, regroup 1 ten as 10 ones.

Subtract the ones. Write how many tens and ones are left.

_2_ tens _8_ ones

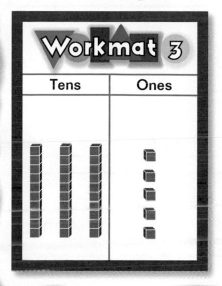

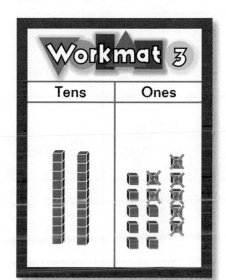

Use Workmat 3 and ▭▭▭ ▫.
Subtract.

	Show the tens and ones.	Subtract.	Are there enough ones to subtract? If not, regroup 1 ten as 10 ones.	Subtract the ones. Write how many tens and ones are left.
1	2 tens 9 ones	4 ones	Yes No	_____ tens _____ ones
2	4 tens 2 ones	6 ones	Yes No	_____ tens _____ ones
3	1 ten 8 ones	9 ones	Yes No	_____ tens _____ ones

Talk About It ● Critical Thinking

How do you know if you need to regroup?

Use Workmat 3 and ▭▭▭▭▭▭▭ ▪.
Subtract.

Show the tens and ones.	Subtract.	Are there enough ones to subtract? If not, regroup 1 ten as 10 ones.	Subtract the ones. Write how many tens and ones are left.
① 4 tens 7 ones	8 ones	Yes (No)	__3__ tens __9__ ones
② 1 ten 4 ones	6 ones	Yes No	_____ tens _____ ones
③ 2 tens 5 ones	9 ones	Yes No	_____ ten _____ ones
④ 3 tens 0 ones	3 ones	Yes No	_____ tens _____ ones
⑤ 2 tens 6 ones	5 ones	Yes No	_____ tens _____ one

Mixed Review

Write the total amount.

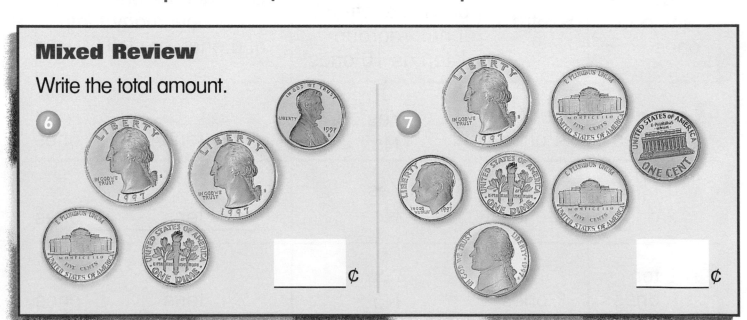

⑥ _____ ¢

⑦ _____ ¢

🏠 **Home Note** Your child regrouped tens as ones.
ACTIVITY Have your child use his or her popcorn bags and single pieces (explained on page 204) to subtract a one-digit number from a two-digit number, for example, 8 from 32.

Modeling One-Digit and Two-Digit Subtraction

24 − 8 = _____

Show 24. Are there enough ones to subtract 8 ones?

Yes   (No)

Do you need to regroup?

(Yes)   No

If so, regroup 1 ten as 10 ones.

Subtract the ones. Write how many are left.

24 − 8 = 16

Use Workmat 3 and .
Subtract.

	Subtract.	Do you need to regroup?	Write how many are left.
1	16 − 7	Yes No	_____
2	28 − 6	Yes No	_____
3	15 − 9	Yes No	_____
4	21 − 7	Yes No	_____

Talk About It • Critical Thinking

What do you do if there are not enough ones to subtract?

Practice

Use Workmat 3 and  ⬛. Subtract.

Subtract.	Do you need to regroup?	Write how many are left.
① 35 − 6	(Yes) No	29
② 43 − 7	Yes No	_____
③ 26 − 4	Yes No	_____
④ 30 − 5	Yes No	_____
⑤ 13 − 8	Yes No	_____
⑥ 44 − 9	Yes No	_____

Problem Solving ● **Visual Thinking**

Use Workmat 3 and ⬛⬛⬛⬛⬛⬛ ⬛. Subtract.

⑦ There were 21 children playing.
Then 3 children went home.
How many children are left?

_____ children

Harcourt Brace School Publishers

Home Note Your child modeled subtracting one-digit numbers from two-digit numbers.
ACTIVITY Give your child 2 dimes and 3 pennies. Ask for 5 pennies. Have your child tell you what he or she would have to do to give you 5 pennies.

Name _____

32 − 7 = _____

Show 32. Subtract 7.

Regroup if you need to.

Subtract the ones. Write how many tens and ones are left.

tens	ones
3	2
−	7
2	5

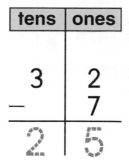

Use Workmat 3 and ▭▭▭▭▭▭ ▪.
Subtract.

1
tens	ones
3	3
−	6

2
tens	ones
2	6
−	7

3
tens	ones
3	9
−	3

4
tens	ones
4	8
−	3

5
tens	ones
5	1
−	8

6
tens	ones
4	0
−	5

7
tens	ones
4	2
−	7

8
tens	ones
5	6
−	9

Talk About It • Critical Thinking

How can regrouping 1 ten as 10 ones help you subtract?

Harcourt Brace School Publishers

22 − 9 = _____

Show 22. Subtract 9.

Regroup if you need to.

Subtract the ones. Write how many tens and ones are left.

tens	ones
2	2
−	9
1	3

tens	ones

tens	ones

tens	ones

Use Workmat 3 and ▭▭▭▭ ▪. Subtract.

1

tens	ones
5	0
−	7

2

tens	ones
3	1
−	4

3

tens	ones
5	6
−	5

4

tens	ones
3	4
−	6

5

tens	ones
2	9
−	5

6

tens	ones
1	9
−	7

7

tens	ones
2	1
−	8

8

tens	ones
4	3
−	6

Problem Solving

Use Workmat 3 and ▭▭▭▭ ▪. Subtract.

9 There are 23 birds at the pond. 9 birds fly away. How many birds are left?

_____ birds

Home Note Your child modeled and recorded subtracting one-digit numbers from two-digit numbers. **ACTIVITY** Ask your child to point out the problems on this page in which he or she regrouped. For each, ask why regrouping was needed.

Name _____

$31 - 18 =$ _____

Show 31. Subtract 18.

Regroup if you need to.

Subtract the ones.
Subtract the tens.
Write the difference.

tens	ones
3	1
−1	8
1	3

Use Workmat 3 and ▭▭▭▭▭▭▭▭▭ ▫.
Find the difference.

1

tens	ones
4	3
−2	7

2

tens	ones
2	2
−1	3

3

tens	ones
2	8
−1	5

4

tens	ones
5	3
−3	5

5

tens	ones
3	0
−1	2

6

tens	ones
2	6
−1	4

7

tens	ones
5	2
−2	6

8

tens	ones
4	4
−2	9

Talk About It ● Critical Thinking

Explain to a classmate the steps you used to subtract.

Harcourt Brace School Publishers

$46 - 29 = \underline{\hspace{1cm}}$

Show 46. Subtract 29.

Regroup if you need to.

Subtract the ones.
Subtract the tens.
Write the difference.

tens	ones
4	6
−2	9
1	7

tens	ones

tens	ones

tens	ones

Use Workmat 3 and 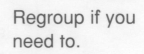.
Find the difference.

1

tens	ones
2	7
−1	8

2

tens	ones
3	5
−1	9

3

tens	ones
4	7
−3	9

4

tens	ones
4	4
−2	1

5

tens	ones
3	6
−2	4

6

tens	ones
5	2
−2	5

7

tens	ones
2	5
−1	7

8

tens	ones
5	0
−3	3

Write About It

9 Write a story about subtracting two numbers.
Both numbers are between 20 and 60.

Math Journal

Harcourt Brace School Publishers

Home Note Your child modeled and recorded subtracting two-digit numbers from two-digit numbers.
ACTIVITY Have your child use his or her popcorn bags and pieces to show you how he or she solved
some of the problems on this page.

Name _____

Understand · Plan · Solve · Look Back

Problem Solving
Choose the Operation

Use Workmat 3 and ▭▭▭▭▭▭ ▯.
Circle add or subtract.
Write + or −. Find the sum or difference.

1. At the Wild Animal Park, Megan sees 38 tigers and 26 bears. How many tigers and bears does she see in all?

   (add)   subtract

tens	ones
3	8
+ 2	6
6	4

2. Julio has 83¢. He spends 65¢ on a pony ride. How much money does he have left?

   add   subtract

   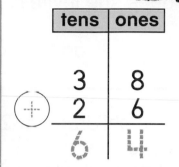

tens	ones
8	3¢
○ 6	5¢

3. Lorna sees 15 big alligators and 19 little alligators. How many alligators does she see in all?

   add   subtract

tens	ones
1	5
○ 1	9

4. Timmy sees 23 seals. 19 seals go into the water. How many seals are left?

   add   subtract

tens	ones
2	3
○ 1	9

Harcourt Brace School Publishers

Chapter 12 • Exploring Two-Digit Subtraction

two hundred thirteen **213**

Use Workmat 3 and .
Circle add or subtract.
Write + or −. Find the sum or difference.

1. Becky invites 26 girls and 14 boys to the park for a picnic. How many more girls than boys does she invite?

   add   (subtract)

tens	ones
2	6
1	4
1	2

2. The children eat 28 chocolate cupcakes and 19 vanilla cupcakes. How many cupcakes do they eat in all?

   add   subtract

tens	ones
2	8
1	9

3. Scott's mom buys orange juice for 43¢ and grape juice for 35¢. How much money does she spend on juice in all?

   add   subtract

tens	ones
4	3¢
3	5¢

4. Mike has 75¢. He spends 49¢ on a balloon. How much money does he have left?

   add   subtract

tens	ones
7	5¢
4	9¢

Home Note Your child chose addition or subtraction to solve problems.
ACTIVITY Make up problems like the ones on the page. Have your child use his or her popcorn bags and pieces to solve the problems.

Harcourt Brace School Publishers

Name _____

Concepts and Skills

Review/Test

Use Workmat 3 and ▨▨▨▨▨▨▨ ▨.
Subtract.

Subtract.	Do you need to regroup? If so, regroup 1 ten as ten ones.	Write how many are left.
1 35 − 6	Yes No	_____

2
tens	ones
3	0
−	7

3
tens	ones
3	6
−	5

4
tens	ones
3	1
−	8

5
tens	ones
5	3
−	6

6
tens	ones
4	2
−2	3

7
tens	ones
4	0
−2	8

8
tens	ones
3	5
−2	3

9
tens	ones
5	6
−3	7

Problem Solving

Use Workmat 3 and ▨▨▨▨▨▨▨ ▨.
Circle add or subtract. Write + or −.
Find the sum or difference.

10 The library has 19 books on flowers and
12 books on trees. How many more books
are there on flowers than on trees?

add   subtract

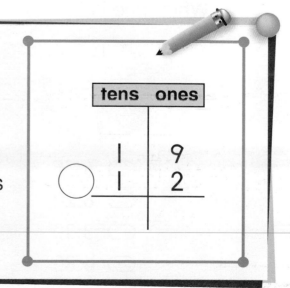

Name _____

Test Prep

Mark the best answer.

① Erika sees 19 red flowers. She sees 15 yellow flowers. How many flowers does she see in all?

- ○ 24
- ○ 25
- ○ 34
- ○ 35

② Is there an even or odd number of buttons?

- ○ even
- ○ odd

③ Look at the clock. What time is it?

- ○ 6:15
- ○ 6:20
- ○ 3:30
- ○ 4:30

④ Ian has 1 half-dollar, 2 dimes, 3 nickels, and 2 pennies. How much money does he have?

- ○ 78¢
- ○ 87¢
- ○ 82¢
- ○ 92¢

⑤ There are 14 children playing soccer. Then 16 children join them. How many children in all are playing soccer?

- ○ 22
- ○ 20
- ○ 30
- ○ 32

⑥ Chris has 86 pennies. He gives 10 pennies to his friend. How many pennies does he have left?

- ○ 96
- ○ 66
- ○ 56
- ○ 76

Harcourt Brace School Publishers

Standardized Test Prep • Chapters 1–12

More Two-Digit Subtraction

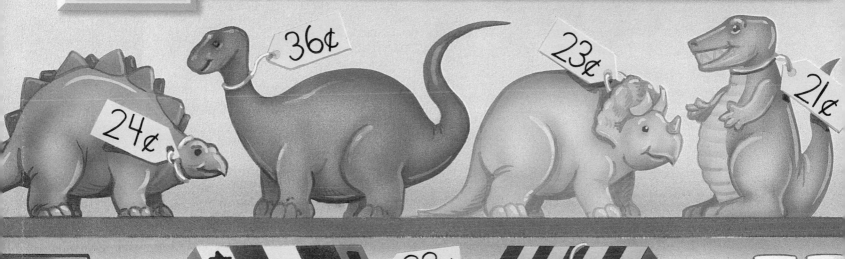

36¢

23¢

21¢

24¢

33¢

22¢

15¢

18¢

19¢   25¢   19¢   25¢   19¢

27¢

40¢

TOY SALE

You have 99¢ to buy a toy.
What will you buy?
How much money will you have left?

Harcourt Brace School Publishers

Home Note In this chapter your child will learn more about two-digit subtraction.
ACTIVITY Have your child write subtraction sentences about the picture.

SCHOOL-HOME CONNECTION

Dear Family,
Today we started Chapter 13. We will look at more ways to subtract two-digit numbers. Here are the new vocabulary words and an activity for us to do together at home.

Love,

_____

Vocabulary

To find the **difference,** or answer, in this subtraction problem, you must **regroup.** To regroup, trade 1 ten for 10 ones to make 11 ones. You can now subtract the ones and write how many are left. Subtract the tens, and write how many tens are left.

tens	ones
3̶4	1̶1̶1
− 2	9
1	2

ACTIVITY

Look through the newspaper with your child to find a sale price for something you buy that costs less than a dollar. Ask your child to find the difference between the sale price and the regular price by subtracting. Have him or her show the two prices, using dimes and pennies. Your child can trade a dime for 10 pennies when he or she needs to regroup.

Visit our Web site for additional ideas and activities.
http://www.hbschool.com

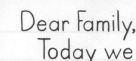

Harcourt Brace School Publishers

Name _____

31 − 8 = _____

Step 1

Show 31.
Look at the ones.
Can you subtract 8?

Yes   (No)

tens	ones
☐	☐
3	1
−	8

Step 2

Regroup 1 ten as 10 ones.
Now there are 11 ones.
Subtract 8 from 11.
Write how many ones are left.

tens	ones
2	11
3	1
−	8
	3

Step 3

Write how many tens are left.

tens	ones
2	11
3	1
−	8
2	3

Use Workmat 3 and ▭▭▭▭▭ ▪.
Subtract. Regroup if you need to.

1
tens	ones
☐	☐
5	6
−	7

2
tens	ones
☐	☐
4	7
−	5

3
tens	ones
☐	☐
2	2
−	9

4
tens	ones
☐	☐
3	0
−	4

Talk About It • Critical Thinking

How do you know if you need to regroup?

Harcourt Brace School Publishers

Practice

Use Workmat 3 and 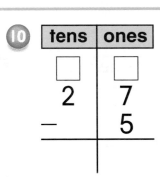 ▮.
Subtract. Regroup if you need to.

1
tens	ones
[5]	[17]
6	7
−	8
5	9

2
tens	ones
☐	☐
7	2
−	4

3
tens	ones
☐	☐
4	5
−	7

4
tens	ones
☐	☐
6	3
−	7

5
tens	ones
☐	☐
9	6
−	8

6
tens	ones
☐	☐
5	4
−	6

7
tens	ones
☐	☐
8	1
−	4

8
tens	ones
☐	☐
3	2
−	6

9
tens	ones
☐	☐
4	3
−	9

10
tens	ones
☐	☐
2	7
−	5

11
tens	ones
☐	☐
7	2
−	3

12
tens	ones
☐	☐
6	0
−	5

Problem Solving

Use Workmat 3 and  ▮.
Solve.

13 John has 45¢. He buys a toy for 8¢. How much money does he have left?

_____ ¢

Home Note Your child modeled and recorded subtraction of one-digit numbers from two-digit numbers.
ACTIVITY Have your child solve a problem such as 43 − 6 and tell why and how he or she regrouped. Your child can use small objects to model the problem.

220 two hundred twenty

Chapter 13

Harcourt Brace School Publishers

Two-Digit Subtraction

$$42 - 15 = \underline{}$$

Step 1
Show 42.
Look at the ones.
Can you subtract 5?

Yes   (No)

tens	ones
□	□
4	2
−1	5

Step 2
Regroup 1 ten as 10 ones.
Now there are 12 ones.
Subtract 5 from 12.
Write how many ones are left.

tens	ones
3	12
4	2
−1	5
	7

Step 3
Subtract the tens.
Write how many tens are left.

tens	ones
3	12
4	2
−1	5
2	7

Use Workmat 3 and  .
Subtract. Regroup if you need to.

① tens	ones		② tens	ones		③ tens	ones		④ tens	ones
□	□		□	□		□	□		□	□
3	8		4	0		2	7		5	1
−1	8		−2	7		−1	3		−3	6

Practice

Use Workmat 3 and
Subtract. Regroup if you need to.

1

tens	ones
6	15
7̷	5̷
−2	9
4	6

2

tens	ones
☐	☐
8	3
−2	7

3

tens	ones
☐	☐
6	5
−2	5

4

tens	ones
☐	☐
7	1
−1	9

5

tens	ones
☐	☐
9	1
−1	6

6

tens	ones
☐	☐
8	0
−4	2

7

tens	ones
☐	☐
5	7
−2	8

8

tens	ones
☐	☐
6	3
−4	7

9

tens	ones
☐	☐
9	5
−4	8

10

tens	ones
☐	☐
3	7
−1	9

11

tens	ones
☐	☐
8	9
−4	8

12

tens	ones
☐	☐
6	2
−3	2

Mixed Review

Write < or > in the circle.

13 26 ◯ 36

14 50 ◯ 49

15 35 ◯ 32

16 94 ◯ 49

17 23 ◯ 27

18 24 ◯ 42

Home Note Your child modeled and recorded subtraction of two-digit numbers.
ACTIVITY Ask your child to tell you how he or she knows when to regroup when subtracting.

Name _____

Alexander had 31 toys. He sold 12 toys at the garage sale. How many toys does he have left?

Step 1
Can you subtract the ones?

$$\begin{array}{r} 31 \\ -12 \\ \hline \end{array}$$

Step 2
Regroup if you need to. Subtract the ones.

$$\begin{array}{r} \overset{2\ 11}{\cancel{31}} \\ -12 \\ \hline 9 \end{array}$$

Step 3
Subtract the tens. Write how many.

$$\begin{array}{r} \overset{2\ 11}{\cancel{31}} \\ -12 \\ \hline 19 \end{array}$$

Alexander had __19__ toys left.

Subtract.

1.
$$\begin{array}{r} 75 \\ -47 \\ \hline \end{array}$$

2.
$$\begin{array}{r} 60 \\ -22 \\ \hline \end{array}$$

3.
$$\begin{array}{r} 58 \\ -39 \\ \hline \end{array}$$

4.
$$\begin{array}{r} 46 \\ -23 \\ \hline \end{array}$$

5.
$$\begin{array}{r} 96 \\ -27 \\ \hline \end{array}$$

6.
$$\begin{array}{r} 92 \\ -57 \\ \hline \end{array}$$

7.
$$\begin{array}{r} 59 \\ -25 \\ \hline \end{array}$$

8.
$$\begin{array}{r} 40 \\ -21 \\ \hline \end{array}$$

9.
$$\begin{array}{r} 33 \\ -18 \\ \hline \end{array}$$

10.
$$\begin{array}{r} 80 \\ -46 \\ \hline \end{array}$$

Talk About It • Critical Thinking

Explain to a classmate how to subtract 2 two-digit numbers.

Practice

Subtract.

Regroup if you need to.

1
$$\begin{array}{r} {\scriptstyle 8\;14} \\ 9\!\!\!/4 \\ -55 \\ \hline 39 \end{array}$$

2
$$\begin{array}{r} 36 \\ -29 \\ \hline \end{array}$$

3
$$\begin{array}{r} 76 \\ -46 \\ \hline \end{array}$$

4
$$\begin{array}{r} 81 \\ -27 \\ \hline \end{array}$$

5
$$\begin{array}{r} 52 \\ -37 \\ \hline \end{array}$$

6
$$\begin{array}{r} 92 \\ -11 \\ \hline \end{array}$$

7
$$\begin{array}{r} 40 \\ -37 \\ \hline \end{array}$$

8
$$\begin{array}{r} 25 \\ -16 \\ \hline \end{array}$$

9
$$\begin{array}{r} 38 \\ -19 \\ \hline \end{array}$$

10
$$\begin{array}{r} 92 \\ -63 \\ \hline \end{array}$$

11
$$\begin{array}{r} 64 \\ -29 \\ \hline \end{array}$$

12
$$\begin{array}{r} 73 \\ -55 \\ \hline \end{array}$$

13
$$\begin{array}{r} 43 \\ -26 \\ \hline \end{array}$$

14
$$\begin{array}{r} 25 \\ -18 \\ \hline \end{array}$$

15
$$\begin{array}{r} 73 \\ -14 \\ \hline \end{array}$$

16
$$\begin{array}{r} 95 \\ -52 \\ \hline \end{array}$$

17
$$\begin{array}{r} 90 \\ -26 \\ \hline \end{array}$$

18
$$\begin{array}{r} 41 \\ -17 \\ \hline \end{array}$$

19
$$\begin{array}{r} 54 \\ -36 \\ \hline \end{array}$$

Write About It

20 Write a subtraction story.
The first number should be between 50 and 99.
The second number should be between 11 and 49.

Math Journal

Harcourt Brace School Publishers

Home Note Your child practiced two-digit subtraction.
ACTIVITY Have your child choose a problem on this page and tell you the steps he or she followed to subtract.

Using Addition to Check Subtraction

Write the difference, 25.
Add the bottom number, 38.
If the sum is the top number, 63,
the subtraction is correct.

Subtract.	Add to check.
5 13	1
63	25
−38	+38
25	63

Subtract.
Add to check.

1
```
  3 11
  4̸1
 −15
  26
```
```
  1
  2̸6
 +15
  4̸1
```

2
```
  74
 −46
```

3
```
  40
 −19
```

4
```
  67
 −35
```

5
```
  83
 −58
```

6
```
  56
 −28
```

Harcourt Brace School Publishers

Practice

Subtract.
Add to check.

1 $\begin{array}{r} {}^{2}\cancel{3}{}^{1}3 \\ 33 \\ -17 \\ \hline 16 \end{array}$ $\begin{array}{r} {}^{1}16 \\ +17 \\ \hline 33 \end{array}$

2 $\begin{array}{r} 70 \\ -43 \\ \hline \end{array}$

3 $\begin{array}{r} 94 \\ -56 \\ \hline \end{array}$

4 $\begin{array}{r} 30 \\ -17 \\ \hline \end{array}$

5 $\begin{array}{r} 48 \\ -25 \\ \hline \end{array}$

6 $\begin{array}{r} 83 \\ -34 \\ \hline \end{array}$

7 $\begin{array}{r} 36 \\ -14 \\ \hline \end{array}$

8 $\begin{array}{r} 53 \\ -26 \\ \hline \end{array}$

9 $\begin{array}{r} 75 \\ -37 \\ \hline \end{array}$

Problem Solving

Subtract. Add to check.

10 Rodney has 87¢. He spends 39¢ on a bear. How much money does he have left?

_____ ¢

Home Note Your child used addition to check subtraction.
ACTIVITY Have your child show you how to check by adding after he or she subtracts.

Chapter 13

Name _____

Add or subtract. Write the sum or difference.

1. How much money would you need to buy a 🧸 and a ⭕ ?

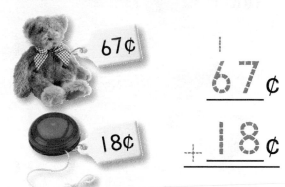

67¢

18¢

$$\begin{array}{r} 67¢ \\ +\ 18¢ \\ \hline \end{array}$$

You would need 85 ¢.

---

2. You have 55¢. You buy a 🧤. How much money do you have left?

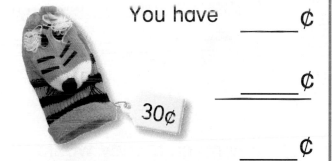

30¢

You have _____ ¢

_____ ¢

_____ ¢

3. How much money would you need to buy a 🚤 and a 🪢 ?

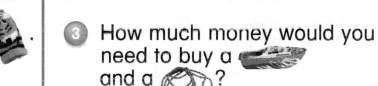

45¢

26¢

_____ ¢

_____ ¢

_____ ¢

---

4. How much money would you need to buy a 🚃 and a 🔴 ?

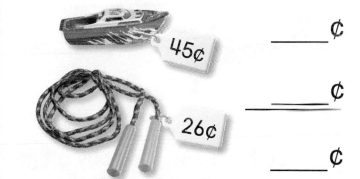

71¢

13¢

_____ ¢

_____ ¢

_____ ¢

5. You have 93¢. You buy a 🧸. How much money do you have left?

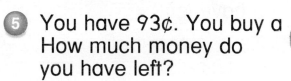

67¢

You have _____ ¢

_____ ¢

_____ ¢

Chapter 13 • More Two-Digit Subtraction

Add or subtract. Write the sum or difference.

1 How much money would you need to buy a and a ?

30¢

30¢
+ 59¢
___
89¢

2 You have 80¢. You buy a . How much money do you have left?

You have _____ ¢

71¢

_____ ¢

_____ ¢

3 You have 90¢. You buy a . How much money do you have left?

You have _____ ¢

59¢

_____ ¢

_____ ¢

4 How much money would you need to buy a and a ?

67¢

_____ ¢

13¢

_____ ¢

_____ ¢

5 You have 75¢. You buy a . How much money do you have left?

You have _____ ¢

18¢

_____ ¢

_____ ¢

6 How much money would you need to buy a and a 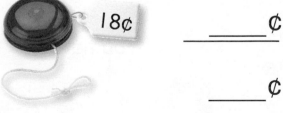?

71¢

_____ ¢

26¢

_____ ¢

_____ ¢

 Home Note Your child chose addition or subtraction to solve problems.
ACTIVITY Have your child model with coins adding the prices of two grocery items that together cost less than 99¢. He or she can also subtract the price of an item from 99¢.

Name _____

Concepts and Skills

Subtract. Regroup if you need to.

1

tens	ones
□	□
9	1
−1	6

2

tens	ones
□	□
8	0
−4	2

3

tens	ones
□	□
5	7
−2	8

4

tens	ones
□	□
6	3
−4	7

5
```
  92
 −57
```

6
```
  59
 −25
```

7
```
  40
 −21
```

8
```
  33
 −18
```

Subtract. Add to check.

9
```
  30
 −17
```

10
```
  48
  25
```

11
```
  83
 −34
```

Problem Solving

Add or subtract. Write the sum or difference.

12 You have 90¢. You buy a .
How much money do
you have left?

You have _____ ¢

_____ ¢

_____ ¢

13 How much money would
you need to buy a
and a 🪢 ?

_____ ¢

_____ ¢

_____ ¢

67¢

26¢

18¢

Name _____

Test Prep

Mark the best answer.

1 Mrs. Fox had 28 pencils. She gave away 15 of them. How many does she have left?

○ 33
○ 43
○ 14
○ 13

2 Craig had 48 baseball cards. Cameron gave him 24 more. How many baseball cards does Craig have now?

○ 62
○ 24
○ 72
○ 28

3 The clock shows when Brooke wakes up in the morning. When does she wake up?

○ 7:15
○ 7:00
○ 7:10
○ 3:35

4 The clock shows the time the football game will start. What time will it start?

○ 10:00
○ 10:05
○ 9:45
○ 10:15

5 Ashley has 64¢. She puts 38¢ in her piggy bank. How much money does she have left?

○ 26¢
○ 98¢
○ 28¢
○ 24¢

6 Martin has 1 half-dollar, 1 quarter, 3 nickels, and 4 pennies. Can he buy a pen that costs 99¢?

○ yes
○ no

Harcourt Brace School Publishers

Name _____

MATH FUN

Secret Message

Subtract. Then use the code to read.

1 – a	6 – f	11 – k	15 – o	19 – s	23 – w
2 – b	7 – g	12 – l	16 – p	20 – t	24 – x
3 – c	8 – h	13 – m	17 – q	21 – u	25 – y
4 – d	9 – i	14 – n	18 – r	22 – v	26 – z
5 – e	10 – j				

```
   17      40      53      47      19      36      39
 –  3    – 19    – 40    – 45    – 14    – 18    – 20
```

14   _____   _____   _____   _____   _____   _____

N   _____   _____   _____   _____   _____   _____

```
   47      54      12      18      10         16      20      26
 – 28    – 34    – 11    –  4    –  6       – 10    –  5    –  8
```

_____   _____   _____   _____   _____   _____   _____   _____

_____   _____   _____   _____   _____   _____   _____   _____

```
   20      24      30      33      39      69      72
 –  8    – 19    – 10    – 13    – 34    – 51    – 53
```

_____   _____   _____   _____   _____   _____   _____ .

 Home Note Your child has been practicing two-digit subtraction.
ACTIVITY You and your child can have fun using codes to write "secret" notes to each other.

Name _____

Write the missing numbers and symbols.
Use a 🖩 to check your answers.

Mrs. Jenkins gave each of her four children 82¢.

1 Jimmy spent 40¢. How much does he have left?

| ON/C | 8 | 2 | − | 4 | 0 | = | 42 |

2 Jenny spent 22¢. How much does she have left?

| ON/C | | | | | | | |

3 Kate spent 50¢. How much does she have left?

| ON/C | | | | | | | |

4 Jared has 62¢. He wants to buy one toy. What toy can he buy and still have 32¢ left? Circle the toy. Draw the keys to show you how you can check your answer.

| ON/C | | | | | | | |

59¢
67¢
26¢
30¢

Busy, Busy Babysitting

Written by Rozanne Lanczak Williams   Illustrated by Bob Holt

 This book will help me review two-digit subtracting.

This book belongs to _____.

Harcourt Brace School Publishers

M om was busy.
The house was a mess.
So I offered to watch
My sister Tess.

I watched little Tess
For one hour and a half.
That's 90 minutes
We played and laughed!

Harcourt Brace School Publishers

B

The first thing we did
Was read a good book.
We spent 10 minutes.
That's what it took.

$$90 - 10$$

With 80 minutes to go,
I played ball with Tess.
Catching and throwing—
We had 13 minutes less.

$$\begin{array}{r} 80 \\ -13 \\ \hline \end{array}$$

We had 67 minutes left.
So we went walking.
We spent 23 minutes,
Walking and talking.

$$\begin{array}{r} 67 \\ -23 \\ \hline \end{array}$$

I subtracted the minutes.
We had 44.
Then for 18 minutes
Tess napped on the floor.

$$\begin{array}{r} 44 \\ -18 \\ \hline \end{array}$$

We had 26 minutes,
So I fixed us a treat.
It took 15 minutes
To make it and eat.

$$\begin{array}{r} 26 \\ -15 \\ \hline \end{array}$$

We had 11 minutes left,
When I looked at the clock.
We spent 11 minutes
Building with blocks.

$$\begin{array}{r} 11 \\ -11 \\ \hline \end{array}$$

With zero minutes left,
My job came to an end.
I handed Tess back
And went off with my friend!

Name _____

Concepts and Skills

Use Workmat 3 and ▭▭▭▭▭▭ ▯.
Subtract.

Subtract.	Do you need to regroup? If so, regroup 1 ten as ten ones.	Write how many are left.
① 25 − 7	Yes No	_____
② 28 − 6	Yes No	_____

Subtract. Regroup if you need to.

③
tens	ones
☐	☐
3	0
−	8

④
tens	ones
☐	☐
4	6
−	5

⑤
tens	ones
☐	☐
2	1
−	9

⑥
tens	ones
☐	☐
5	3
−	7

⑦
tens	ones
☐	☐
8	5
−	3

⑧
tens	ones
☐	☐
7	2
−	6

⑨
tens	ones
☐	☐
9	4
−	5

⑩
tens	ones
☐	☐
6	0
−	9

⑪
tens	ones
☐	☐
4	2
−1	3

⑫
tens	ones
☐	☐
5	0
−2	8

⑬
tens	ones
☐	☐
3	5
−1	9

⑭
tens	ones
☐	☐
3	7
−2	6

15	tens	ones		16	tens	ones		17	tens	ones		18	tens	ones
	□	□							□	□				
	7	6			9	4			8	8			6	7
	−2	3			−1	7			−4	3			−2	8

19
```
  42
−16
```

20
```
  58
−38
```

21
```
  38
−23
```

22
```
  60
−32
```

23
```
  73
−52
```

24
```
  82
−66
```

25
```
  56
−45
```

26
```
  95
−56
```

Problem Solving

Use  .
Choose the operation. Write + or −.

27 Josie has 70¢. She buys some balloons for 39¢. How much money does she have left?

tens	ones
7	0¢
○ 3	9¢

28 How much money would you need to buy popcorn for 55¢ and juice for 26¢?

tens	ones
5	5¢
○ 2	6¢

Name _____

Performance Assessment

Use Workmat 3 and 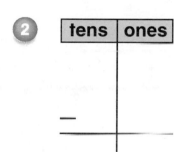.
Build a number between 50 and 99.
Subtract from that number
a number between 11 and 49.

Draw a picture to show the difference.

1

tens	ones
−	

Workmat 3

Tens	Ones

2

tens	ones
−	

Workmat 3

Tens	Ones

3

tens	ones
−	

Workmat 3

Tens	Ones

4

tens	ones
−	

Workmat 3

Tens	Ones

Write About It

5 How do you know if you need to regroup
to subtract?

Math Journal

Name _____

Fill in the ⬭ for the correct answer.

1
12
− 4
○ 5
○ 6
○ 7
○ 8

2
4
3
+6
○ 7
○ 13
○ 14
○ 15

3 Which is the number?

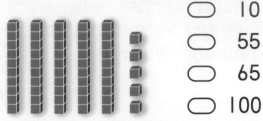

○ 10
○ 55
○ 65
○ 100

4 Count on. Which is the total amount?

○ 31¢   ○ 43¢
○ 46¢   ○ not here

5 Which is the rule for this number pattern?

15, 18, 21, 24, 27

○ Count by twos.
○ Count by threes.
○ Count by fives.
○ Count by tens.

6
59
+32

○ 81
○ 91
○ 97
○ not here

7
85
−45

○ 30
○ 35
○ 45
○ not here

8 Add or subtract.
You have 90¢. You buy a

How much money do you have left?

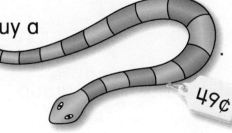

49¢

○ 41¢
○ 51¢
○ 59¢
○ not here

Organizing Data

**What are some
ways you could
sort the toys?**

Home Note In this chapter your child will learn about organizing data.
ACTIVITY Have your child show you different ways to sort the objects on this page.

Harcourt Brace School Publishers

SCHOOL-HOME CONNECTION

Dear Family,
  Today we started Chapter 14. We will learn how to make and use tally tables and how to take a survey. Here are the new vocabulary words and an activity for us to do together at home.

Love,

_____

Vocabulary

One way to count things is by using **tally marks**. You can show information gathered with tally marks in a **table** like the one below. It is easier to compare numbers when the information is shown in a table.

Favorite Pets	
bird	IIII
cat	⊞II III
dog	⊞II ⊞II
hamster	II

ACTIVITY

Help your child make a tally table to count the cars, trucks, vans, and buses you see on a walk through your neighborhood. Make a tally mark in the table for each one you see of each kind.

 Visit our Web site for additional ideas and activities.
http://www.hbschool.com

Name _____

This table shows one way these leaves can be sorted and counted.

Leaf Shapes	
broad leaf	ЖН III
narrow leaf	IIII
needle leaf	II

I stands for I. ЖН stands for 5. These are tally marks.

Use the table to answer the questions.

1 Which group has the most leaves? broad leaf

2 Which group has the fewest leaves? _____

3 How many more broad leaves than narrow leaves are there?

4 How many broad and narrow leaves are there together?

5 How many leaves are there in all? _____

Talk About It • Critical Thinking

Without counting, how can you tell which group has the fewest leaves?

Use the table to answer the questions.

Rock Shapes	
round	⊞⊞ I
flat	II
bumpy	III

1. How many round and flat rocks are there together?

   ⟨8⟩

2. Are there more bumpy rocks or flat rocks?

3. How many more round rocks than bumpy rocks are there?

4. How many more bumpy rocks than flat rocks are there?

5. How many rocks are there in all?

Write About It

6. Write a question to ask about the table. Answer the question.

Math Journal

Home Note Your child interpreted tally tables.
ACTIVITY Have your child sort some objects in several ways and make tally tables.

Harcourt Brace School Publishers

Name _____

How many children were absent from school in 1 week? Use the table to find out.

_____	
Monday	⊬⊬⊬
Tuesday	|||
Wednesday	||||
Thursday	|||
Friday	⊬⊬⊬	

1. Write a title for the table.

2. How many more children were absent on Wednesday than on Tuesday?

   1 more

3. On which day were the most children absent?

4. On which two days were the same number absent?

5. On which day were twice as many absent as on Tuesday?

How many are in the families
of the children in Mrs. Jackson's class?
Use the table to find out.

two	⊥⊥⊥⊥ I
three	⊥⊥⊥⊥
four	⊥⊥⊥⊥ I
five	III
six	II

1. Write a title for the table.

2. How many families have two people?   _____

3. How many families have fewer than four people? _____

4. How many families have more than four people? _____

5. How many children are in Mrs. Jackson's class? _____

Write About It

6. Write a question to ask about this table.
Answer the question.

Home Note Your child used a table to interpret data.
ACTIVITY Have your child make a tally table to show the kinds of weather for one week.

Harcourt Brace School Publishers

Name _____

Ask 10 classmates these questions.
Fill in tally marks.
Then answer the questions at the bottom.

1 Are you a boy or a girl?

boy	
girl	

2 How many children are in your family?

one	
two	
more	

3 What is your age?

seven	
eight	
nine	

4 Did you talk to more girls or boys? _____

5 Do more families have 2 children or 1? _____

6 Which age group has the most people? _____

Talk About It ● Critical Thinking

Do you think you would get the same answers with a
different group of classmates? Why or why not?

Harcourt Brace School Publishers

Ask 10 classmates these questions.
Fill in tally marks.
Then answer the questions at the bottom.

1 What is your favorite color?

blue	
red	
yellow	

2 What is your favorite animal?

horse	
dog	
cat	
rabbit	

3 Which favorite color did the most classmates choose? _____

4 How many chose red as their favorite color? _____

5 How many liked horses or dogs best? _____

6 Did more classmates like cats or rabbits best? _____

Harcourt Brace School Publishers

Home Note Your child took surveys and used information from them.
ACTIVITY Have your child take a survey at home and use tally marks to show the answers to his or her questions.

Name _____

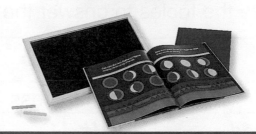

Use the tables to answer the questions.

Favorite School Subjects	
Ms. Krieger's Class	
reading	ЖЖ IIII
math	ЖЖ ЖЖ
science	ЖЖ ЖЖ I
social studies	III

Favorite School Subjects	
Mr. Farley's Class	
reading	ЖЖ ЖЖ
math	ЖЖ ЖЖ II
science	ЖЖ II
social studies	IIII

1. In which class do more children like math best?

   Mr. Farley's

2. In which class do more children like science best?

   _____

3. Which subject got the most votes? _____

4. Do more people in Ms. Krieger's class like reading
   and math best or social studies and science?

   _____

5. How many children are in each class? _____

Practice

Use the tables to answer the questions.

Favorite Colors	
Mr. Cushman's Class	
red	~~IIII~~ II
blue	~~IIII~~ IIII
purple	~~IIII~~ I
orange	III

Favorite Colors	
Ms. Nakitani's Class	
red	~~IIII~~ ~~IIII~~
blue	~~IIII~~ ~~IIII~~
purple	~~IIII~~ I
orange	II

1. Which class gave the same number of votes to two colors?

   Ms. Nakitani's

2. Which color got the same number of votes in each class?

3. In which class did purple get twice as many votes as orange?

4. Which color got the fewest votes in both classes?

Mixed Review

Add or subtract.

5.
$$73 - 19$$ $$66 + 16$$ $$38 - 17$$ $$39 + 5$$ $$37 + 44$$ $$42 - 19$$

Harcourt Brace School Publishers

 Home Note Your child compared information in tables.
ACTIVITY Have your child sort objects in two ways and make two tally tables. Invite him or her to compare the information in the tables.

Concepts and Skills

Favorite Zoo Animals	
bear	ЖЖ
giraffe	|||
lion	|||
monkey	ЖЖ ||
tiger	ЖЖ ЖЖ

1 Which animal got twice as many votes as the bear?

_____

2 Which animals got the same number of votes?

_____

Use the tables to answer the questions.

Favorite Lunches Room 238	
sandwich	ЖЖ ЖЖ ||
salad	ЖЖ
hamburger	ЖЖ	

Favorite Lunches Room 246	
sandwich	ЖЖ ||
salad	ЖЖ	
hamburger	ЖЖ ЖЖ

3 How many children are in each room? _____

4 In Room 246, how many like a hamburger best for lunch? _____

5 In which room do more children like a sandwich best? _____

Name _____

Test Prep

Mark the best answer.

1 The tally table shows the favorite pets of second graders. How many children like dogs the best?

Favorite Pets	
cats	ЖН II
dogs	ЖН ЖН I
hamsters	IIII
frogs	ЖН

- ◯ 5
- ◯ 4
- ◯ 11
- ◯ 7

2 Which number does the model show?

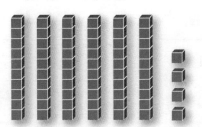

- ◯ 46
- ◯ 64
- ◯ 83
- ◯ 44

3 Which is the missing number in this pattern?

2, 4, 6, 8, ___, 12, 14

- ◯ 9
- ◯ 11
- ◯ 13
- ◯ 10

4 Murray has 97 pennies. He puts them in groups of ten. How many pennies will be left over?

- ◯ 87
- ◯ 7
- ◯ 9
- ◯ 16

5 Mr. Potter had 91¢. He bought an apple for 29¢. How much money does Mr. Potter have now?

- ◯ 62¢
- ◯ 70¢
- ◯ 39¢
- ◯ 26¢

Standardized Test Prep • Chapters 1-14

CHAPTER 15

Making and Reading Graphs

Make a graph to show the rain gear.

Home Note In this chapter your child will learn to make and read graphs.
ACTIVITY Have your child show you some different ways to sort the rain gear.

SCHOOL-HOME CONNECTION

Dear Family,
  Today we started Chapter 15. We will learn how to make and read different kinds of graphs. Here are the new vocabulary words and an activity for us to do together at home.

  Love,

  _____

Vocabulary

pictograph

Favorite Peanut Butter	
smooth	🧍 🧍 🧍
crunchy	🧍 🧍

Each 🧍 stands for 2 children.

bar graph

Favorite Peanut Butter
smooth
crunchy

0 1 2 3 4 5 6 7 8

ACTIVITY

Work with your child to graph the number of times he or she cleans his or her room each week.

 Visit our Web site for additional ideas and activities.
http://www.hbschool.com

Harcourt Brace School Publishers

Name _____

Picture Graphs

Use the graph to answer the questions.

A graph makes it easy to compare groups.

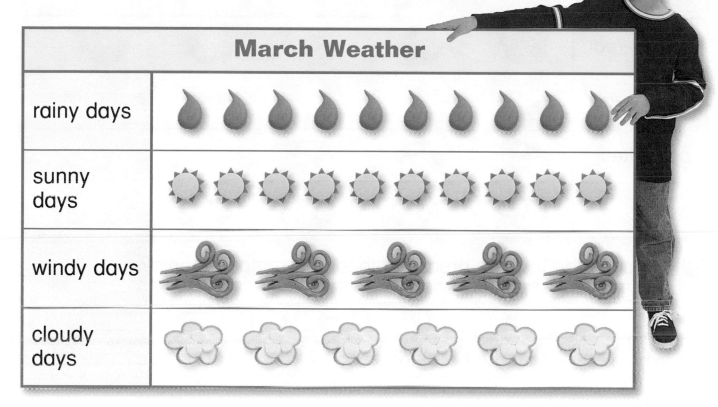

March Weather

rainy days	🌧🌧🌧🌧🌧🌧🌧🌧🌧🌧
sunny days	☀☀☀☀☀☀☀☀☀☀
windy days	🌀🌀🌀🌀🌀
cloudy days	☁☁☁☁☁☁

1. How many sunny days were there in March?

10

2. How many rainy days were there? _____

3. How many cloudy days were there? _____

4. Were there more windy days or cloudy days?

_____

5. Were there fewer cloudy days or rainy days?

_____

Talk About It • Critical Thinking

How many days are in March? How do you know?

Harcourt Brace School Publishers

Practice

Use the graph to answer the questions.

Favorite Breakfast Food					
cold cereal	🥣	🥣	🥣	🥣	🥣
hot cereal	🥣				
pancakes	🥞	🥞	🥞		
waffles	🧇	🧇	🧇	🧇	

① Which is the favorite breakfast food of the most people?

cold cereal

② Which is the favorite breakfast food of the fewest people?

_____

③ How many more like pancakes than hot cereal best? _____

④ How many fewer like hot cereal than cold cereal best? _____

⑤ How many in all like pancakes and waffles best? _____

⑥ How many in all were asked about their favorite breakfast food? _____

Mixed Review

⑦ Count on by tens.

24, _____, _____, 54, _____, 74, _____, _____

⑧ Count back by tens.

_____, 77, _____, 57, _____, _____, 27, _____

 Home Note Your child used information from picture graphs to answer questions.
ACTIVITY Have your child explain how he or she used each graph to answer the questions.

252 two hundred fifty-two

Chapter 15

Harcourt Brace School Publishers

Name _____

Children Who Walk to School	
Tosha's Class	ⵑ卌 卌 卌
Linda's Class	卌 卌
Carolyn's Class	卌 卌 卌 卌 卌
Barb's Class	卌 卌 卌 卌

A pictograph uses pictures.
Each picture stands
for more than 1 thing.

Use the tally table to fill in the pictograph.
Draw 1 🧍 for every 5 children.

Children Who Walk to School

Tosha's Class	🧍 🧍 🧍
Linda's Class	🧍 🧍
Carolyn's Class	
Barb's Class	

Each 🧍 stands for 5 children.

1. How many walkers are there in Tosha's class?

   _____
   _____

2. How many children in Tosha's class and Linda's class walk to school?

   _____
   _____

3. Which class has the most walkers?

   _____

4. Write a question to ask about the graph.

   _____
   _____

Practice

Children Who Have Pets	
birds	I I I I
cats	⊞⊞ I I I
dogs	⊞⊞ ⊞⊞ I I I I
fish	⊞⊞ I

Use the tally table to fill in the pictograph.
Draw I 🚶 for every 2 children.

Children Who Have Pets	
birds	🚶 🚶
cats	
dogs	
fish	

Each 🚶 stands for 2 children.

1 How many more children have dogs
than cats?

_____
_ _ _ _ _ _ _ _ _ _ _ _ _
_____
_ _ _ _ _ _ _ _ _ _ _ _ _

2 Which pet do the fewest children have?   _____

3 Write a question to ask about the graph.

_____
_ _ _ _ _ _ _ _ _ _ _ _ _
_____

Home Note Your child made and read pictographs.
ACTIVITY Tell your child that the graph is for the whole school and that each picture stands for 10
children. Have him or her answer questions I and 2 again.

Harcourt Brace School Publishers

Name _____

Use the tally table to fill in the bar graph.

Our Favorite Sandwiches	
peanut butter	IIII
ham and cheese	IIII
hamburger	IIII IIII
tomato	II
tuna	III

Color the boxes to make a bar graph.

Our Favorite Sandwiches

	0	1	2	3	4	5	6	7	8	9	10
peanut butter		▓	▓	▓							
ham and cheese											
hamburger											
tomato											
tuna											

1. How many more people like tuna sandwiches than tomato the best? _____

2. How many more like a hamburger than a ham and cheese sandwich the best? _____

3. Which sandwich is the favorite of the most people? _____

4. Which sandwich is the favorite of the fewest people? _____

Talk About It • Critical Thinking

How is a bar graph different from a pictograph?

Use the tally table to fill in the bar graph.

Our Favorite Cookies

chocolate chip	~~IIII~~ ~~IIII~~
oatmeal raisin	IIII
spice	I
sugar	~~IIII~~

Our Favorite Cookies

	0	1	2	3	4	5	6	7	8	9	10
chocolate chip											
oatmeal raisin											
spice											
sugar											

1. How many people like chocolate chip cookies the best? _____

2. How many fewer people like spice cookies than chocolate chip cookies the best? _____

3. How many more people like chocolate chip cookies than like sugar cookies the best? _____

Write About It

4. Which cookie is the favorite of the most people? How do you know?

Harcourt Brace School Publishers

Home Note Your child made and interpreted horizontal bar graphs.
ACTIVITY Have your child ask family members about other favorite things and make graphs to show what he or she learns.

Name _____

Which season do your classmates like best? Make a graph to find out.

1 Ask ten people which season is their favorite. Fill in the tally table to show their answers.

2 Use the tally table to fill in the graph.

Favorite Seasons

winter	
spring	
summer	
fall	

10
9
8
7
6
5
4
3
2
1
0

3 Which season do the most people like best?

_____

_____

4 Do more people like winter or summer best?

_____

_____

5 Do more people like fall or spring best?

_____

_____

Harcourt Brace School Publishers

Practice

Which day of the week do your classmates like best?
Make a graph to find out.

1 Ask ten people which day of
the week is their favorite.
Fill in the tally table to show
their answers.

2 Use the tally table to fill in
the graph.

Favorite Days of the Week	
Sunday	
Monday	
Tuesday	
Wednesday	
Thursday	
Friday	
Saturday	

10
9
8
7
6
5
4
3
2
1
0

3 Which day do the most people like
best? _____

4 Do more people like Saturday or
Sunday best? _____

5 Do more people like Monday or
Friday best? _____

6 Which day is liked by the fewest
people? _____

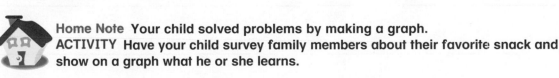

Home Note Your child solved problems by making a graph.
ACTIVITY Have your child survey family members about their favorite snack and
show on a graph what he or she learns.

Harcourt Brace School Publishers

Name _____

Concepts and Skills

Review/Test

Use the pictograph to answer the questions.

Ways We Come to School	
bus	♦ ♦ ♦
walk	♦ ♦
car	♦

Each ♦ stands for 5 children.

1. How many more children come by bus than by car? _____

2. How many fewer children come by car than walk? _____

Use the tally table to fill in the bar graph.

Lunches	
bring lunch	ℍℍ ℍℍ
buy lunch	ℍℍ ℍℍ II

	_____											
_____												
_____												

0 1 2 3 4 5 6 7 8 9 10 11 12

3. How many children bring their lunch? _____

4. How many more children buy lunch than bring lunch? _____

Name _____

Test Prep

Mark the best answer.

1 The graph shows favorite colors. How many children like blue the best?

Our Favorite Colors

red	♟♟♟♟
blue	♟♟♟♟♟
green	♟♟

Each ♟ stands for 3 children.

- ○ 12
- ○ 9
- ○ 15
- ○ 5

2 The clock shows the time Barry's piano lesson starts. What time does it start?

- ○ 6:15
- ○ 6:45
- ○ 5:45
- ○ 9:30

3 Fran had 23 pieces of bread. She fed 16 pieces to the ducks. How many pieces are left?

- ○ 7
- ○ 39
- ○ 9
- ○ 42

4 Ryan had 46¢. His friend gave him 38¢. How much money does he have now?

- ○ 8¢
- ○ 18¢
- ○ 84¢
- ○ 74¢

5 Gilda has 1 quarter, 6 dimes, 2 nickels, and 1 penny. How much money does she have?

- ○ 81¢
- ○ 61¢
- ○ 36¢
- ○ 96¢

Standardized Test Prep • Chapters 1–15

Harcourt Brace School Publishers

Data and Predictions

Which color toy are you more likely to get?

Home Note In this chapter your child is learning about data and predictions.
ACTIVITY Help your child think of and answer questions that involve making predictions.

SCHOOL-HOME CONNECTION

Dear Family,
    Today we started Chapter 16. We will learn how to look at information and say what is most likely and least likely to happen. Here are the new vocabulary words and an activity for us to do together at home.

Love,

_____

Vocabulary

The child in the picture is **most likely** to hook a blue car because there are more blue cars than red cars or green cars.

The child is **least likely** to hook a green car because there are fewer green cars than blue cars or red cars.

ACTIVITY

Gather 10 socks in 3 colors. Ask your child to count and write down how many socks there are of each color. Put all the socks in a paper bag. Have your child tell which color he or she thinks is **most likely** and which **least likely** to be pulled from the bag and why. Make a tally table. Have your child pull a sock from the bag 10 times without looking and then put it back, shaking the bag to mix up the socks. Mark the tally table each time. Talk about which color was pulled out most often and which least often.

 Visit our Web site for additional ideas and activities.
http://www.hbschool.com

Name _____

Use the picture. Circle the groups of boats
that you are certain to find in this picture.
Cross out the groups of boats that are
impossible to find in this picture.

Something is certain
if it is sure to happen.
Something is impossible if
it cannot happen.

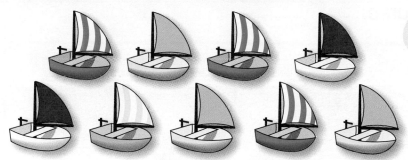

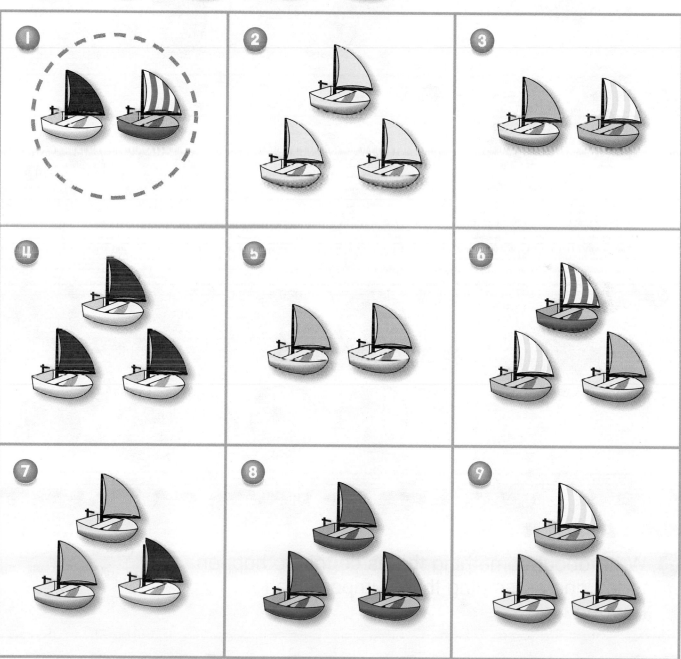

Harcourt Brace School Publishers

Practice

Use the picture.
Circle the groups of coins that
you are certain to find in the purse.
Cross out the groups of coins that
are impossible to find in the purse.

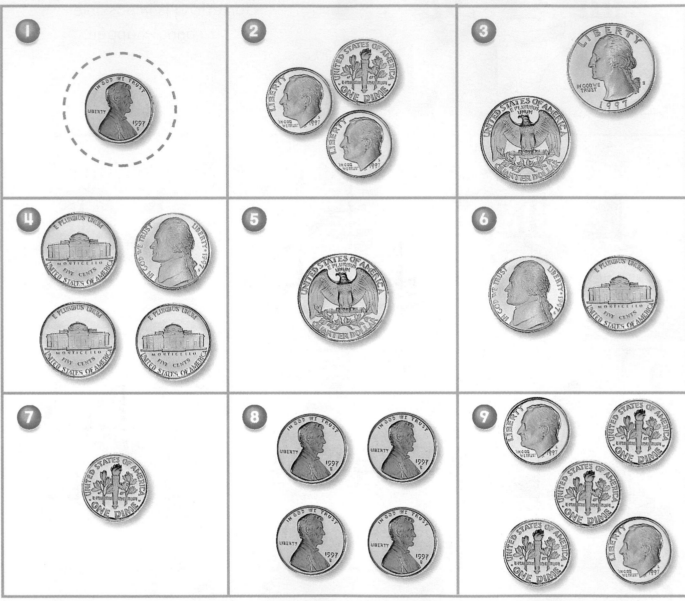

Write About It

10 Write about something that is certain to happen
today and something that is impossible to
happen today.

Home Note Your child determined whether an event is certain or impossible.
ACTIVITY Give your child the coins shown in the purse. Have him or her use them to act out these
problems.

Harcourt Brace School Publishers

Name _____

This table shows
the outcomes of 10 spins.

Color	Tally Marks
blue	⌿⌿⌿⌿ |||
red	||

1 On what colors could the spinner stop?

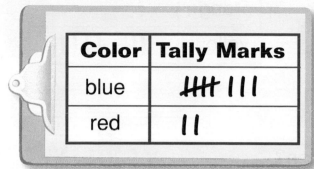
blue or red

2 Which color did the spinner stop on more often? _____

3 Which color did the spinner stop on less often? _____

This table shows
the outcomes of 10 spins.

Color	Tally Marks
blue	|||
red	⌿⌿⌿⌿ ||

4 Which color did the spinner stop on more often? _____

5 Which color did the spinner stop on less often? _____

Talk About It ● **Critical Thinking**

Compare the outcomes for both sets of spins.
Why do you think the outcomes are different?

Practice

This table shows the outcomes of 10 pulls from the bag.

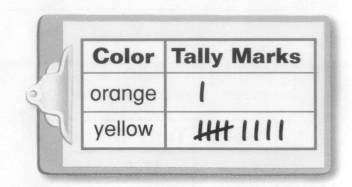

Color	Tally Marks
orange	I
yellow	IIII IIII

1 Which color was pulled out more often?

yellow

2 Which color was pulled out less often?

3 Do you think there are more orange or yellow cubes in the bag?

This table shows the outcomes of 10 pulls from the bag.

Color	Tally Marks
orange	IIII II
yellow	III

4 Which color was pulled out more often?

5 Do you think there are more orange or yellow cubes in the bag?

Mixed Review

Subtract. Add to check.

6
```
  83
- 58
____
```

7
```
  56
- 28
____
```

Harcourt Brace School Publishers

Home Note Your child interpreted outcomes of games.
ACTIVITY Place in a bag a group of objects, alike except for color—for example, 6 red buttons and 2 white buttons. Have your child pull out an object 10 times and make a tally table to show the outcomes.

Chapter 16

Name _____

You will need: 9 ■, 3 ■, 3 ■, 1 bag

Part 1

① Put all the ■, ■, and ■ in the bag.
Pull out 1 tile.
Make a tally mark to show which color you pulled out.

② Put the tile back into the bag. Shake. Do this 9 more times.

③ Make a prediction.
If you do this 10 more times, which color do you think you are most likely to pull?

_____

- - - - - - - - - - - - - - - - - - - -

_____

Color	Tally Marks
yellow	
blue	
red	

Part 2

④ Do this 10 more times.
Make a tally mark each time.

⑤ Which color tile did you pull out most often?

_____

- - - - - - - - - - - - - - - - - - - -

_____

⑥ Why do you think this happened?

_____

- - - - - - - - - - - - - - - - - - - -

_____

- - - - - - - - - - - - - - - - - - - -

Talk About It • Critical Thinking

Explain to a classmate how you know which color is most likely to be pulled out of the bag.

Practice

You will need: 6 ■, 4 ■, 2 ■, I bag

Color	Tally Marks
yellow	
blue	
red	

Part I

1. Put all the ■, ■, and ■ in the bag. Pull out I tile.

2. Make a tally mark to show which color you pulled out. Put the tile back. Shake. Do this 9 more times. Record each color on the tally table.

3. Make a prediction. If you do this 10 more times, which color do you think you are most likely to pull?

_____

- - - - - - - - - - - - - -

_____

Part 2

4. Do this 10 more times. Make a tally mark each time.

5. Which color tile did you pull out most often?

_____

- - - - - - - - - - - - - -

_____

6. Why do you think this happened?

_____

- - - - - - - - - - - - - -

_____

_____

Problem Solving

Solve.

7. Jenny pulled a red tile from her bag 15 times. She pulled out a blue tile 3 times, and a yellow tile 2 times. Which color tile do you think there is most of in her bag?

_____

- - - - - - - - - - - - - -

Draw a picture to show what might be in her bag.

Harcourt Brace School Publishers

Home Note Your child learned to predict which event is most likely.
ACTIVITY Have your child make and test predictions using groups of small objects and a paper bag.

Name _____

You will need:

4 ⊗ and ▭, ▭, and ▭.

Part 1

1 Make a prediction. Circle the ⊗ that you think is less likely to stop on blue.

Color	Tally Marks
blue	
red	

2 Use 2 ⊗.
Spin each ⊗ 10 times.
Make a tally mark each time.

Color	Tally Marks
blue	
red	

3 Was your prediction correct? _____

Part 2

4 Make a prediction. Circle the ⊗ that you think is less likely to stop on yellow.

Color	Tally Marks
yellow	
red	

5 Use 2 ⊗.
Spin each ⊗ 10 times.
Make a tally mark each time.

Color	Tally Marks
yellow	
red	

6 Was your prediction correct? _____

Harcourt Brace School Publishers

Practice

You will need:
2 paper bags, 7 ■, 7 ■, 8 ■, 8 ☐

Part 1

1. Make a prediction. Circle the bag from which you think it is less likely to pull .

Color	Tally Marks
red	
green	

2. Pull out 1 cube 10 times. Make a tally mark each time.

Color	Tally Marks
red	
green	

3. Was your prediction correct? _____

Part 2

4. Make a prediction. Circle the bag from which you think it is less likely to pull ■.

Color	Tally Marks
yellow	
purple	

5. Pull out 1 cube 10 times. Make a tally mark each time.

Color	Tally Marks
yellow	
purple	

6. Was your prediction correct? _____

 Home Note Your child predicted which event is less likely.
ACTIVITY Have your child make a spinner that is less likely to stop on orange than on green.

Harcourt Brace School Publishers

Name _____

Concepts and Skills

Use the picture.
Circle the groups of coins that you
are certain to find in the purse.
Cross out the groups of coins that are
impossible to find in the purse.

1

2

3

This table shows
the outcomes
of 10 spins.

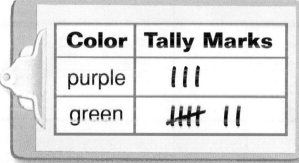

Color	Tally Marks
purple	III
green	IIII II

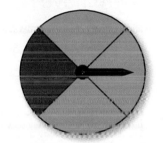

4 On what colors could the spinner stop? _____

_____

5 Which color did the spinner stop on more often? _____

_____

6 Which color did the spinner stop on less often? _____

7 Circle the spinner
that you think would
stop on blue less
often.

Name _____

Test Prep

Mark the best answer.

1 On which color is the spinner more likely to stop?

○ green
○ blue

2 Use the tally table. How many green beads does Myra have?

Myra's Beads	
🔴	‖‖‖ III
🔵	‖‖‖ ‖‖‖ I
⚪	‖‖‖

○ 2
○ 5
○ 8
○ 24

3 On Tuesday, 48 second graders rode the bus to school. On Wednesday, 39 second graders rode the bus to school. How many more students rode the bus on Tuesday?

○ 9
○ 10
○ 19
○ 87

4 Which numbers come next?

48, 51, 54, 57, ___, ___

○ 58, 59
○ 60, 63
○ 56, 55
○ 60, 61

5 Which shape comes next?

6 Count on. What is the total amount?

○ 81¢
○ 86¢
○ 66¢
○ 96¢

Harcourt Brace School Publishers

Name _____

You will need:
pencil, clear tape, magnifying glass

Fingerprint Detective

All fingerprints have one of the three patterns shown in the table.

Fingerprint Patterns in Ms. Taylor's Class		
arch		ⅢⅢ ⅢⅢ I I
loop		ⅢⅢ I I
whorl		I I I I

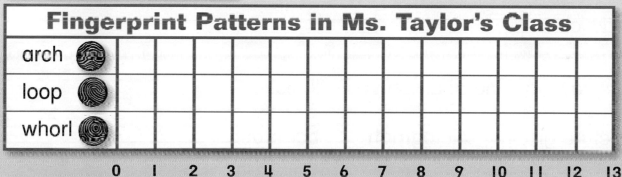

Fingerprint Patterns in Ms. Taylor's Class

		0	1	2	3	4	5	6	7	8	9	10	11	12	13
arch															
loop															
whorl															

1 Use the tally table to fill in the bar graph.

2 How many fingerprints have an arch pattern? ☐

3 How many fingerprints have a whorl pattern? _____

4 Roll your finger over the box you filled in with a pencil. Put tape over that finger.

5 Peel the tape from your finger and put the tape on the other box.

6 Use a magnifying glass to look at your fingerprint pattern.

7 Add your fingerprint to the table and the graph.

Use a pencil to fill in this box.

My Fingerprint

Home Note Your child has learned to organize, display, and interpret data.
ACTIVITY Have your child graph the fingerprint patterns of family members.

Harcourt Brace School Publishers

Name _____

Calculator   **Computer**

1 Ask 10 people to name their favorite lunch food. Fill in tally marks.

Favorite Foods	
hot dog	
hamburger	
pizza	
sandwich	

2 Circle what kind of graph you will make.

   picture graph   pictograph   bar graph

3 Use a computer to make the graph.

4 Print the graph.

Use the graph you made to answer the questions.

5 Which favorite food did the most people choose?

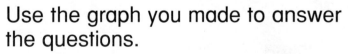

6 Which favorite food did the fewest people choose?

7 Were there any foods that the same number chose?

Harcourt Brace School Publishers

Hector's friends

written by Ann Lee
illustrated by Holly Cooper

 This book will help me review *certain* and *impossible*.

This book belongs to _____.

A

On Monday when Hector came home
from school, he said to his mother.
"Today I met a lion. He wants to come
to my house and play with me."

Harcourt Brace School Publishers

"That is <u>impossible</u>," said Hector's mother. "Lions are ferocious animals that live on the plains of Africa. It is impossible for a lion to come home and play with you."

Harcourt Brace School Publishers

The next day when Hector came home
from school, he said to his mother, "Today
I met a boy named Juan. I want him to
come to my house to play with me."

D

"That is <u>certain</u>," said Hector's mother. "I will call Juan's mother to see when he can come and play with you."

On Friday when Hector came home from school, he said to his mother, "Today I met a tiger. He wants to come to my house to play with me."

Harcourt Brace School Publishers

"That is <u>impossible</u>," said Hector's mother. "Tigers live in rain forests and cold, snowy forests. They also live in grasslands and swamps. A tiger cannot come home and play with you. But today I met someone, and she wants to play with you."

G

"That is <u>certain</u>!" said Hector.
"Yes, it is certain that I want to
play with her!"

Name _____

Concepts and Skills

Use the table for questions 1 and 2.

Favorite Crayons	
green	ЖЖ ЖЖ
red	IIII
purple	ЖЖ II
blue	IIII

1 Which crayon got the most votes?

_____

_____

2 Which crayons got the same number of votes?

_____

Use the tables for questions 3 and 4.

Favorite Snack – Room A	
apple	ЖЖ III
cookie	IIII
carrot	II
grapes	ЖЖ I

Favorite Snack – Room B	
apple	IIII
cookie	ЖЖ II
carrot	ЖЖ I
grapes	III

3 In Room B, how many children liked carrots the best? _____

4 In which room did apples get twice as many votes as cookies? _____

Use the graph for questions 5 and 6.

Color of Our Shirts	
blue	웃
green	웃 웃 웃
brown	웃 웃

Each 웃 stands for 5 children.

5 How many children have brown shirts?

_____ children

6 How many more children have green shirts than brown shirts?

_____ more children

7 Use the tally table to fill in the graph.

Children in Our Class	
girls	~~HHHH~~ ~~HHHH~~ II
boys	~~HHHH~~ IIII

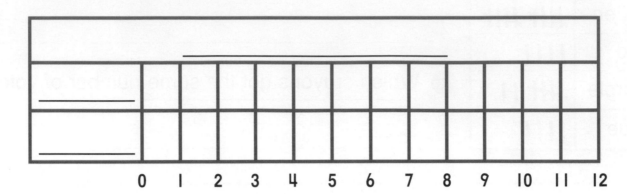

```
_____
_____
       0  1  2  3  4  5  6  7  8  9  10  11  12
```

8 How many boys are there? _____ boys

9 How many more girls than boys are there? _____ more girls

Use the picture.
Circle the groups of cars you are certain to find on the shelf.
Cross out the groups of cars that are impossible to find on the shelf.

10

11

12

The table shows
the outcomes of
10 spins.

Color	
blue	~~HHHH~~ III
pink	II

13 On what colors could the spinner stop? _____

14 Which color did the spinner stop on less often? _____

Performance Assessment

Use a .
Write 1, 2, or 3 on each face of the .
Use each number at least once.

1 What numbers did you write?

_____

2 Toss the cube 20 times.
Make a tally mark for each toss.

Numbers Tossed	
1	
2	
3	

3 Color the graph to match the tally marks.

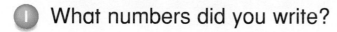

Numbers Tossed												
1												
2												
3												

0 1 2 3 4 5 6 7 8 9 10 11 12

4 Write the three numbers you are certain could come up when you toss the cube.

___, ___, ___

5 Write three numbers it is impossible to get when you toss the cube.

___, ___, ___

Write About It

6 Use a red and a yellow crayon. Color the spinner so that yellow is more likely. Explain how you know.

Name _____

Fill in the ⬭ for the correct answer.

1 6
   +6
   ◯ 11
   ◯ 12
   ◯ 13
   ◯ 14

2 16
   − 7
   ◯ 8
   ◯ 9
   ◯ 10
   ◯ 11

3 Is 15 an even or odd number?

◯ even   ◯ odd

4 Which is the total amount?

◯ 28¢   ◯ 31¢
◯ 46¢   ◯ not here

5 School starts at .

Jan gets there at .

Is Jan early or late?
◯ early   ◯ late

6 16
  +28
  ◯ 34
  ◯ 43
  ◯ 44
  ◯ 45

7 27
  − 14
  ◯ 13
  ◯ 31
  ◯ 41
  ◯ 42

8 Which color is the spinner likely to stop on more often?

◯ green
◯ yellow

9 Which fruit got the most votes?
◯ apple   ◯ banana
◯ grapes   ◯ orange

10 Which fruit got the same number of votes as apple?
◯ apple   ◯ banana
◯ grapes   ◯ orange

Favorite Fruit	
apple	ⅢⅢ ‖
banana	ⅢⅢ ‖‖
grapes	‖‖
orange	ⅢⅢ ‖

Cumulative Review • Chapters 1–16

Harcourt Brace School Publishers

Solid and Plane Figures

What solid figures do you see in the picture?

Home Note In this chapter your child will learn about solid and plane figures.
ACTIVITY Have your child find examples of solid figures at home.

Harcourt Brace School Publishers

SCHOOL-HOME CONNECTION

Dear Family,
    Today we started Chapter 17. We will identify and use solid figures. Here are the new vocabulary words and an activity for us to do together at home.

Love,

_____

Vocabulary

rectangular prism

sphere

cone

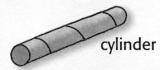
cylinder

pyramid

cube

ACTIVITY

Play a game of I Spy with your child. Look around the room for an object that is shaped like one of the solid figures shown at the left. Give your child clues about the object you have in mind. For example, you might say that you spy an object that rolls, has no corners, and is orange. Your child should name the object and tell you what solid figure it is, using the correct math word.

Visit our Web site for additional ideas and activities.
http://www.hbschool.com

Harcourt Brace School Publishers

Identifying Solids

These are solid figures.

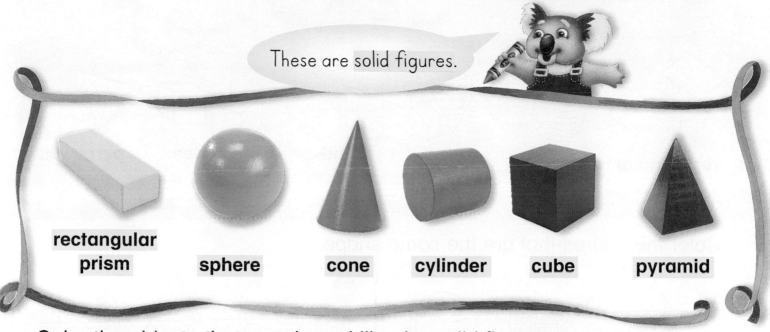

rectangular
prism

sphere

cone

cylinder

cube

pyramid

Color the objects that are shaped like the solid figure.
Cross out the objects that are not shaped like the solid figure.

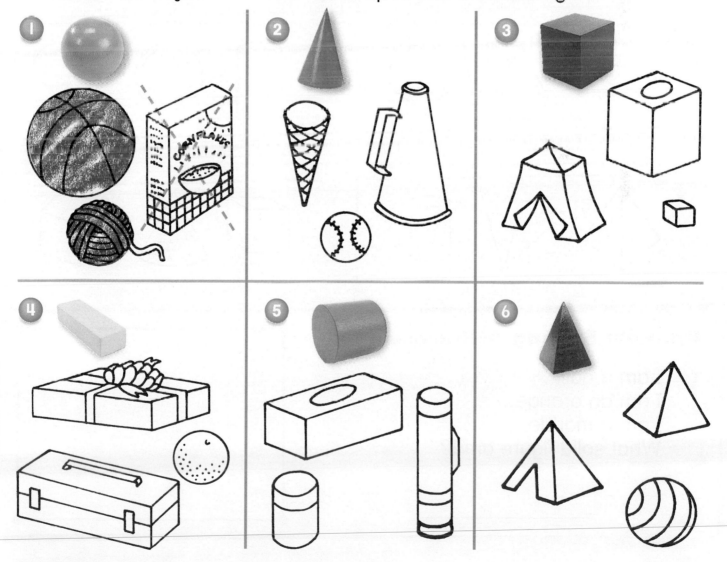

Talk About It ● Critical Thinking

What do you notice about each solid figure?

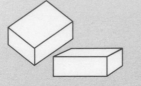 rectangular prisms

 sphere

 cones

 cylinders

 cubes

pyramids

Color the figures that are the same shape.

1

2

3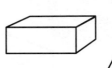

4

5

6

Problem Solving ● Reasoning

7 I am a ball.
I am an orange.
I am a marble.
What solid figure am I?

_____

Home Note Your child learned to identify solid figures.
ACTIVITY Have your child point out objects that are shaped like the solid figures he or she has learned about.

Name _____

A flat surface can also be called a face.

Cubes can be stacked.

Color all the solid figures that fit the rule.

1. It has six faces. It can be stacked.

2. It has only two faces. It can be stacked.

   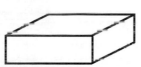

3. It has no faces. It can roll, but it cannot slide.

  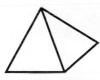 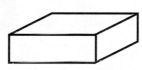

4. It has 6 faces. It can slide, and it can be stacked.

  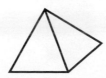 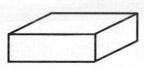

Talk About It • Critical Thinking

Describe the faces. Tell how many each figure has. Tell which figures can stack, roll, or slide.

Practice

Circle the solid figure that is missing.

1

2

3

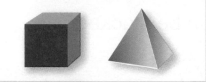

4

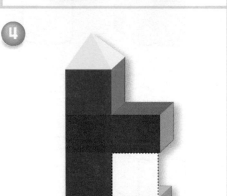

5

6

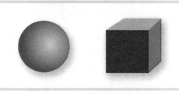

Write About It

7 Write about the solid figure.
Tell how many faces it has.
Tell if it can be stacked.
Tell if it can roll and if it can slide.

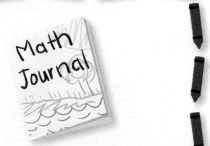

 Home Note Your child learned to sort solid figures.
ACTIVITY Find objects that are shaped like solid figures. With your child, count the faces. Talk
about which figures can be stacked, which can roll, and which can slide.

Name _____

Understand • Plan • Solve • Look Back

There is a mistake in each pattern.
Cross out the mistake.
Circle the solid figure that belongs.

1

2

3

4

5

6

Chapter 17 • Solid and Plane Figures

There is a mistake in each pattern.
Cross out the mistake.
Circle the solid figure that belongs.

Home Note Your child used the strategy Look for a Pattern to solve problems.
ACTIVITY Set out objects in a pattern. Change one of the objects so that there is a mistake in the
pattern. Have your child find and correct the mistake.

Name _____

The faces of solid figures are plane figures.

Trace the faces of the solid figure.
Then circle the plane figure you
can trace from the solid figure.

1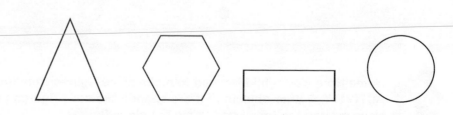

2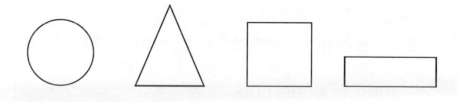

3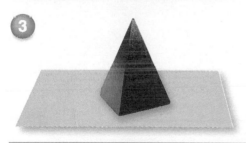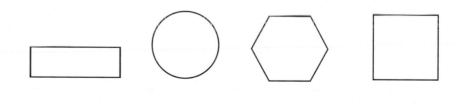

4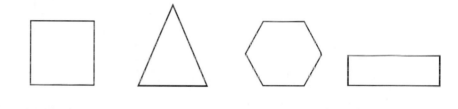

5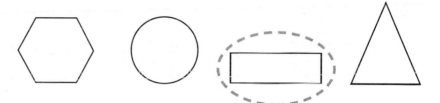

Chapter 17 • Solid and Plane Figures

Practice

Look at the faces on the
solid figure.
Circle the solid figure you
can use to trace the faces.

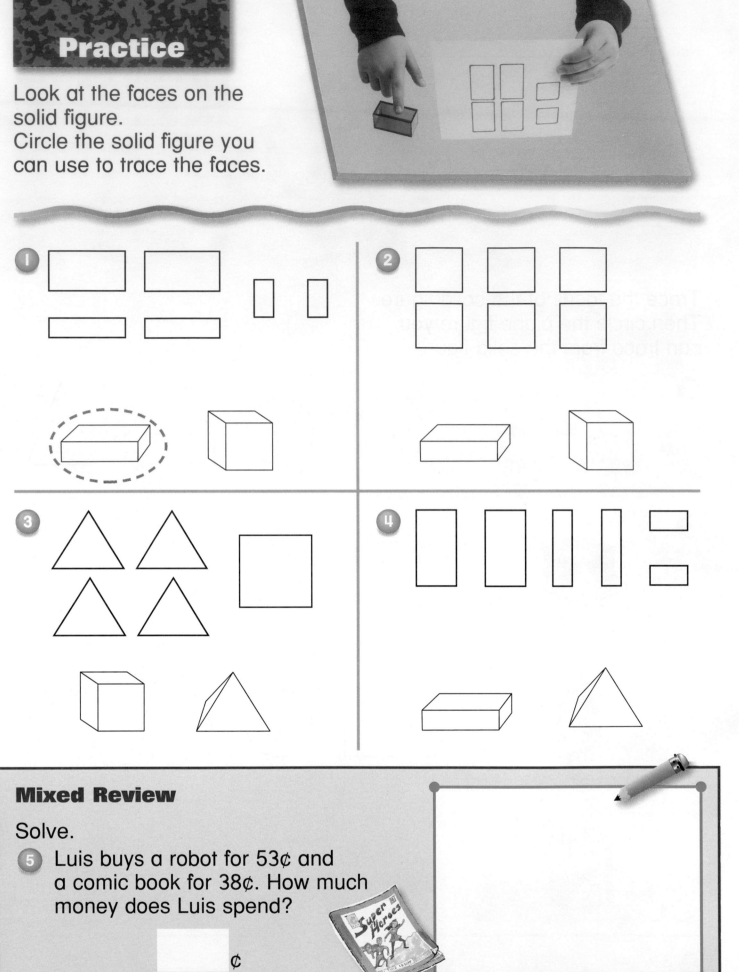

1

2

3

4

Mixed Review

Solve.

5 Luis buys a robot for 53¢ and
a comic book for 38¢. How much
money does Luis spend?

_____ ¢

Home Note Your child learned to make plane figures from the faces of solid figures.
ACTIVITY Gather objects that are shaped like solid figures your child knows. Have him or her
trace around the faces and name the plane figures.

Harcourt Brace School Publishers

Concepts and Skills

Color the objects that are shaped like the solid figure.
Cross out the objects that are not shaped like the solid figure.

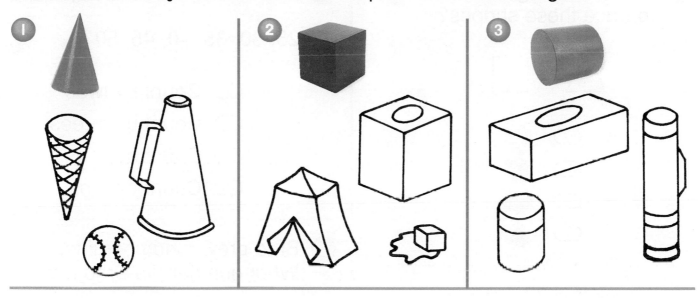

Color all the solids that fit the rule.

4 It has six square faces. It can be stacked.

Circle the plane figure you can trace from the solid figure.

5

Problem Solving

Cross out the mistake in the pattern.
Circle the solid figure that belongs.

6

Name _____

Test Prep

Mark the best answer.

1 Which solid figure can be used to trace these shapes?

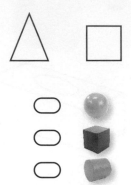

○
○
○
○

2 Chuck has 47 pictures. Julie has 35 pictures. How many pictures do they have in all?

○ 70
○ 82
○ 72
○ 90

3 Babs had 50 pennies in her purse. She put 31 of the pennies in her piggy bank. How many pennies are in Babs' purse now?

○ 19
○ 81
○ 21
○ 29

4 What is the rule for the pattern?

25, 30, 35, 40, 45, 50

○ Count by twos.
○ Count by threes.
○ Count by fives.
○ Count by tens.

5 Brad drew a number line. What number did Brad mark?

25   40

_____

○ 25
○ 33
○ 38
○ 40

6 Julian's alarm clock goes off at

What time is that?

○ 6:15
○ 7:15
○ 8:05
○ 3:30

Harcourt Brace School Publishers

Plane Figures

CHAPTER
18

What plane figures can you find?

Home Note In this chapter your child will learn about plane figures.
ACTIVITY Have your child find plane figures at home.

SCHOOL-HOME CONNECTION

Dear Family,
    Today we started Chapter 18. We will learn about and make plane figures. Here are the new vocabulary words and an activity for us to do together at home.

Love,

_____

Vocabulary

square

triangle

rectangle

circle

These two triangles are **congruent** because they are the same size and shape.

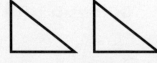

ACTIVITY

Help your child make a table to tally the plane figures (flat shapes) found on your street. Go for a walk around the block. Have your child make a tally mark for each circle, triangle, square, and rectangle he or she sees.

Visit our Web site for additional ideas and activities.
http://www.hbschool.com

Harcourt Brace School Publishers

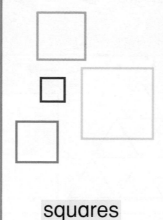 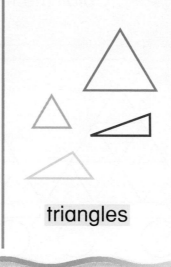 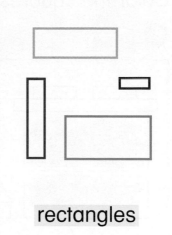

| circles | squares | triangles | rectangles |

1 Color the circles.
Cross out the figures that are not circles.

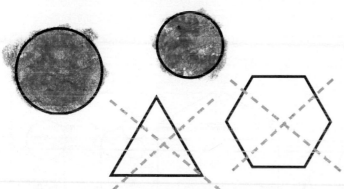

2 Color the squares.
Cross out the figures that are not squares.

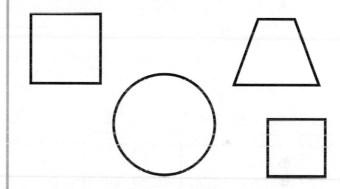

3 Color the triangles.
Cross out the figures that are not triangles.

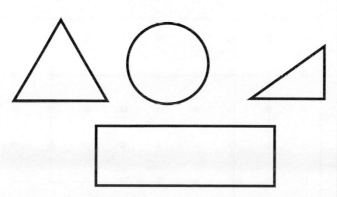

4 Color the rectangles.
Cross out the figures that are not rectangles.

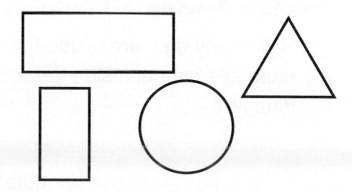

Talk About It ● Critical Thinking

Tell one thing about triangles that makes them different from circles, squares, and rectangles. Do the same for the other figures.

Harcourt Brace School Publishers

Color the squares . Color the triangles . Color the circles .

1

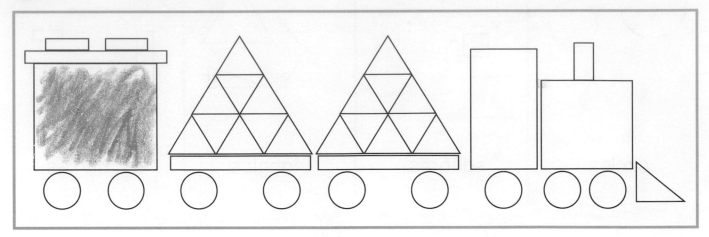

Color the rectangles . Color the triangles .
Color the circles .

2

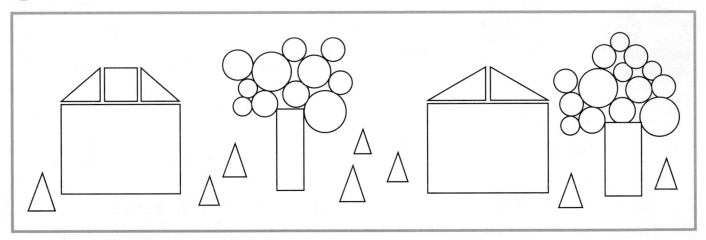

Problem Solving ● **Reasoning**

3 How many dots are inside the rectangle but not inside the triangle?

_____ dots

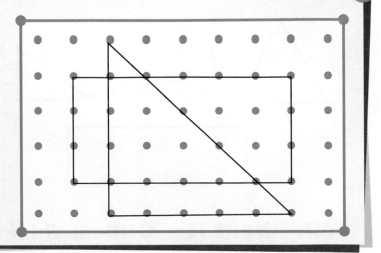

 Home Note Your child identified circles, squares, triangles, and rectangles.
ACTIVITY Have your child draw a picture made up of plane figures.

Harcourt Brace School Publishers

Sides and Corners

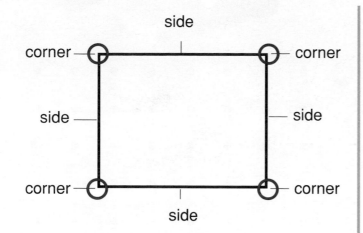

corner — side — corner

side — side

corner — side — corner

This figure has 4 sides
and 4 corners.

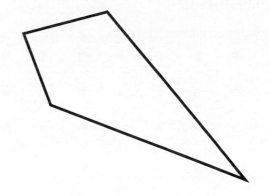

This figure has __4__ sides

and __4__ corners.

Write how many sides and corners.

1

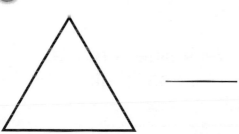

_____ sides

_____ corners

2

_____ sides

_____ corners

3

_____ sides

_____ corners

4

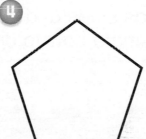

_____ sides

_____ corners

5

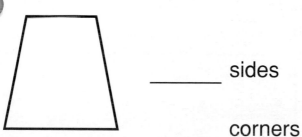

_____ sides

_____ corners

6

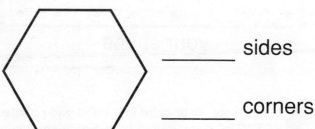

_____ sides

_____ corners

Practice

Draw the figure.

 1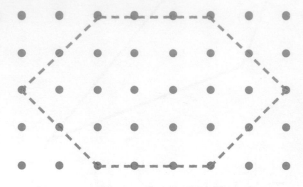

6 sides 6 corners

 2

3 sides 3 corners

3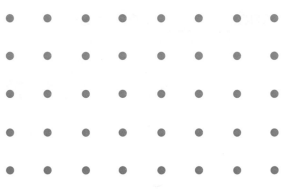

4 sides   4 corners
2 sides are long.
2 sides are short.

 4

4 sides   4 corners
All 4 sides are the
same length.

Problem Solving • Visual Thinking

Draw a figure that has sides and corners.
Cover it. Tell a classmate how to draw it.

5

your shape

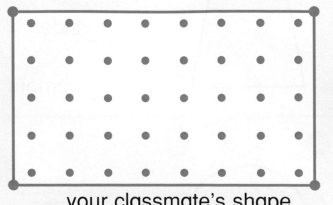

your classmate's shape

 Home Note Your child identified and counted sides and corners of plane figures.
ACTIVITY Give your child a matching number of sides and corners, such as 4 sides and 4 corners.
Have him or her draw the figure.

Chapter 18

Name _____

I square

2 triangles

Trace the line or lines.
Write how many rectangles, triangles,
or squares you made.

1

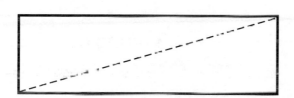

2 triangles

2

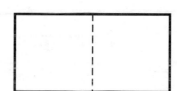

3

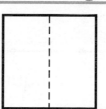

4

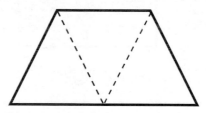

5

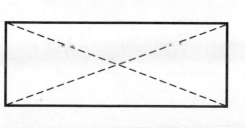

6

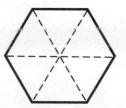

Harcourt Brace School Publishers

Practice

Draw a line or lines to make the new figures.

1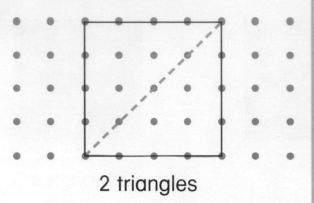

2 triangles

2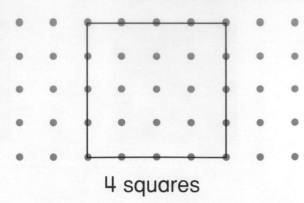

4 squares

3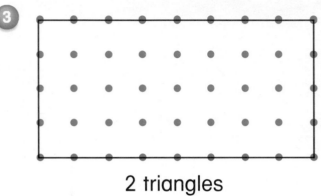

2 triangles

4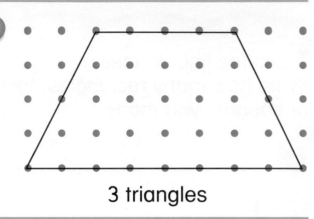

3 triangles

5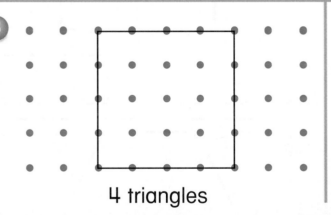

4 triangles

6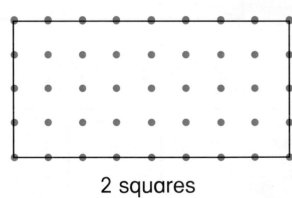

2 squares

Mixed Review

Add or subtract.

7

$$\begin{array}{r} 63¢ \\ -47¢ \\ \hline \end{array} \qquad \begin{array}{r} 52¢ \\ -37¢ \\ \hline \end{array} \qquad \begin{array}{r} 22 \\ +16 \\ \hline \end{array} \qquad \begin{array}{r} 18 \\ +9 \\ \hline \end{array} \qquad \begin{array}{r} 51 \\ -19 \\ \hline \end{array} \qquad \begin{array}{r} 37 \\ -28 \\ \hline \end{array}$$

 Home Note Your child separated plane figures to make new plane figures.
ACTIVITY Draw and cut out a figure. Have your child draw lines on your figure and cut it apart to make and name new figures.

Congruent Figures

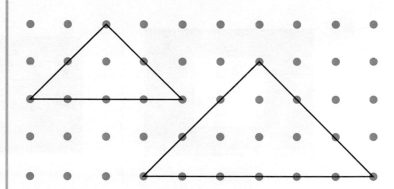

These figures are the same size and shape. They are **congruent**.

These figures are the same shape but not the same size. They are not congruent.

Draw a figure that is the same size and shape.

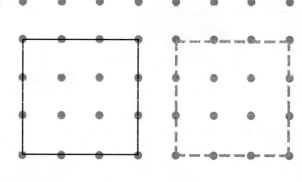

1

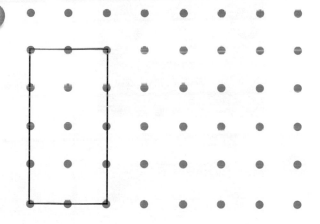

2

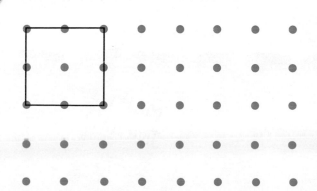

3

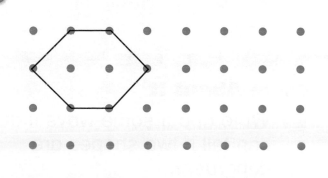

4

Talk About It ● Critical Thinking

How can you tell that two figures are the same size and shape?

Practice

Circle the figure that fits.

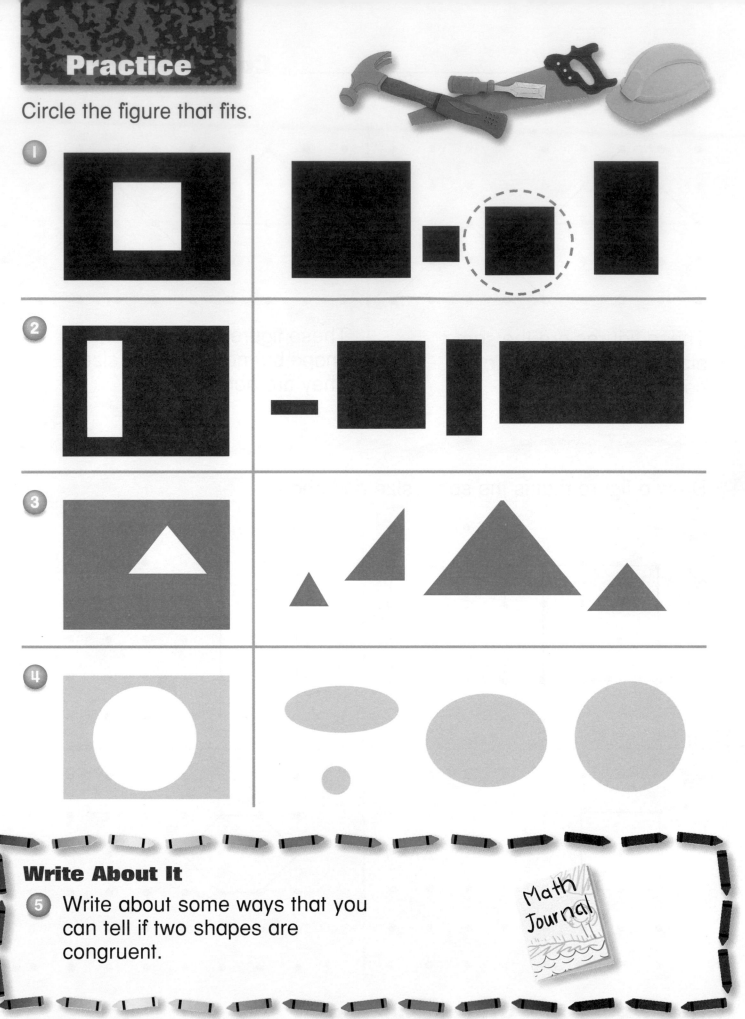

Write About It

5 Write about some ways that you can tell if two shapes are congruent.

Math Journal

Harcourt Brace School Publishers

Home Note Your child identified and drew congruent figures.
ACTIVITY Draw and cut out a figure. Have your child use your figure to draw and cut out a figure that is the same size and shape.

Name _____

Concepts and Skills

Color the circle .
Color the square .
Color the triangle .

1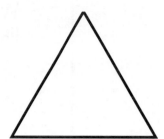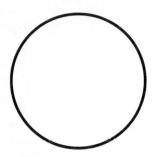

Write how many sides and corners.

2

_____ sides	_____ sides	_____ sides
_____ corners	_____ corners	_____ corners

Trace the line.
Circle the name of the figures you made.

3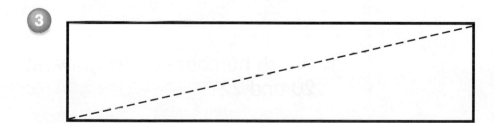

squares

triangles

rectangles

Circle the figure that fits.

4

Harcourt Brace School Publishers

Name _____

Test Prep

Mark the best answer.

1 How many sides does the plane figure have?

- ○ 4
- ○ 3
- ○ 2
- ○ 6

2 Martha has 36¢. Which coins could she have?

- ○ 2 dimes, I nickel, I penny
- ○ I quarter, I dime, I penny
- ○ I quarter, I dime, I nickel
- ○ I dime, 2 nickels, I penny

3 Which solid figure can roll?

- ○
- ○
- ○
- ○

4 Todd has a bag with 15 red crayons and 5 green crayons. Which color crayon is he less likely to pull?

- ○ red
- ○ green

5 Which sentence matches the picture?

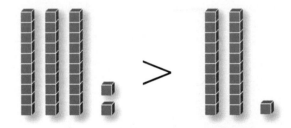

- ○ 32 is greater than 21.
- ○ 32 is the same as 21.
- ○ 21 is greater than 32.
- ○ 32 is less than 21.

6 Which number comes between 20 and 22?

- ○ 19
- ○ 21
- ○ 23
- ○ 12

Standardized Test Prep • Chapters 1-18

Harcourt Brace School Publishers

Symmetry

Which butterfly has both sides the same?

Home Note In this chapter your child will learn about symmetry.
ACTIVITY Have your child find objects in your home where both sides look the same.

SCHOOL-HOME CONNECTION

Dear Family,
 Today we started Chapter 19. We will look at shapes that have symmetry. We will also learn some ways to move shapes. Here are the new vocabulary words and an activity for us to do together at home.

Love,

_____

Vocabulary

line of symmetry

This butterfly has **symmetry** because both sides are exactly the same.

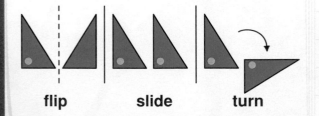

flip   slide   turn

ACTIVITY

With your child, look around the house for patterns, such as those in wallpaper, in which shapes slide, flip, and turn. Then have him or her cut out a shape from construction paper. Work with your child to make an interesting pattern on another paper. Turn, flip, and slide the shape, tracing it each time. Your child may wish to color the design you make together.

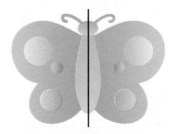

 Visit our Web site for additional ideas and activities.
http://www.hbschool.com

Harcourt Brace School Publishers

Name _____

This house has a line of symmetry.
Both sides are the same.

This house does not have
a line of symmetry.
The sides are not the same.

Find the pictures that have symmetry. Draw the line.
Cross out the pictures that do not have symmetry.

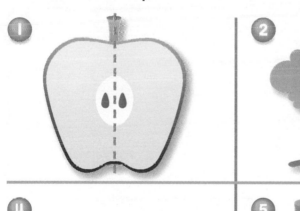

1

2

3

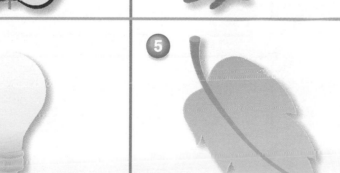

4

5

6

Talk About It • Critical Thinking

What do you notice about the two parts
of a picture that has a line of symmetry?

Draw the line of symmetry.

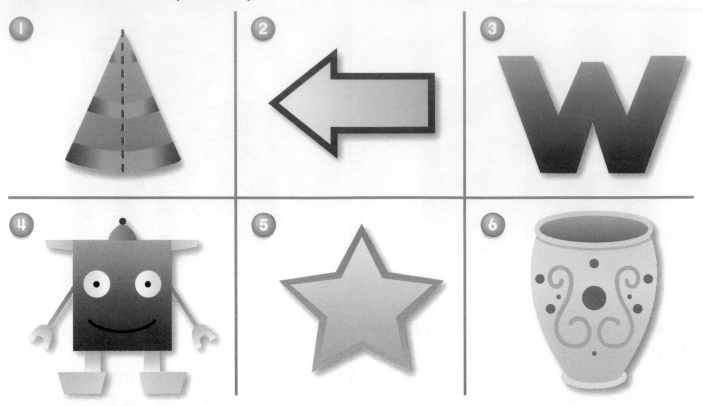

1.

2.

3.

4.

5.

6.

Mixed Review

Solve.

7. Kay has 15 pennies. Ira has 47 pennies. How many more pennies does Ira have?

_____ more pennies

8. Paul has 35 pennies. Norma has 26 pennies. How many pennies do they have altogether?

_____ pennies

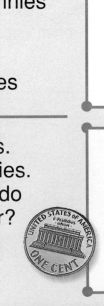

Home Note Your child learned to identify and draw lines of symmetry.
ACTIVITY Find or draw an object that has symmetry. Have your child trace the line of symmetry with a finger or draw the line.

More Symmetry

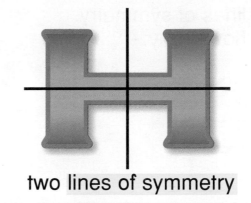

one line of symmetry

two lines of symmetry

Draw one line of symmetry.

1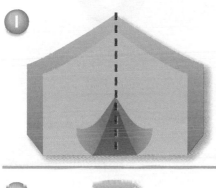

2

3

4

5

6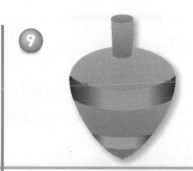

Draw one or two lines of symmetry.

7

8

9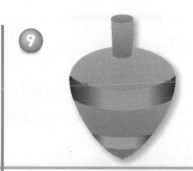

10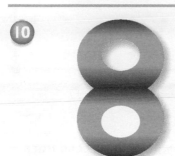

11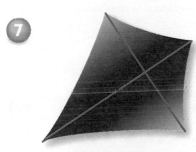

12

Practice

Draw lines of symmetry.
Write how many.

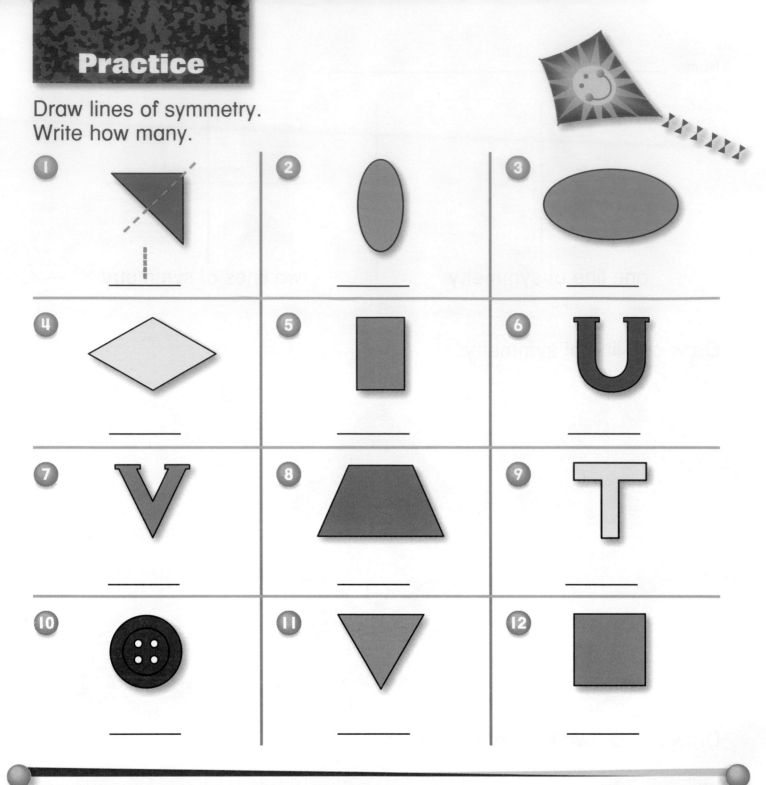

1 _____

2 _____

3 _____

4 _____

5 _____

6 _____

7 _____

8 _____

9 _____

10 _____

11 _____

12 _____

Problem Solving ● **Visual Thinking**

13 Draw a figure that has more than two lines of symmetry. Draw the lines.

Harcourt Brace School Publishers

Home Note Your child learned to draw lines of symmety.
ACTIVITY Find or draw an object that has more than one line of symmetry. Have your child trace the lines of symmetry with a finger.

Name _____   **Moving Figures**

You can move your box of crayons by turning and flipping it.

You can turn.   You can flip.

Use ▲.
Put your ▲ on top of the first one.
Do not lift your ▲. Turn it to fit on top
of the second ▲. Trace the figure.

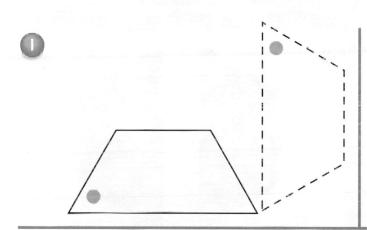 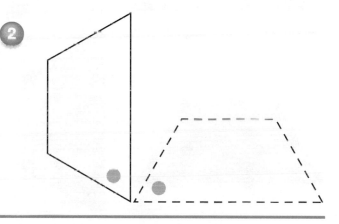

Put your ▲ on top of the first one.
Flip it to fit on top of the second ▲.
Trace the figure.

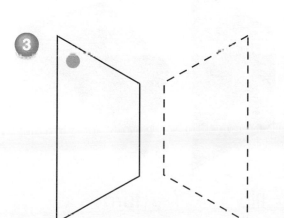 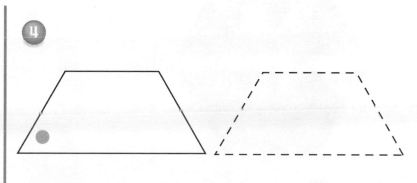

Talk About It ● Critical Thinking

How is a turn different from a flip?

Practice

Use 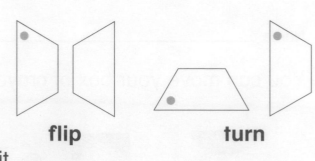.
Move the ▰ the same way
as shown in the picture.
Circle turn or flip to tell how you moved it.

flip **turn**

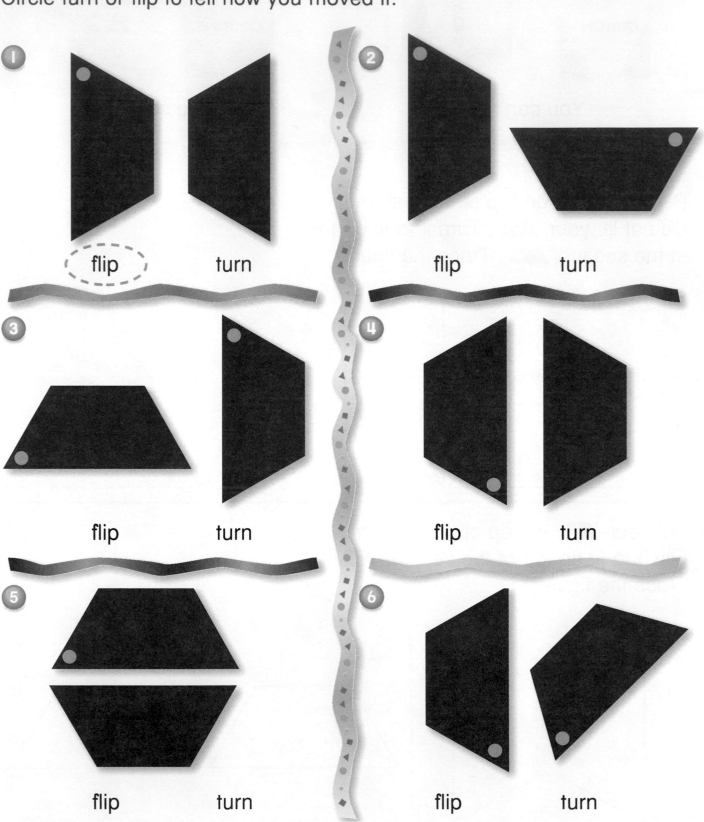

1. flip   turn

2. flip   turn

3. flip   turn

4. flip   turn

5. flip   turn

6. flip   turn

 Home Note Your child learned to move figures by flipping and turning.
ACTIVITY Ask your child to draw and cut out a figure. Have him or her show how to flip and turn
the figure.

Chapter 19

More About Moving Figures

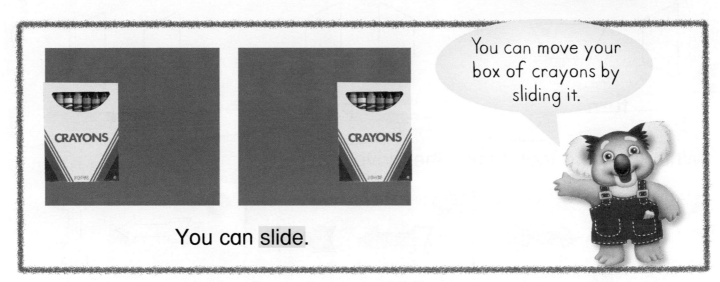

You can move your box of crayons by sliding it.

You can slide.

Use ▓.
Put your ▓ on top of the first one.
Slide it to fit on top of the second ▓.
Trace the figure. Draw the dot.

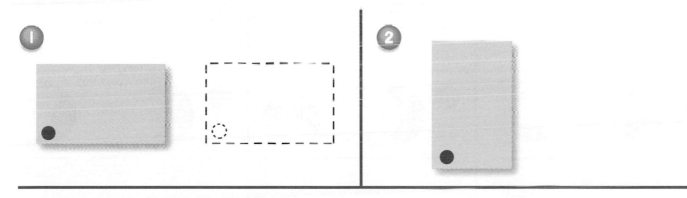

Use ▲.
Put your ▲ on top of the one shown.
Slide your ▲ to a different place.
Trace to show the new place. Draw the dot.

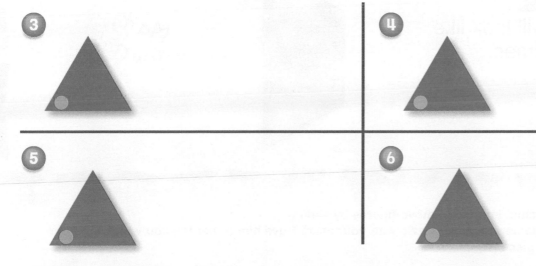

Chapter 19 • Symmetry

Practice

turn   **flip**   **slide**

Write the word that names the move.

1

flip

2

3

4

5

6

7

8

9

Write About It

10 Look at the ◣.
Draw what it will look like
if you flip it 2 times.

Math Journal

Harcourt Brace School Publishers

 Home Note Your child learned to move figures by sliding.
ACTIVITY Put together a jigsaw puzzle with your child. Have him or her tell you which kind of
move made each piece fit.

Concepts and Skills

Draw the line of symmetry.
Cross out the figures that do not have symmetry.

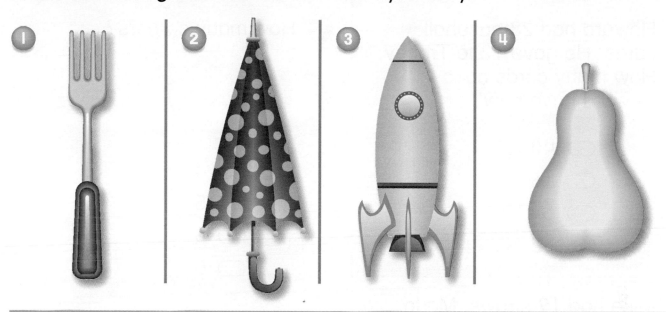

① ② ③ ④

Draw the lines of symmetry.

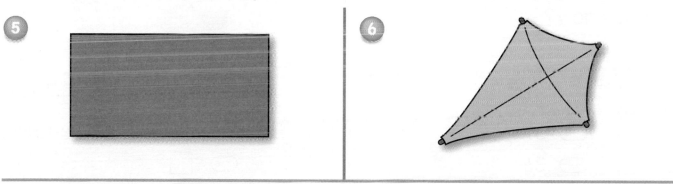

⑤ ⑥

Circle the word that names the move.

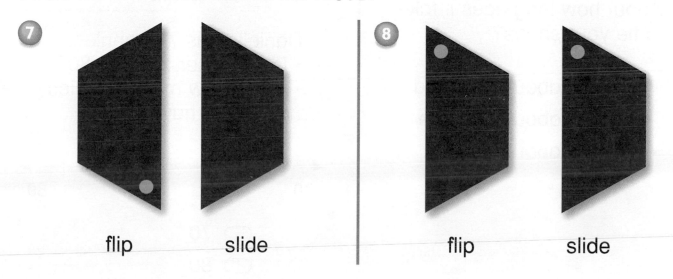

⑦

flip   slide

⑧

flip   slide

Name _____

Test Prep

Mark the best answer.

1 Howard had 28 baseball cards. He gave 12 to Tracey. How many cards does Howard have now?

- ◯ 40
- ◯ 16
- ◯ 39
- ◯ 42

2 Mike had 19 straws. Marlo gave him 17 straws. How many straws does Mike have now?

- ◯ 27
- ◯ 26
- ◯ 37
- ◯ 36

3 About how long does it take to tie your shoes?

- ◯ about 1 second
- ◯ about 1 minute
- ◯ about 1 hour

4 How many corners?

- ◯ 4
- ◯ 5
- ◯ 6
- ◯ 0

5 Which is a face on this solid?

- ◯ trapezoid
- ◯ triangle
- ◯ square
- ◯ circle

6 Danielle has 72 pennies.
- Is 72 closer to 70 or 80?
- About how many pennies does she have?

70   80

- ◯ 70
- ◯ 80

Harcourt Brace School Publishers

MATH FUN

Hidden Picture

Green

right A - 1 up
right B - 1 up
right C - 1 up
right D - 1 up
right E - 1 up
right F - 1 up
right G - 1 up

Black

right D - 7 up
right C - 6 up
right D - 6 up
right E - 6 up
right B - 5 up
right C - 5 up
right D - 5 up
right E - 5 up
right F - 5 up
right A - 4 up
right G - 4 up

Red

right B - 4 up
right C - 4 up
right D - 4 up
right E - 4 up
right F - 4 up
right B - 3 up
right D - 3 up
right F - 3 up
right B - 2 up
right C - 2 up
right D - 2 up
right E - 2 up
right F - 2 up

1. Color the squares to make a picture.

2. Draw the line of symmetry.

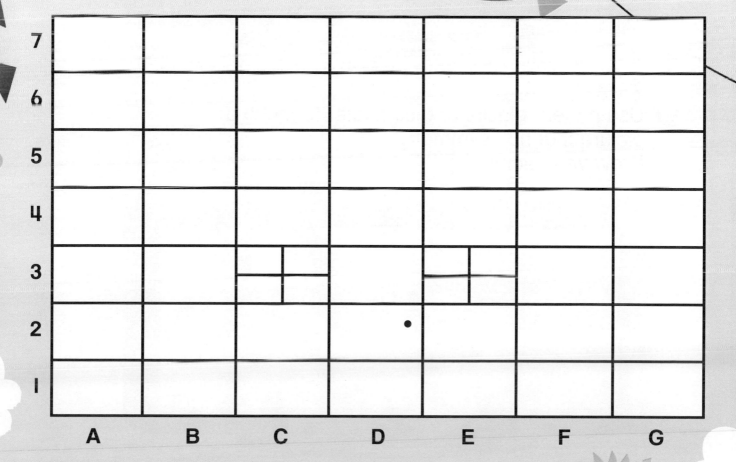

Home Note Your child has been learning about shapes and symmetry.
ACTIVITY Help your child look for objects that have symmetry.

Name _____

Calculator

Computer

You can use a 🖥 to make a picture that has symmetry.

1 Use pattern blocks to complete the picture.
Draw the blocks.

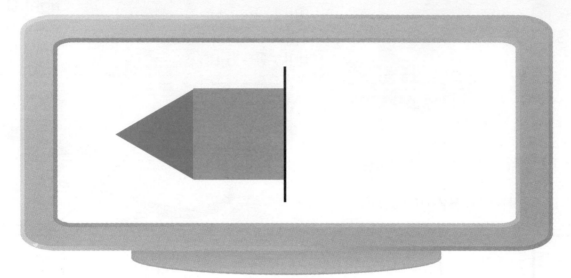

2 Use pattern blocks or a computer to make a picture that has symmetry.
Draw your picture.

Have a classmate draw the line of symmetry.

Technology

Sam's Adventures

written by F. R. Robinson
illustrated by Ken Spengler

This book will help me review solid figures.

This book belongs to _____.

A

Sam is learning about solid figures. He thinks about them day and night. Sam also likes to pretend. He likes to pretend that he is a great adventurer. Sometimes Sam includes what he is learning about solid figures with what he is pretending.

B

Harcourt Brace School Publishers

Today Sam pretends he is a great explorer. He climbs a very high mountain. It is a very dangerous climb. Near the top, he finds a cave filled with cones. He puts on his hat with a light and goes inside to search for cones.

Point to the cones Sam finds.

C

Now Sam pretends he is a sea diver.
Today he goes down in his diving cage.
At the bottom of the sea, he finds the
wreckage of an old ship. In the wreckage,
Sam discovers a lot of cubes.

Point to the cubes Sam discovers.

Harcourt Brace School Publishers

Sam pretends he is a space pilot. He blasts off into space and leaves Earth far behind. Soon Sam notices that there are many spheres in space. As he zooms through space, he passes many spheres.

Point to the spheres Sam finds.

E

Today Sam pretends he is in a circus. He rides a horse in the circus ring. He and the horse do many tricks. The people clap and cheer. Then Sam does his final trick. He rides the horse around the cylinders.

Point to the cylinders Sam rides around.

Sam pretends he is in the dry, hot desert.
For several days he rides a camel in search
of lost pyramids. Finally, there in the sand,
he finds the pyramids.

Point to the pyramids Sam finds.

G

Name each figure Sam found.

H

Name _____

Concepts and Skills

Circle the objects that are shaped like the solid figure. Cross out the objects that are not shaped like the solid figure.

 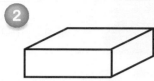 

3 Circle the solid figure that fits this rule. It has two faces. It can be stacked.

   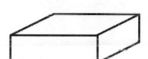 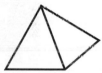

11 Circle the plane figure you can trace from the solid figure.

    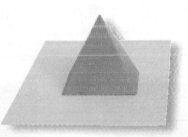

5 Color the circle blue.
Color the rectangle red.
Color the triangle yellow.

6 Write how many sides and corners.

_____ sides _____ corners

7 Draw a line to make 2 triangles.

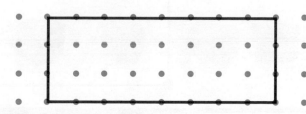

8 Draw a figure that is the same size and shape.

Circle the figure that has symmetry.
Draw the line of symmetry.
Cross out the figure that does not have symmetry.

9

10

Circle the word that names the move.

11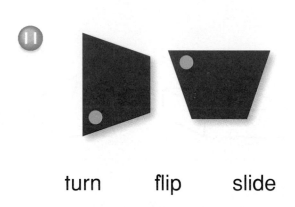

turn   flip   slide

12

turn   flip   slide

13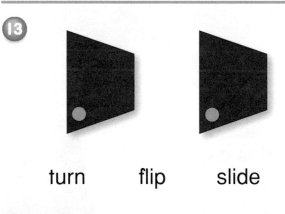

turn   flip   slide

14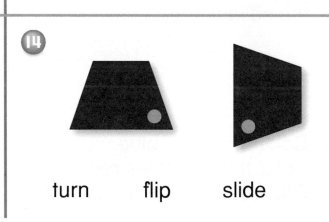

turn   flip   slide

Problem Solving

15 Cross out the mistake in the pattern.
Circle the solid figure that belongs.

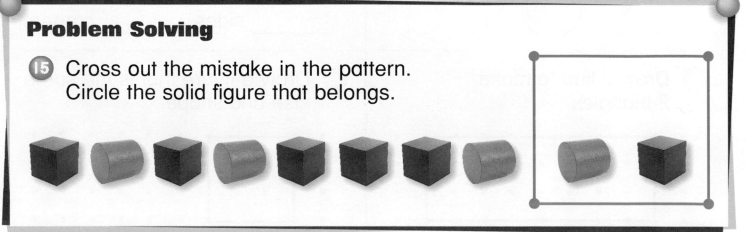

Harcourt Brace School Publishers

Name _____

Performance Assessment

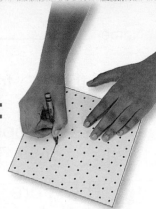

Use shapes.
Choose a plane figure with sides and corners.

1 Draw the figure.
How many sides and corners?

_____ sides   _____ corners

2 Draw another figure that is the same size and shape.

Draw the line of symmetry in the figure.

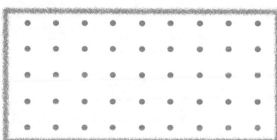

3 Trace the figure and draw a dot in a corner.

Use a flip, a turn, or a slide to move the figure to a different place.

Trace to show the new place.

Circle the move you used.

    turn   flip   slide

Write About It

4 Write a sentence that tells one thing about the figure you used that is different from a circle.

5 Write a sentence that tells one thing about the figure you used that is the same as a circle.

Harcourt Brace School Publishers

Name _____

Fill in the ⬭ for the correct answer.

Choose the operation.
Write + or −. Then solve.

1 There are 15 girls playing tag.
Then 8 girls stop. How many
girls are still playing tag?

15 ◯ 8 = _____

⬭ 7 girls   ⬭ 8 girls
⬭ 23 girls   ⬭ not here

2 Which is the rule for
these numbers?

15, 25, 35, 45, 55

⬭ Count by twos.
⬭ Count by threes.
⬭ Count by fives.
⬭ Count by tens.

3 Karen has 53 stickers.
• Is 53 closer to 50 or 60?
• About how many stickers
  does Karen have?

⬭ 50 stickers
⬭ 60 stickers

4 You have

How much money do you have?

⬭ 46¢   ⬭ 56¢

5

$$25$$
$$+16$$

⬭ 11
⬭ 31
⬭ 41
⬭ 51

6

$$42$$
$$-17$$

⬭ 15
⬭ 25
⬭ 35
⬭ 45

7 Which figure has the same
shape as this figure?

  ⬭
  ⬭

8 Which figure is a
rectangle?

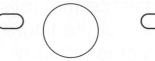

⬭ ◯   ⬭ △
⬭ ▭   ⬭ ⬡

Cumulative Review • Chapters 1–19

Harcourt Brace School Publishers

Length: Customary Units

This little dinosaur was 20 inches long. Was it shorter or longer than its name spelled with 1-inch blocks? How do you know?

Home Note In this chapter your child will learn to measure length using nonstandard and customary units.
ACTIVITY Have your child measure his or her math book with an inch ruler.

Harcourt Brace School Publishers

Dear Family,
   Today we started Chapter 20. We will look at ways to measure length. Here are the new vocabulary words and an activity for us to do together at home.

Love,
_____

Vocabulary

inch ruler

1 inch

inches

12 inches = **1 foot**.

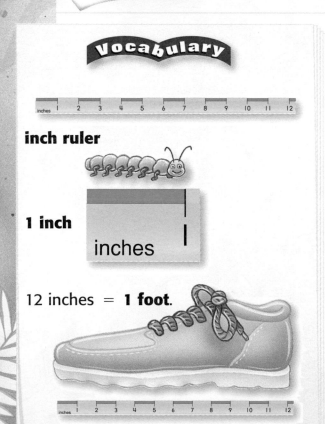

ACTIVITY

Have your child practice measuring length by finding the height of each family member. First, use a ruler, a yardstick, or a tape measure to measure how tall your child is in inches. Write the measurement. Next, help your child measure and write how tall you are. Together, measure other family members and write their heights.

 Visit our Web site for additional ideas and activities.
http://www.hbschool.com

Name _____

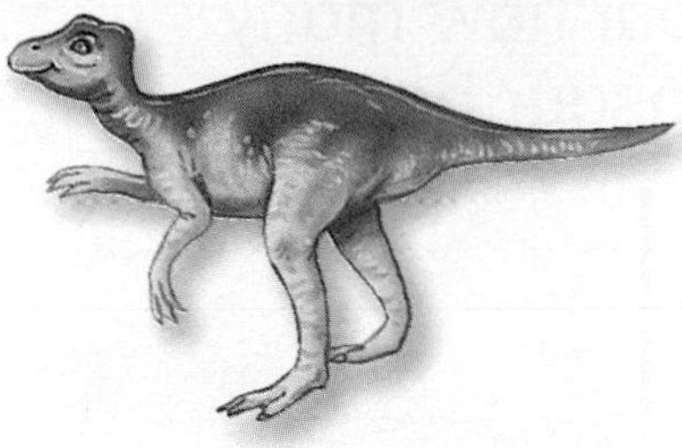

Use ⊂═⊃ to measure.
About how many ⊂═⊃ long
is the dinosaur bone?

1

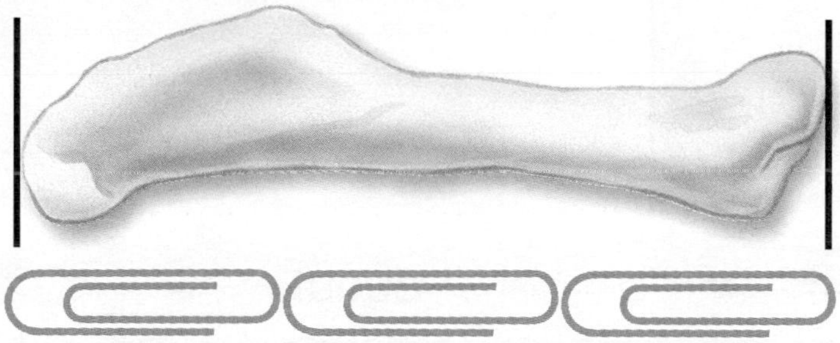

about ___3___ ⊂═⊃

2

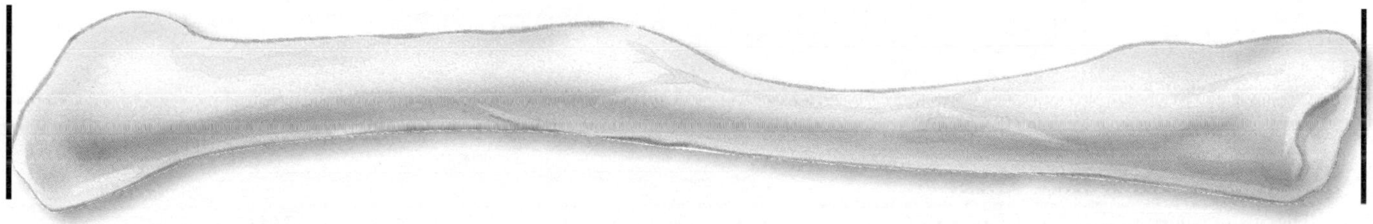

about _____ ⊂═⊃

3

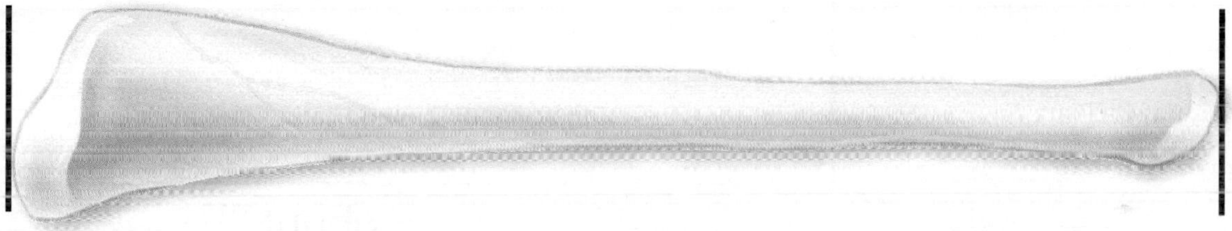

about _____ ⊂═⊃

4

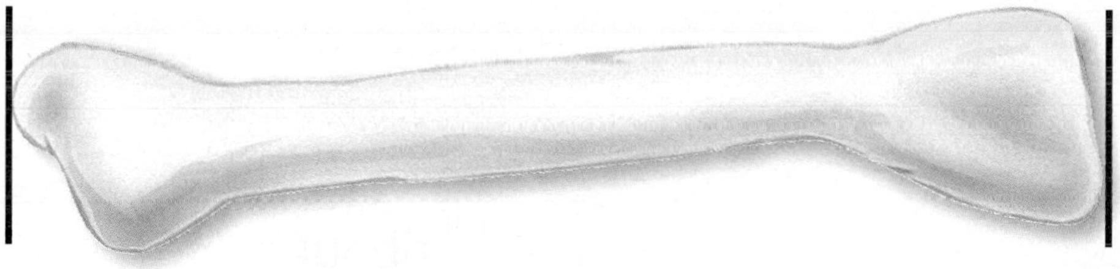

about _____ ⊂═⊃

5

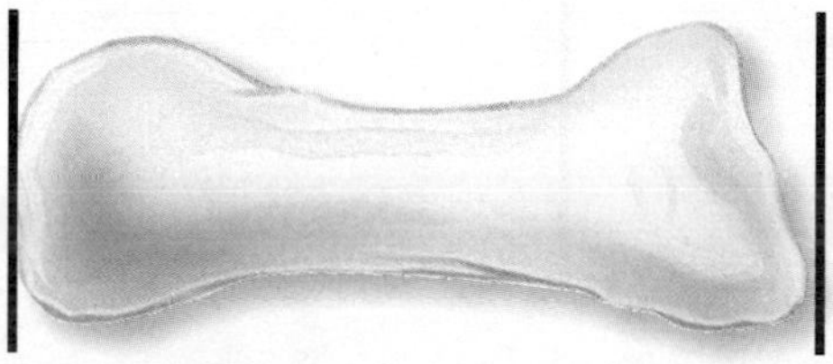

about _____ ⊂═⊃

Talk About It ● Critical Thinking

Would you get different answers if you used a longer
paper clip? How do you know?

Practice

Use 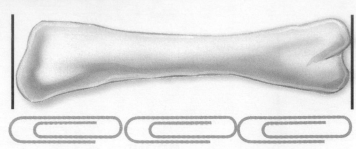 to measure.
About how many long is the
dinosaur bone?

 1

about ___3___

2

about _____

 3

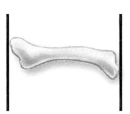

about _____

4

about _____

5

about _____

Home Note Your child learned to measure length using nonstandard units.
ACTIVITY Have your child use other small items that are all alike to measure each dinosaur bone.

Chapter 20

Name _____

This dinosaur is about 3 inches long.

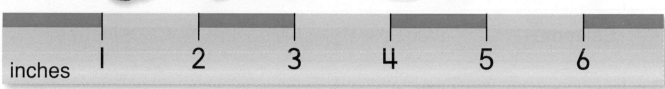

inches | 1 | 2 | 3 | 4 | 5 | 6

Use your inch ruler.
Write the length of the dinosaur.

1

about __2__ inches

2

about _____ inches

3

about _____ inch

4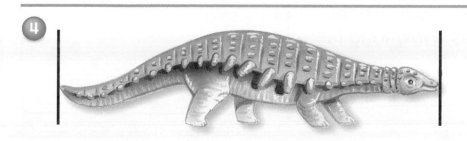

about _____ inches

Talk About It • Critical Thinking

Name some things that are about 1 inch long.

Estimate. Then use your inch ruler to measure.

1

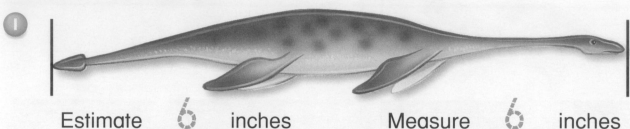

Estimate __6__ inches   Measure __6__ inches

2

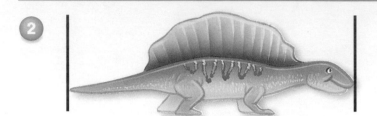

Estimate _____ inches   Measure _____ inches

3

Estimate _____ inches   Measure _____ inches

4

Estimate _____ inches   Measure _____ inches

Problem Solving

5 3 dinosaurs are lined up nose to tail to make a dinosaur parade. The lengths of the dinosaurs are 3 inches, 5 inches, and 8 inches. How long is the dinosaur parade?

_____ inches

Home Note Your child learned to measure length in inches.
ACTIVITY Tell your child a number of inches from 1 to 12, and have him or her find an object that is about that long.

Name _____

Use your inch ruler. Write the length of the tool.

Be sure to place your ruler correctly. This tool is 3 inches long.

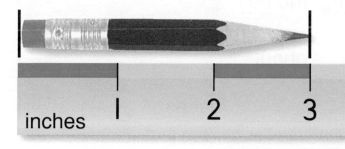

inches | 1 | 2 | 3

1. __3__ inches

2. _____ inches

3. _____ inches

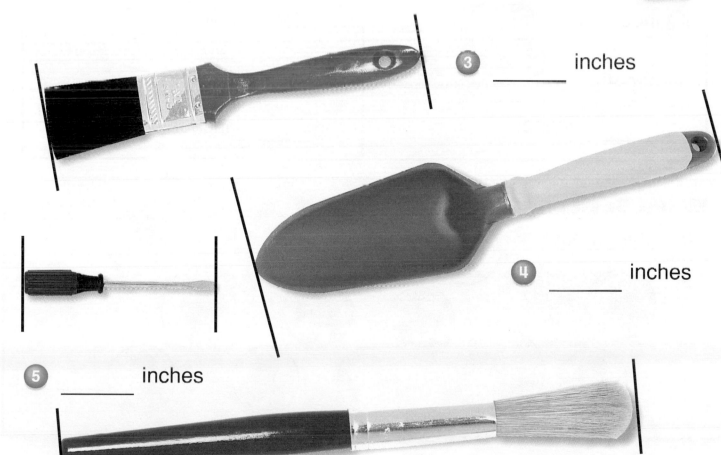

4. _____ inches

5. _____ inches

6. _____ inches

Work with a partner.
Use an inch ruler to measure.

Measuring Me

1 little finger

about

_____ inches

2 thumb

about

_____ inches

3 ear

about

_____ inches

4 hand

about

_____ inches

5 heel to toe

about

_____ inches

6 elbow to wrist

about

_____ inches

Mixed Review

Write the amount

7

_____ ¢

Home Note Your child learned to use an inch ruler to measure length.
ACTIVITY Have your child use an inch ruler to measure small objects to the nearest inch.

Harcourt Brace School Publishers

Name _____

Use a ruler to measure real things like these.
Circle the things that are more than 1 foot.
Cross out the things that are less than 1 foot.

I foot is 12 inches long.

1

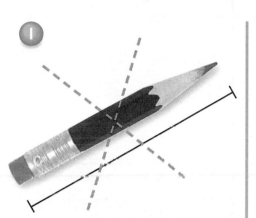

pencil

2

paper

3

bookcase

4

desk

5

chalkboard

6

wastebasket

7

lunch box

8

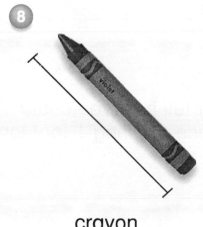

crayon

9

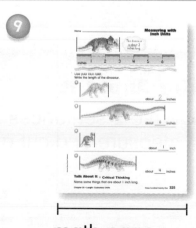

math page

Harcourt Brace School Publishers

Practice

Look around your classroom.
Draw pictures of things that are less than,
the same as, and more than 1 foot.
Draw two or more pictures for each.

1.

Less Than	Same As	More Than

Write About It

2. Write 2 sentences that tell how you could measure and cut a piece of string 1 foot long.

Home Note **Your child learned to measure with a 1-foot ruler.
ACTIVITY Have your child find things that are less than, the same as, and more than 1 foot long.
Then ask your child to explain how he or she decided.**

Understand · **Plan** · **Solve** · **Look Back**

Problem Solving
Guess and Check

How long is the path? Guess the length.
Then check your guess with a ruler.

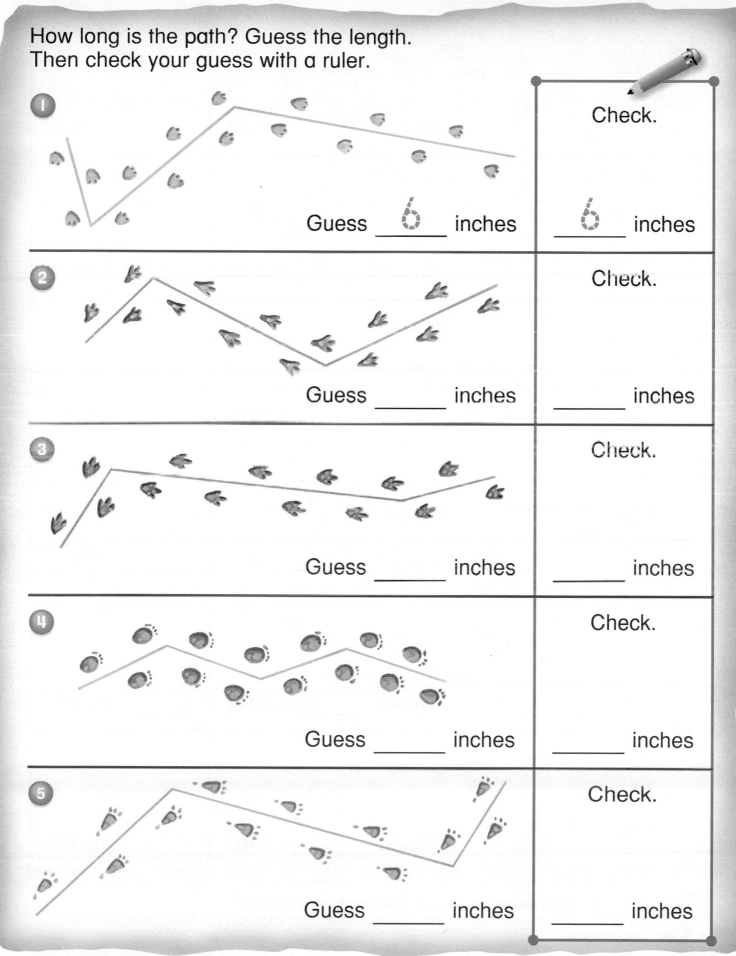

1

Guess ___6___ inches

Check.

___6___ inches

2

Guess _____ inches

Check.

_____ inches

3

Guess _____ inches

Check.

_____ inches

4

Guess _____ inches

Check.

_____ inches

5

Guess _____ inches

Check.

_____ inches

Practice

How long is the path? Guess the length. To check, put yarn along the path and measure the yarn.

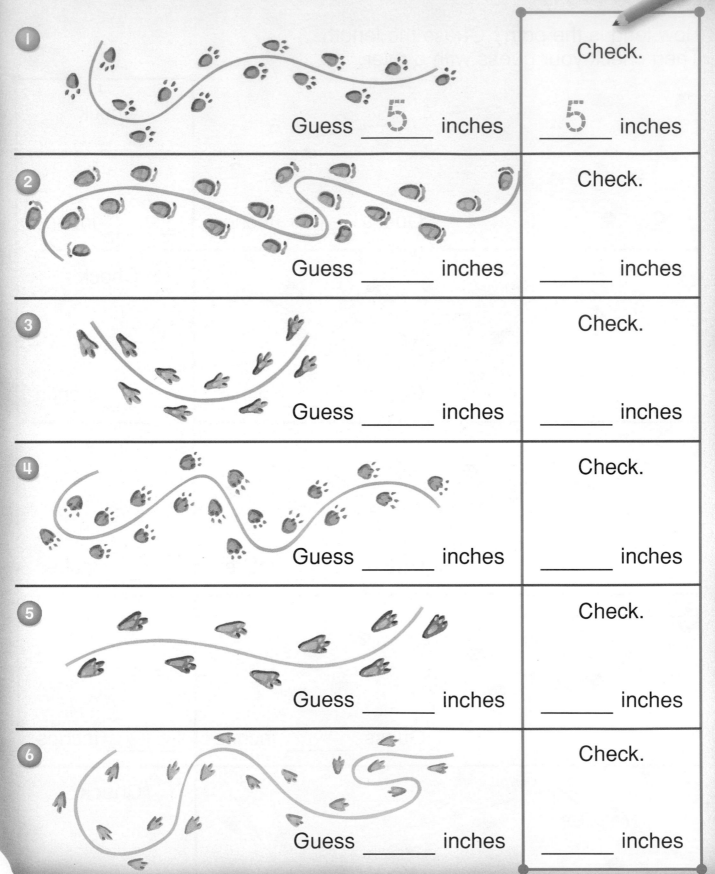

1 Guess __5__ inches

Check.

__5__ inches

2 Guess _____ inches

Check.

_____ inches

3 Guess _____ inches

Check.

_____ inches

4 Guess _____ inches

Check.

_____ inches

5 Guess _____ inches

Check.

_____ inches

6 Guess _____ inches

Check.

_____ inches

Home Note Your child learned to guess and check to solve problems.
ACTIVITY Have your child guess the lengths of some small objects. Then have him or her use a ruler to check.

Harcourt Brace School Publishers

Name _____

Concepts and Skills

Use your inch ruler. Write the length.

1

about _____ inches

_____

2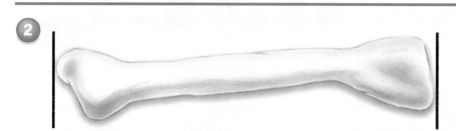

about _____ inches

_____

Use a ruler to measure real things like these.
Circle the things that are more than 1 foot.
Cross out the things that are less than 1 foot.

3

pencil

4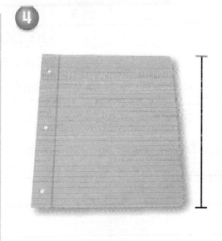

paper

5

chair

Problem Solving

How long is the path?
Guess the length.
Then check your guess with a ruler.

6

Guess. _____ inches

Check. _____ inches

Name _____

Test Prep

Mark the best answer.

1 Greg has these coins

Maria has these coins

Who has more money?

◯ Greg

◯ Maria

2 Tasha buys a hot dog for 55¢. Which 2 coins can she use to pay?

◯ quarter and nickel

◯ half-dollar and nickel

◯ quarter and dime

◯ half-dollar and dime

3 About how long does it take you to brush your teeth?

◯ about 1 second

◯ about 1 minute

◯ about 1 hour

4 Which plane figures come next in the pattern?

◯ ● ■

◯ ■ ▲

◯ ▲ ●

◯ ▲ ■

5 There were 53 children in the park. Then 39 more children came. How many children were in the park?

◯ 14

◯ 24

◯ 92

◯ 95

6 Linda had 24 pencils. She gave 9 pencils to Bob. How many pencils does Linda have now?

◯ 20

◯ 33

◯ 17

◯ 15

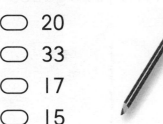

Harcourt Brace School Publishers

CHAPTER 21

Length, Perimeter, and Area

Harcourt Brace School Publishers

How tall is the flower?
How can you tell?

Home Note In this chapter your child will learn about length, perimeter, and area.
ACTIVITY Have your child measure things with a centimeter ruler.

SCHOOL-HOME CONNECTION

Dear Family,
   Today we started Chapter 21. We will learn how to measure using the metric system. We will also find out about perimeter and area. Here are the new vocabulary words and an activity for us to do together at home.

Love,

_____

Vocabulary

3 centimeters

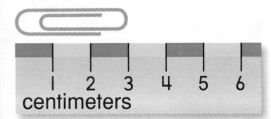

centimeters

The distance around a plane figure is called the **perimeter.**

3 + 3 + 3 + 3 = 12 centimeters

ACTIVITY

Help your child cut a piece of string 10 centimeters long. Ask him or her to use it to find objects that are close to 1 decimeter, or 10 centimeters, long. Then have your child sort these into groups of objects less than 10 centimeters long and more than 10 centimeters long.

Visit our Web site for additional ideas and activities.
http://www.hbschool.com

Harcourt Brace School Publishers

Centimeters

Use a centimeter ruler.
Write how long.

You can measure short
lengths in centimeters.

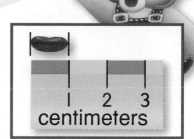

1

centimeters

about __10__ centimeters

2

about _____ centimeters

3

about _____ centimeters

4

about _____ centimeters

5

about _____ centimeters

Practice

Use a centimeter ruler
to draw lines.
Start your lines at the dots.

① 4 centimeters

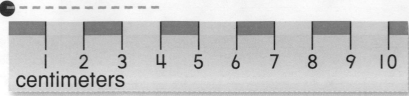

centimeters

② 7 centimeters ●

③ 5 centimeters ●

④ 10 centimeters ●

⑤ 8 centimeters ●

⑥ 6 centimeters ●

⑦ 3 centimeters ●

Mixed Review

⑧ Trace the lines.
Circle the name of
the figures you made.

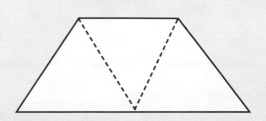

squares

triangles

rectangles

Harcourt Brace School Publishers

🏠 **Home Note** Your child measured length in centimeters.
ACTIVITY Have your child use a centimeter ruler to measure small objects.

Name _____

This ruler is 10 centimeters long.
It is 1 decimeter long.

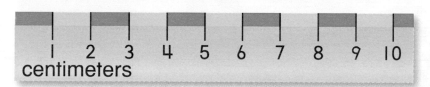

centimeters 1 2 3 4 5 6 7 8 9 10

Look around your classroom.
Draw pictures of things that are less than,
the same as, and more than 1 decimeter long.

Less Than	The Same As	More Than
	Crayons	

Talk About It ● **Critical Thinking**

Name some things that are about 1 decimeter long.

Use a centimeter ruler. Write how long.
Circle less than, the same as, or more
than I decimeter.

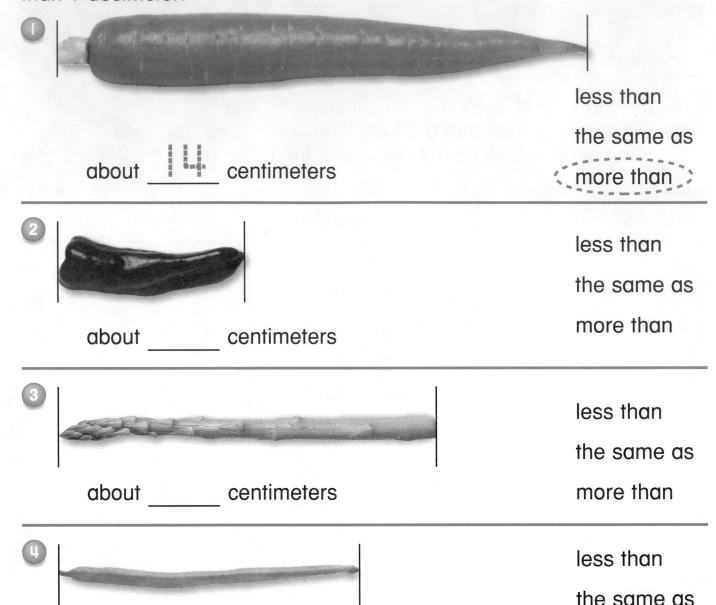

1
about __14__ centimeters

less than

the same as

(more than)

2
about _____ centimeters

less than

the same as

more than

3
about _____ centimeters

less than

the same as

more than

4
about _____ centimeters

less than

the same as

more than

Write About It

5 Use a centimeter ruler to measure your pencil.
Write the number of centimeters. Write if it is less
than, the same as, or more than I decimeter.

Math Journal

Home Note Your child estimated and measured length using decimeters.
ACTIVITY Have your child sort objects into groups that are less than, equal to, and more than
I decimeter.

Name _____

Measure each side.
Write how many centimeters.
Then write how many
centimeters around the figure.

The distance around a
figure is called the
perimeter.

1

<u>4</u> + <u>2</u> + <u>4</u> + <u>2</u> = <u>12</u> centimeters

2

_____ + _____ + _____ = _____ centimeters

3

_____ + _____ + _____ + _____ = _____ centimeters

4

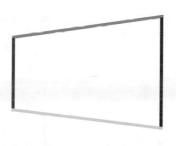

_____ + _____ + _____ + _____ = _____ centimeters

Talk About It • **Critical Thinking**
Can two figures look different and have the same perimeter?

Measure each side.
Write how many centimeters.
Then write how many centimeters around the figure.

$\underline{3} + \underline{3} + \underline{3} = \underline{9}$ centimeters

②

_____ + _____ + _____ + _____ = _____ centimeters

③

_____ + _____ + _____ + _____ = _____ centimeters

Problem Solving ● **Visual Thinking**

④ Draw a different figure that has the same perimeter.

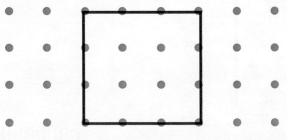 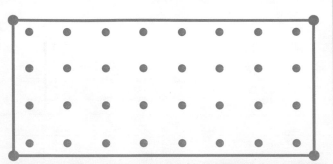

 Home Note Your child measured perimeter.
ACTIVITY Have your child use string to measure the distance around the top of a small table. Then have him or her measure the string with a ruler.

Name _____

Understand • Plan • Solve • Look Back

Use 1-inch squares.
How many squares will fit in the figure?
Write your guess.
Then use the squares to check.

1 inch square

1

Guess. _____ squares

Check. __4__ squares

2

Guess. _____ squares

Check. _____ squares

3

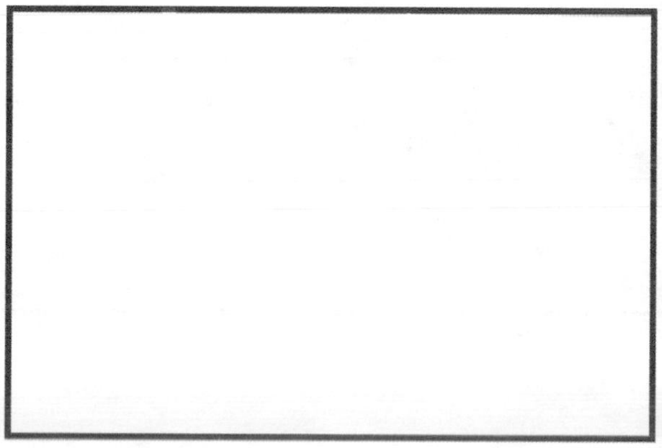

Guess. _____ squares

Check. _____ squares

4

Guess. _____ squares

Check. _____ squares

Harcourt Brace School Publishers

Chapter 21 • Length, Perimeter, and Area

Use 1-inch squares.
How many squares will fit in the figure?
Write your guess. Then use the squares to check.

1

Guess. _____ squares

Check. _____ square

2

Guess. _____ squares

Check. _____ squares

3

Guess.

_____ squares

Check.

_____ squares

4

Guess. _____ squares

Check. _____ squares

Home Note Your child used the strategy guess and check to solve problems.
ACTIVITY Cut some 1-inch squares of paper. Have your child estimate how many would cover an envelope and then check.

Name _____

Concepts and Skills

Use a centimeter ruler. Write how long.

1

about _____ centimeters

Use a centimeter ruler to draw a line.
Start your line at the dot.

2 8 centimeters

Measure with a centimeter ruler. Write how long.
Circle less than, the same as, or more than 1 decimeter.

less than

the same as

3 _____ centimeters   more than

Measure each side. Write how many centimeters.
Then write how many centimeters around the figure.

4

_____ + _____ + _____ = _____ centimeters

Problem Solving

5 Use 1-inch squares.
How many squares will fit
in the figure? Write your
guess. Then use the
squares to check.

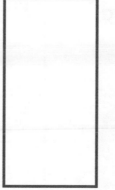

Guess. _____ squares

Check. _____ squares

Harcourt Brace School Publishers

Name _____

Test Prep

Mark the best answer.

1. Jean has 4 goldfish. Matt has 7 goldfish. How many goldfish do the children have in all?

   ○ 11
   ○ 13
   ○ 16
   ○ 26

2. Which is the total amount?

   ○ 50¢   ○ 53¢
   ○ 68¢   ○ 70¢

3. Laura had 93 pennies. She gave 48 to Corbett. How many pennies does Laura have left?

   ○ 31
   ○ 41
   ○ 45
   ○ 141

4. Which takes about 1 second?

   ○ eating lunch
   ○ clapping your hands
   ○ walking to school
   ○ brushing teeth

5. Which is the rule for the number pattern?
   18, 21, 24, 27, 30

   ○ Count by twos.
   ○ Count by threes.
   ○ Count by fives.
   ○ Count by tens.

6. How many children have two pets?

Number of Pets	
0 pets	ЖЖ
1 pet	I I I
2 pets	I I I I

   ○ 4
   ○ 5
   ○ 15
   ○ 20

Harcourt Brace School Publishers

Capacity, Weight and Temperature

Do you think the temperature is hot or cold? How do you know?

Home Note In this chapter your child will learn how to measure capacity, weight, and temperature.
ACTIVITY Have your child draw pictures to illustrate different temperatures.

SCHOOL-HOME CONNECTION

Dear Family,
   Today we started Chapter 22. We will begin to measure how much things hold, how much things weigh, and how hot or cold it is. Here are the new vocabulary words and an activity for us to do together at home.

Love,

_____

Vocabulary

2 cups fill **1 pint**.

2 pints fill **1 quart**.

ACTIVITY

Look for an unopened grocery item that weighs one pound. Let your child hold the item to get an idea of how that amount of weight feels. Then have him or her choose 10 other grocery items and sort them into groups of less than 1 pound, about 1 pound, and more than 1 pound. Check your child's estimates by using a scale or by reading the weight on the packages.

Visit our Web site for additional ideas and activities.
http://www.hbschool.com

Harcourt Brace School Publishers

Name _____

I cup | I pint | I quart

 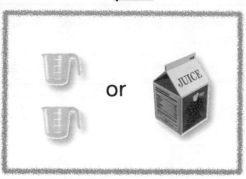 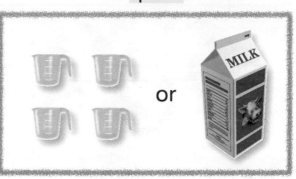

2 cups = I pint   4 cups = I quart

Color cups to show how many hold the same amount.

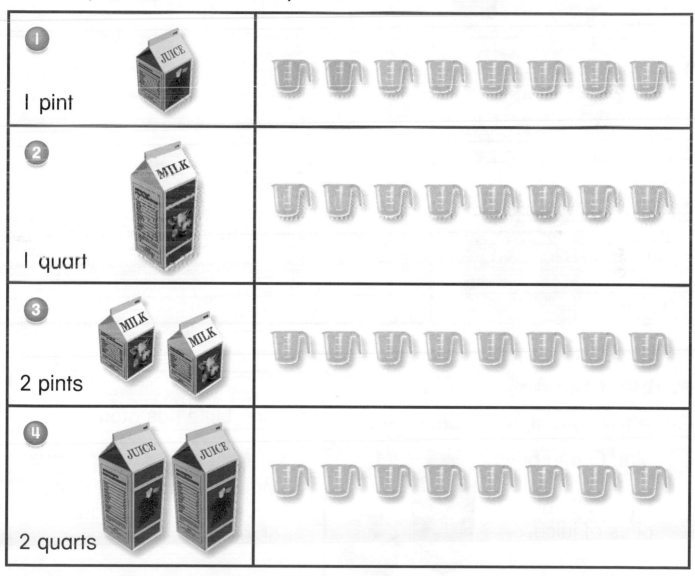

1 I pint	
2 I quart	
3 2 pints	
4 2 quarts	

Talk About It • Critical Thinking

What do you notice about I quart and 2 pints?

Practice

Color cups to show how many hold the same amount.

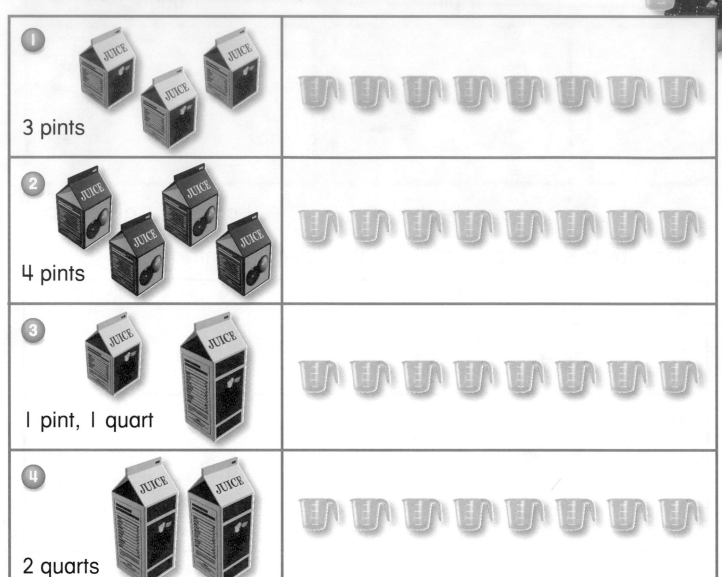

1 JUICE JUICE JUICE 3 pints	
2 JUICE JUICE JUICE JUICE 4 pints	
3 JUICE JUICE 1 pint, 1 quart	
4 JUICE JUICE 2 quarts	

Problem Solving

Circle the correct sentence.

5 Mrs. Green buys 2 quarts of juice. Mrs. Little buys 4 pints of juice.

a. Mrs. Little has more juice.

b. Mrs. Little and Mrs. Green have the same amount of juice.

Harcourt Brace School Publishers

Home Note Your child determined how many cups fill pint and quart containers.
ACTIVITY Have your child use a measuring cup to find containers that hold the same amounts of water.

Name _____

These objects weigh about 1 pound.

1 Circle the objects that weigh less than 1 pound.

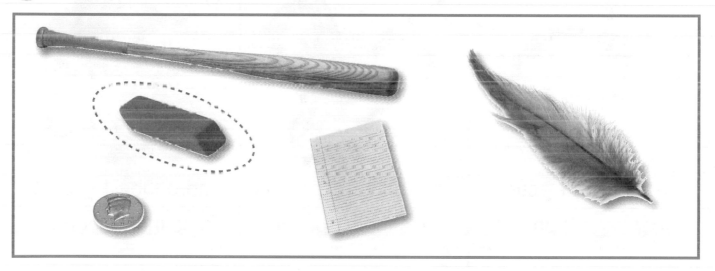

2 Circle the objects that weigh more than 1 pound.

Harcourt Brace School Publishers

Circle about how much each object weighs.

①  (more than I pound) less than I pound	②  more than I pound less than I pound	③  more than I pound less than I pound
④  more than I pound less than I pound	⑤  more than I pound less than I pound	⑥  more than I pound less than I pound
⑦  more than I pound less than I pound	⑧  more than I pound less than I pound	⑨  more than I pound less than I pound

 Home Note Your child determined whether objects weigh more or less than I pound.
ACTIVITY Have your child compare the weights of three objects and put them in order from lightest to heaviest.

Chapter 22

Using a Thermometer

We use a thermometer to measure the temperature.

We say 75 degrees Fahrenheit.

We write 75°F.

Read the thermometer.
Write the temperature.

1

30 °F

2

_____ °F

3

_____ °F

4

_____ °F

Talk About It • Critical Thinking

What temperature do you think would show
on the thermometer outside today?

Chapter 22 • Capacity, Weight, and Temperature

Read the temperature.
Use a red crayon to color in the thermometer
to show the temperature.

1 80°F   **2** 25°F   **3** 40°F   **4** 95°F

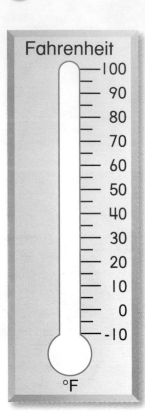

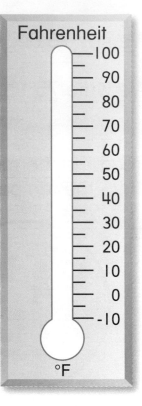

Mixed Review

Measure each side and write how many centimeters.
Then write how many centimeters around the figure.

5

_____ + _____ + _____ + _____ = _____ centimeters

 Home Note Your child read a Fahrenheit thermometer.
ACTIVITY Have your child read a thermometer and tell you the temperature.

Harcourt Brace School Publishers

Name _____

Choosing the Appropriate Tool

I can use a ruler!

I can use a cup!

I can use a thermometer!

Write the name of the tool you would use.

1	to find out how long a piece of string is		ruler
2	to find out how much water is in a bottle		_____
3	to find out the temperature on a sunny day		_____
4	to find out how much milk is in a pitcher		_____
5	to find out how long a piece of wood is		_____

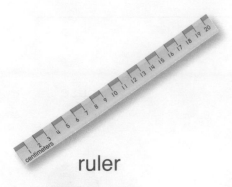

cup   ruler   thermometer

Write the name of the tool you would use.

① to find out the temperature on a cold day 	_____
② to find out how much juice is in a glass 	_____
③ to find out how long a piece of ribbon is 	_____
④ to find out the temperature of the classroom 	_____

Write About It

⑤ Write 1 sentence about each tool. Tell what each measures.

Home Note Your child chose the appropriate measuring tool.
ACTIVITY Make up some stories in which a tool is needed to measure. Have your child tell you which tool he or she would use and why.

Chapter 22

Name _____

Concepts and Skills

Review/Test

Color cups to show how many hold the same amount.

1 1 pint

---

2 Circle the object that weighs less than a pound.

3 Circle the object that weighs more than a pound.

Read the thermometer. Write the temperature.

4
Fahrenheit
—100
—90
—80
—70
—60
—50
—40
—30
—20
—10
—0
—-10
°F

_____ °F

5
Fahrenheit
—100
—90
—80
—70
—60
—50
—40
—30
—20
—10
—0
—-10
°F

_____ °F

6
Fahrenheit
—100
—90
—80
—70
—60
—50
—40
—30
—20
—10
—0
—-10
°F

_____ °F

Problem Solving

7 Write the name of the tool you would use to find out how much juice is in a bottle.

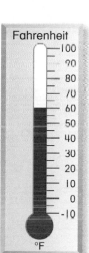 cup

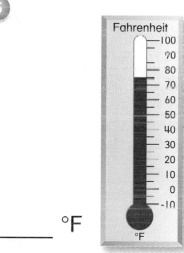 ruler

 thermometer

_____

_____

Name _____

Test Prep

Mark the best answer.

1 Does a goldfish weigh more or less than 1 pound?

○ more than 1 pound
○ less than 1 pound

2 There were 82 ants under a log. Then 48 ants went away. How many ants are left?

○ 24
○ 34
○ 46
○ 30

3 Brad played tag for 15 minutes. Then he played ball for 15 minutes. How many minutes did Brad play?

○ 20
○ 35
○ 25
○ 30

4 About how many centimeters long is the paper clip?

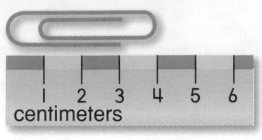

centimeters

○ 1
○ 2
○ 3
○ 4

5 Which number is greater than 63?

○ 76
○ 36
○ 46
○ 26

6 What is the temperature?

○ 40° F
○ 70° F
○ 80° F
○ 85° F

358 three hundred fifty-eight

Standardized Test Prep • Chapters 1–22

Harcourt Brace School Publishers

Fractions

**What fraction do you
see on the quilt?**

Home Note In this chapter your child is learning about fractions.
ACTIVITY Ask your child to draw their own quilts that show fractions.

SCHOOL-HOME CONNECTION

Dear Family,
   Today we started Chapter 23. We will look at fractions. We will learn ways to find equal parts of wholes and groups. Here are the new vocabulary words and an activity for us to do together at home.

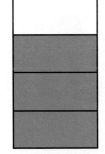

Love,

_____

Vocabulary

halves   **fourths**

2 equal parts   4 equal parts

$\frac{1}{2}$ is green $\frac{3}{4}$ is blue

ACTIVITY

Help your child learn about fractions at snack time. For example, you might spread 2 out of 6 crackers with peanut butter and the other 4 crackers with cheese. Have your child draw a picture and write the fraction for each part of the snack.

 Visit our Web site for additional ideas and activities.
http://www.hbschool.com

Halves and Fourths

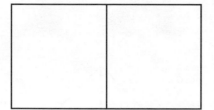

2 equal parts

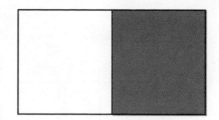

1 of 2 equal parts.
One-half is brown.

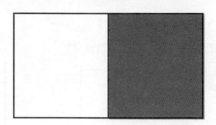

$\frac{1}{2}$ 1 brown part
2 equal parts

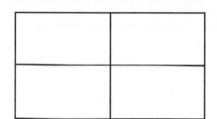

4 equal parts

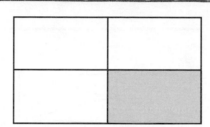

1 of 4 equal parts.
One-fourth is yellow.

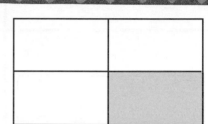

$\frac{1}{4}$ 1 yellow part
4 equal parts

Find the figures that show halves. Color $\frac{1}{2}$.

Find the figures that show fourths. Color $\frac{1}{4}$.

Talk About It • Critical Thinking

Is $\frac{1}{2}$ always the same size?

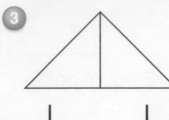

Practice

Color one part .
Circle the fraction.

1

$\frac{1}{2}$ $\boxed{\frac{1}{4}}$

2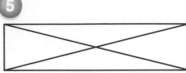

$\frac{1}{2}$ $\frac{1}{4}$

3

$\frac{1}{2}$ $\frac{1}{4}$

4

$\frac{1}{2}$ $\frac{1}{4}$

5

$\frac{1}{2}$ $\frac{1}{4}$

6

$\frac{1}{2}$ $\frac{1}{4}$

7

$\frac{1}{2}$ $\frac{1}{4}$

8

$\frac{1}{2}$ $\frac{1}{4}$

9

$\frac{1}{2}$ $\frac{1}{4}$

Problem Solving

10 Draw a picture. Solve.

Tony ate $\frac{1}{4}$ of his cookie.

Karen ate $\frac{1}{2}$ of her cookie.

Circle the one who ate the greater amount.

Tony   Karen

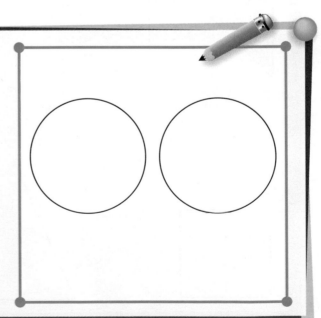

 Home Note Your child identified halves and fourths.
ACTIVITY Invite your child to divide food items into halves and fourths and name each part.

Harcourt Brace School Publishers

Thirds and Sixths

 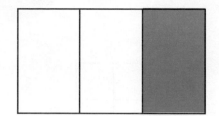 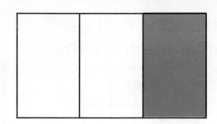

| 3 equal parts | 1 of 3 equal parts. One-third is green. | $\frac{1}{3}$ | 1 green part 3 equal parts |

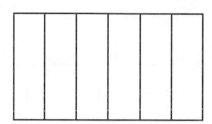  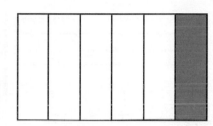

| 6 equal parts | 1 of 6 equal parts. One-sixth is orange. | $\frac{1}{6}$ | 1 orange part 6 equal parts |

Find the figures that show thirds. Color $\frac{1}{3}$ 🖍.

Find the figures that show sixths. Color $\frac{1}{6}$ 🖍.

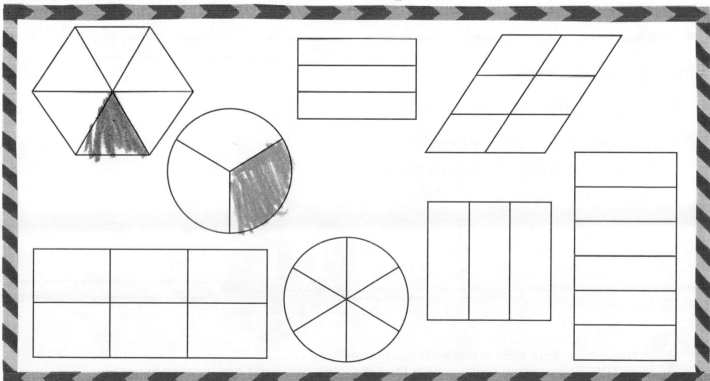

Harcourt Brace School Publishers

Practice

Color one part .
Circle the fraction.

1

$\frac{1}{2}$ $\frac{1}{3}$ $\left(\frac{1}{6}\right)$

2

$\frac{1}{2}$ $\frac{1}{3}$ $\frac{1}{4}$

3

$\frac{1}{3}$ $\frac{1}{4}$ $\frac{1}{6}$

4

$\frac{1}{2}$ $\frac{1}{6}$ $\frac{1}{3}$

5

$\frac{1}{2}$ $\frac{1}{4}$ $\frac{1}{3}$

6

$\frac{1}{2}$ $\frac{1}{3}$ $\frac{1}{6}$

7

$\frac{1}{2}$ $\frac{1}{4}$ $\frac{1}{3}$

8

$\frac{1}{2}$ $\frac{1}{4}$ $\frac{1}{6}$

9

$\frac{1}{2}$ $\frac{1}{3}$ $\frac{1}{6}$

Problem Solving

Solve. Circle the fraction.

10 6 children share a pizza.
Each one gets an equal part.
What part does each child get?

$\frac{1}{2}$ $\frac{1}{3}$ $\frac{1}{6}$

 Home Note Your child identified thirds and sixths.
ACTIVITY Invite your child to divide food into thirds and sixths and name each part.

Chapter 23

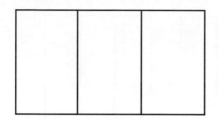
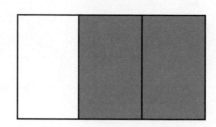
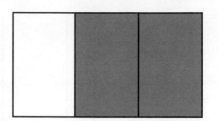

3 equal parts   2 of 3 equal parts. $\frac{2}{3}$ 2 green parts
                       Two-thirds is green.   3 equal parts

Color to show the fraction.

 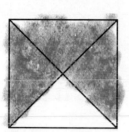

$\frac{3}{4}$

$\frac{1}{2}$

 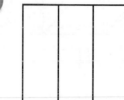

$\frac{2}{3}$

 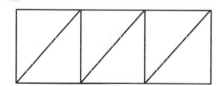

$\frac{2}{6}$

 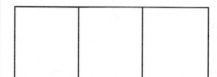

$\frac{2}{3}$

 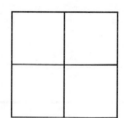

$\frac{1}{4}$

 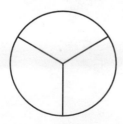

$\frac{2}{3}$

 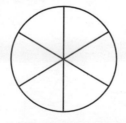

$\frac{1}{6}$

 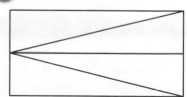

$\frac{3}{4}$

Practice

Color to show the fraction .

1.
$$\frac{2}{4}$$

2.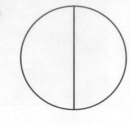
$$\frac{1}{2}$$

3.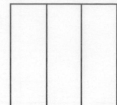
$$\frac{2}{3}$$

4.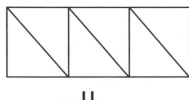
$$\frac{4}{6}$$

5.
$$\frac{2}{3}$$

6.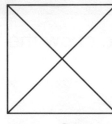
$$\frac{3}{4}$$

7.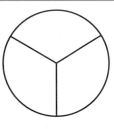
$$\frac{1}{3}$$

8.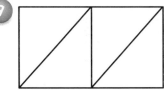
$$\frac{3}{6}$$

9.
$$\frac{1}{4}$$

Mixed Review

10. Write the time.

____:____

11. Write the amount.

____ ¢

Home Note Your child identified fractions that represent more than 1 equal part.
ACTIVITY Invite your child to divide food items into thirds, fourths, and sixths and tell you the fraction for one part and more than one part.

Parts of Groups

group of 4

2 equal parts

Red part is $\frac{1}{2}$.

Color to show the fraction.

1
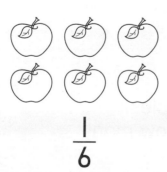

$\frac{1}{2}$

2
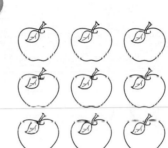

$\frac{2}{3}$

3
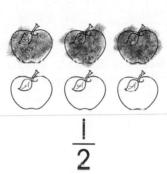

$\frac{1}{4}$

4
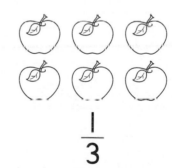

$\frac{1}{3}$

5
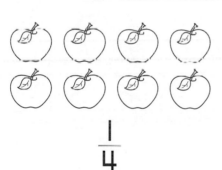

$\frac{1}{6}$

6
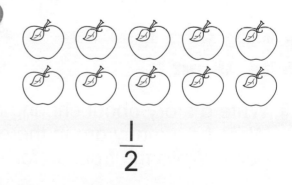

$\frac{1}{2}$

Talk About It ● Critical Thinking

How do you know if you have an equal part of a group?

Color to show the fraction.

1  $\dfrac{2}{3}$

2  $\dfrac{2}{3}$

3 $\dfrac{2}{4}$

4  $\dfrac{1}{2}$

5  $\dfrac{2}{3}$

6  $\dfrac{2}{4}$

Write About It

7 Write a story about sharing a group of apples. Write how many are in the group. Write how many parts. Write the fraction for each part.

Math Journal

Home Note Your child identified and recorded equal parts of groups.
ACTIVITY Invite your child to divide a group of objects into halves, thirds, or fourths.

Harcourt Brace School Publishers

Name _____

Understand · Plan · Solve · Look Back

Use fraction circles.
Make and draw a model to solve.

① Larry and Sandra cut a pizza in thirds.
Larry ate 1 piece. Sandra ate 2 pieces.
What part of the pizza did Sandra eat?

$\frac{1}{3}$ $\frac{2}{3}$ $\frac{3}{4}$

② Mike cut a pie in fourths.
Then he ate two pieces.
What part did Mike eat?

$\frac{1}{3}$ $\frac{2}{3}$ $\frac{2}{4}$

③ Caryn cut a waffle in fourths.
Then she ate one piece.
What part did Caryn eat?

$\frac{1}{3}$ $\frac{1}{4}$ $\frac{3}{4}$

④ LaToya cut a cake in sixths.
Then she ate 2 pieces.
What part did LaToya eat?

$\frac{1}{4}$ $\frac{2}{6}$ $\frac{1}{6}$

⑤ Kevin cut a grapefruit in fourths.
Then he ate 3 pieces.
What part did Kevin eat?

$\frac{1}{3}$ $\frac{1}{4}$ $\frac{3}{4}$

Chapter 23 • Fractions

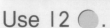

Practice

Use 12 .
Make and draw a model to solve.

1. Two children are sharing a bag of
6 marbles. Each child has an equal
part. What part does one child have?

   $\boxed{\frac{1}{2}}$ $\frac{1}{3}$ $\frac{1}{4}$

2. Three children are sharing a bag of
9 marbles. Each one has an equal
part. What part does one child have?

   $\frac{1}{2}$ $\frac{1}{3}$ $\frac{1}{4}$

3. Three children are sharing a bag of
12 marbles. Each child has an equal
part. What part does one child have?

   $\frac{1}{3}$ $\frac{2}{3}$ $\frac{2}{4}$

4. Four children are sharing a bag of
8 marbles. Each child has an equal
part. What part does one child have?

   $\frac{1}{3}$ $\frac{2}{3}$ $\frac{1}{4}$

5. Six children are sharing a bag of
12 marbles. Each child has an equal
part. What part does one child have?

   $\frac{1}{2}$ $\frac{1}{6}$ $\frac{2}{6}$

 Home Note Your child used the strategy Make a Model to solve problems.
ACTIVITY Make up problems similar to the ones on this page. Have your child use objects to model
and solve them.

Harcourt Brace School Publishers

Name _____

Concepts and Skills

Color one part . Circle the fraction.

1

$\frac{1}{3}$ $\frac{1}{2}$ $\frac{1}{4}$

2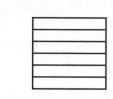

$\frac{1}{2}$ $\frac{1}{3}$ $\frac{1}{6}$

3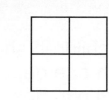

$\frac{1}{3}$ $\frac{1}{2}$ $\frac{1}{4}$

Color to show the fraction.

4

$\frac{3}{4}$

5

$\frac{4}{6}$

6

$\frac{2}{3}$

Color to show the fraction.

7

$\frac{1}{2}$

8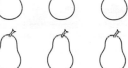

$\frac{1}{3}$

Problem Solving

Use fraction circles.
Make and draw a model to solve.

9 Jack cut a pizza in thirds. Then he ate two pieces. What part did Jack eat?

$\frac{1}{2}$ $\frac{1}{3}$ $\frac{2}{3}$

Name _____

Test Prep

Mark the best answer.

1 Six children share a cake. Each one gets an equal part. What part does each child get?

○ $\frac{2}{3}$

○ $\frac{1}{2}$

○ $\frac{1}{4}$

○ $\frac{1}{6}$

2 Four children are sharing a bag of 8 marbles. Each child has an equal part. What part does one child have?

○ $\frac{1}{4}$ ○ $\frac{2}{3}$

○ $\frac{1}{2}$ ○ $\frac{1}{6}$

3 What time is it?

○ 11:10

○ 12:00

○ 12:10

○ 2:00

4 There were 97 birds on a wire. Then 59 flew away. How many birds are left?

○ 32

○ 38

○ 42

○ 156

5 Ian has 8 blue cars, 4 red cars, and 3 black cars. How many cars does Ian have?

○ 7

○ 12

○ 15

○ 18

6 What is the temperature?

○ 25°F

○ 30°F

○ 45°F

○ 60°F

Harcourt Brace School Publishers

Name _____

Fabulous Flags

Flags are used to stand for countries.

1 Use a centimeter ruler.
Find the perimeter of the flag.

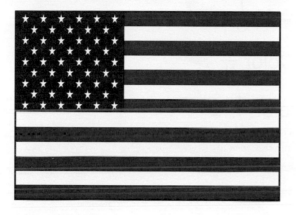

_____ + _____ + _____ + _____ = _____ centimeters

---

2 What part of the flag is green?

$\dfrac{1}{2}$ $\dfrac{1}{3}$ $\dfrac{1}{4}$

---

3 Make up your own flag.
Tell what fractions you used.

Harcourt Brace School Publishers

Home Note Your child has been learning about fractions and measurement.
ACTIVITY Have your child design a flag for your family and tell what fractions he or she used.

Math Fun

Name _____

Calculator

Computer

You can use a 🖥 to make figures that show fractions.

1 Find the figure that shows thirds. Color $\frac{1}{3}$ 🖍.

Find the figure that shows fourths. Color $\frac{1}{4}$ 🖍.

Find the figure that shows sixths. Color $\frac{1}{6}$ 🖍.

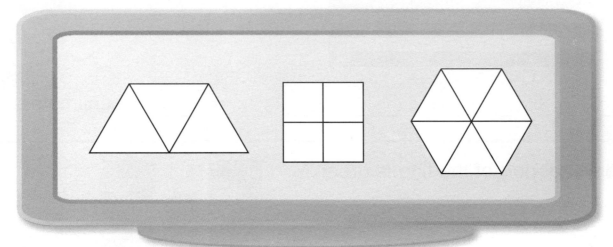

2 Use pattern blocks or a 🖥 to make figures that show halves, fourths, thirds, and sixths. Draw your figure.

3 Have a classmate find which figure shows fourths and which figure shows sixths.

SHOPPING FOR DINNER

written by Rozanne Lanczak Williams and Kathryn Corbett
illustrated by Fian Arroyo

 This book will help me review measurement and fractions.

This book belongs to _____.

Harcourt Brace School Publishers

"Patty!" called Rex. "Come over here
And see what I have found!
Fresh carrots in a crunchy bunch,
The finest ones around!"

72¢

50¢

B

"Juice! Let's buy some juice!" said Rex.
"What kind do you like?
How many quarts will our family need?
Tell me what you think."

"Cakes!" said Rex. "How I love cake!
We could get one of these
And have it with our orange juice—
A party, if you please!"

"What fun!" said Patty. "The biggest cake
Is the one that we should pick.
With six for dinner, we'll cut it so
That each of us gets one sixth."

"Shopping for dinner is fun!" said Rex.
"Yes!" said Patty. "It's neat!
But the best part of shopping for dinner,"
she said, "Is when we sit down to eat!"

Name _____

Concepts and Skills

1 Use your inch ruler. Write the length.

about _____ inches

2 Circle the things that are more than 1 foot.
Cross out the things that are less than 1 foot.

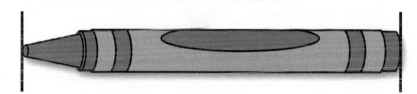

3 Use a centimeter ruler. Write how long.

about _____ centimeters

4 Circle the worm that is about 1 decimeter long.

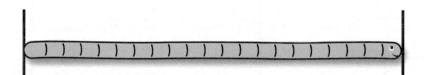

5 Measure each side. Write how many centimeters.
Then write how many centimeters around the figure.

_____ + _____ + _____ + _____ = _____ centimeters

Color cups to show how many hold the same amount.

6 **1 quart**

Circle the answer.

7 Which object weighs less than a pound?

8 Which object weighs more than a pound?

Color to show the fraction.

9

$\dfrac{1}{3}$

10

$\dfrac{3}{4}$

11

$\dfrac{2}{6}$

Problem Solving

Write the name of the tool you would use.

12 to find out how warm it is

cup   ruler   thermometer

_____

_ _ _ _ _ _ _ _ _ _ _ _ _

_____

Harcourt Brace School Publishers

Name _____

Performance Assessment

1. Use an inch ruler to draw a figure.
Write how many inches around the figure.

_____ inches

2. Use a centimeter ruler to draw a line.
Start the line at the dot. Write how many
centimeters long.

●

_____ centimeters

3. Use pattern blocks to make a picture with
equal parts. Draw the picture.
Write how many equal parts.

_____ equal parts

Write About It

4. Write the name of one thing that weighs
more than 1 pound and one thing that
weighs less than 1 pound.

This object weighs about 1 pound.

Harcourt Brace School Publishers

Name _____

Fill in the ⬭ for the correct answer.

1 Count on. Which is the total amount?

- ⬭ 29¢
- ⬭ 50¢
- ⬭ 51¢
- ⬭ not here

2 Which weighs less than I pound?

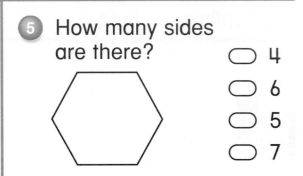

3
7
3
+5

- ⬭ 11
- ⬭ 13
- ⬭ 14
- ⬭ 15

4
46
−24

- ⬭ 12
- ⬭ 22
- ⬭ 32
- ⬭ 70

5 How many sides are there?

- ⬭ 4
- ⬭ 6
- ⬭ 5
- ⬭ 7

Our Favorite Fruit

apple										
banana										
orange										

0 1 2 3 4 5 6 7 8 9 10

6 How many like oranges the best?

- ⬭ 6
- ⬭ 7
- ⬭ 8
- ⬭ not here

7 How many more like apples than bananas?

- ⬭ 2
- ⬭ 4
- ⬭ 6
- ⬭ not here

8 Find the mistake in the pattern. Which solid figure belongs in the pattern?

Numbers to 1,000

How many squares
would it take to cover
the rabbit's paper?

Home Note In this chapter, your child will learn to model and read numbers to 1,000.
ACTIVITY Have your child count the number of squares across and then the number of rows.
Discuss the idea of groups of ten.

SCHOOL-HOME CONNECTION

Dear Family,
Today we started Chapter 24. We will learn ways to build and read numbers to 1,000. Here is the new vocabulary and an activity for us to do together at home.

Love,

_____

Vocabulary

In the number 243, the 2 stands for the number of **hundreds**, the 4 stands for the number of tens, and the 3 stands for the number of ones. 243 is made up of 2 hundreds, 4 tens, and 3 ones.

hundreds	tens	ones
2	4	3

ACTIVITY

Have your child count out small marshmallows into groups of ten. Have him or her put 10 groups of ten in sandwich bags until not enough groups of 10 are left to make a hundred. Then have your child put the remaining groups of 10 together and any extra marshmallows in a third group. Have your child tell how many hundreds, tens, and ones there are and write the number.

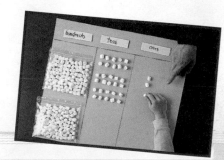

 Visit our Web site for additional ideas and activities.
http://www.hbschool.com

Name _____

You can show 100 as hundreds, tens, or ones.

 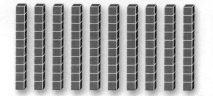 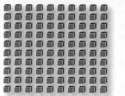

1 hundred   =   10 tens   =   100 ones

Circle groups of hundreds.
Write how many hundreds, tens, and ones.

1

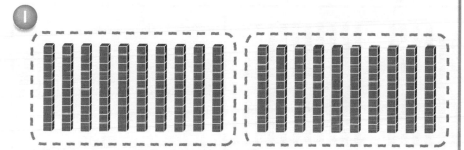

_____2_____ hundreds
_____20_____ tens
_____200_____ ones

2

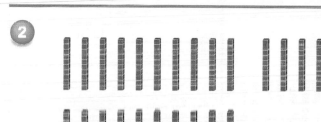

_____ hundreds

_____ tens

_____ ones

3

_____ hundreds

_____ tens

_____ ones

4

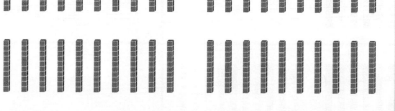

_____ hundreds

_____ tens

_____ ones

Circle groups of hundreds.
Write how many hundreds, tens, and ones.

1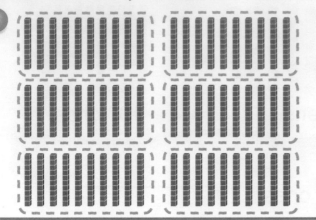

_____6_____ hundreds

_____60_____ tens

____600_____ ones

2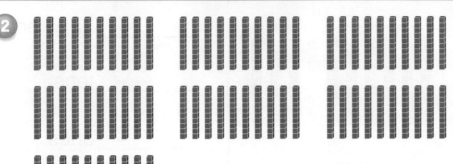

_____ hundreds

_____ tens

_____ ones

3

_____ hundreds

_____ tens

_____ ones

4

_____ hundreds

_____ tens

_____ ones

 Home Note Your child modeled and recorded large quantities.
ACTIVITY Have your child count by tens to 100.

Numbers to 500

Use Workmat 5 and 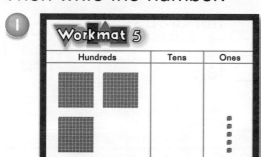.
Write how many hundreds, tens, and ones.
Then write the number.

1

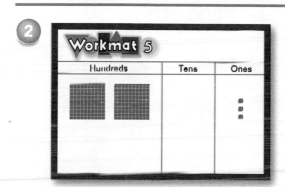

_____ **3** hundreds

_____ **0** tens

_____ **5** ones

2

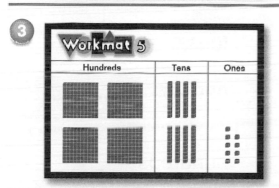

_____ hundreds

_____ tens

_____ ones

3

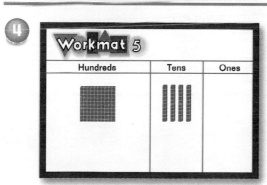

_____ hundreds

_____ tens

_____ ones

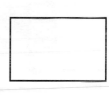

4

_____ hundred

_____ tens

_____ ones

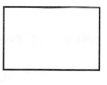

5

_____ hundreds

_____ tens

_____ ones

Practice

Use Workmat 5 and 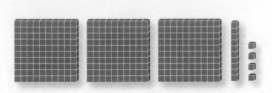.
Write how many hundreds, tens, and ones.
Then write the number.

 1

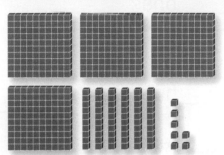

_____ **3** hundreds

_____ **1** ten

_____ **4** ones

 **314**

 2

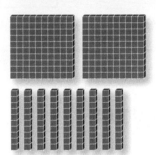

_____ hundreds

_____ tens

_____ ones

 3

_____ hundreds

_____ tens

_____ ones

 4

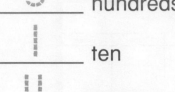

_____ hundreds

_____ tens

_____ ones

Mixed Review

Add or subtract.

5
$$\begin{array}{r} 42 \\ -23 \\ \hline \end{array}$$

6
$$\begin{array}{r} 56 \\ +39 \\ \hline \end{array}$$

7
$$\begin{array}{r} 70 \\ -58 \\ \hline \end{array}$$

8
$$\begin{array}{r} 37 \\ +23 \\ \hline \end{array}$$

 Home Note Your child modeled and recorded three-digit numbers.
ACTIVITY Say a number between 100 and 500, and have your child tell how many hundreds, tens, and ones make up that number.

Harcourt Brace School Publishers

Name ______________________

Numbers to 1,000

Write the number the model shows.

1. 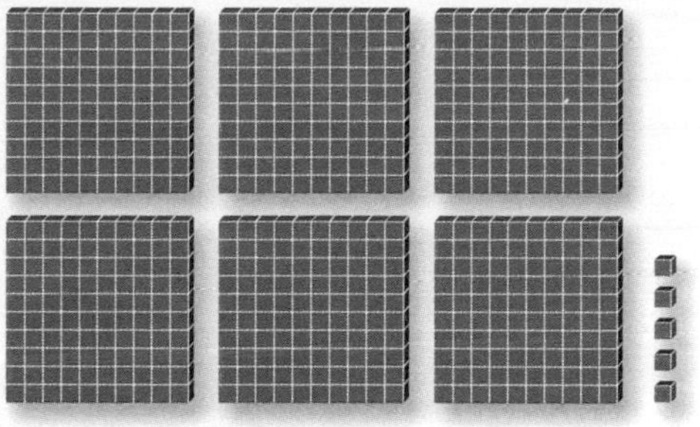

605

2. 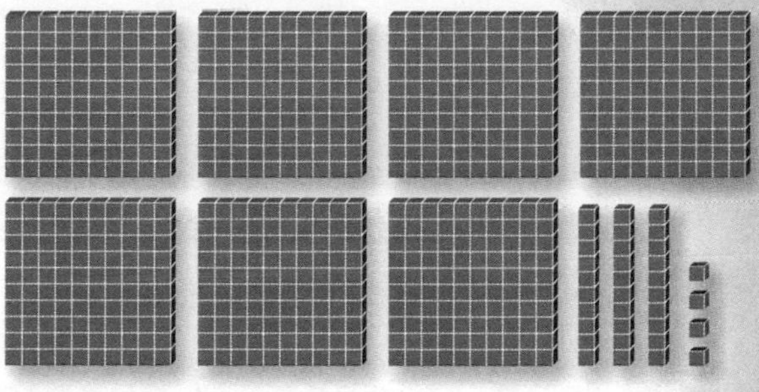

______

3. 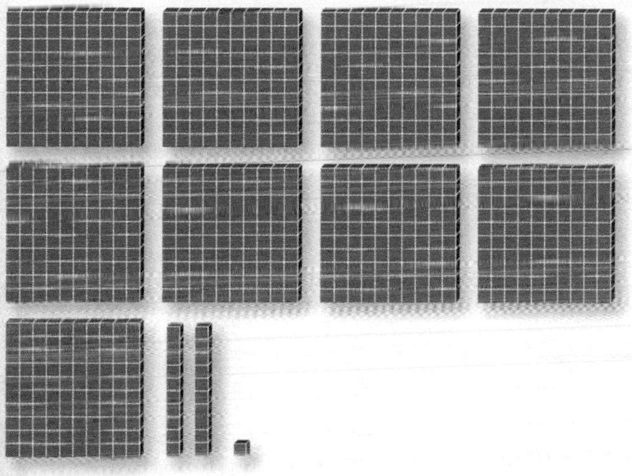

______

4. 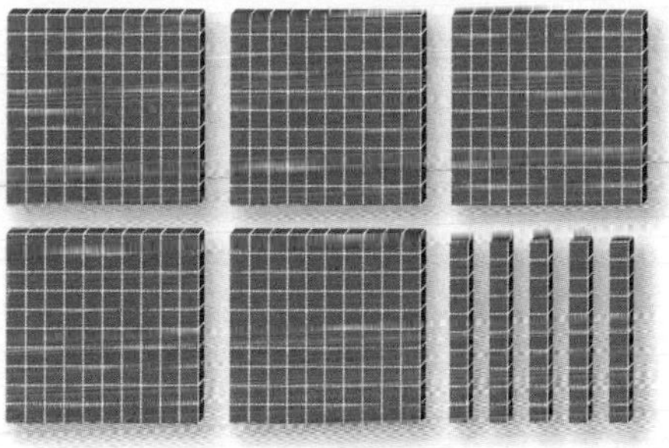

______

5. 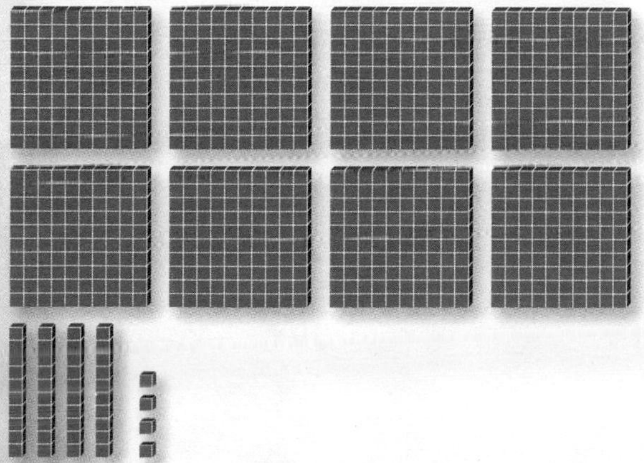

______

6. 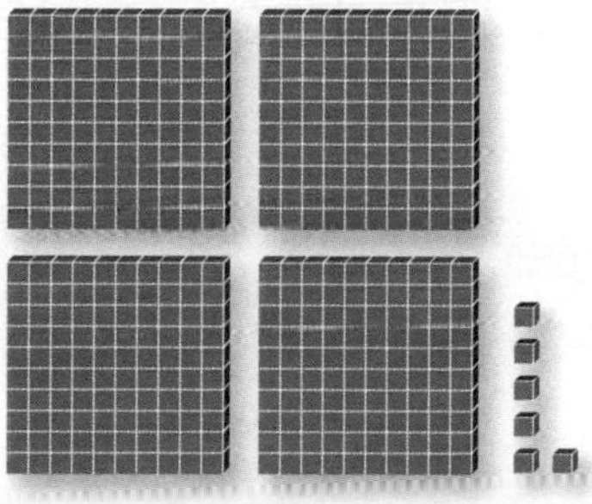

______

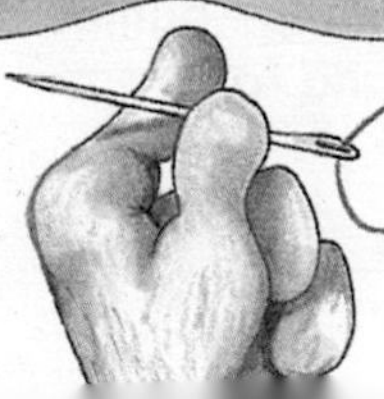

Write the number.

① 6 ones   5 hundreds   9 tens = 596

② 8 hundreds   1 ten   0 ones   = _____

③ 8 tens   5 ones   7 hundreds = _____

④ 6 hundreds   2 tens   3 ones = _____

⑤ 1 one   9 hundreds   0 tens   = _____

⑥ 6 hundreds   9 tens   8 ones = _____

⑦ 4 tens   4 ones   5 hundreds = _____

⑧ 9 ones   9 hundreds   9 tens = _____

Write About It

⑨ Write a sentence that tells how 106 is different from 16. Draw a model for each number.

Home Note Your child modeled and recorded three-digit numbers to 1,000.
ACTIVITY Have your child look for three-digit numbers and read them to you, telling you how many hundreds, tens, and ones they stand for.

Harcourt Brace School Publishers

Understand • Plan • Solve • Look Back

Circle the models that show the number.
Write the number.

1. Jason has 0 tens, 3 hundreds, and 6 ones. What number is Jason showing?

   306

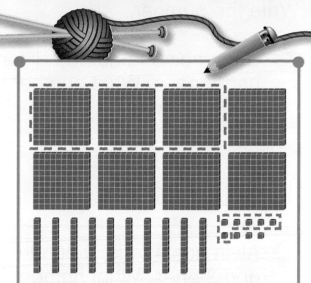

2. Rachel has 7 hundreds, 0 ones, and 2 tens. What number is Rachel showing?

   _____

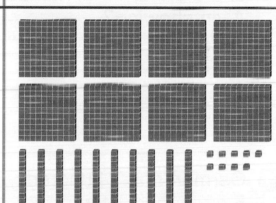

3. Jose has 8 ones, 6 hundreds, and 2 tens. What number is Jose showing?

   _____

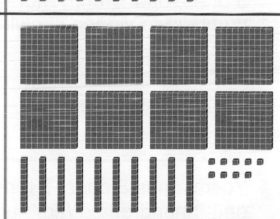

4. Rita has 1 hundred, 9 ones, and 4 tens. What number is Rita showing?

Harcourt Brace School Publishers

Circle the models that show the number.
Write the number.

1. Sean has 3 hundreds, 1 ten,
   and 9 ones. What number is
   Sean showing?

   3 1 9

   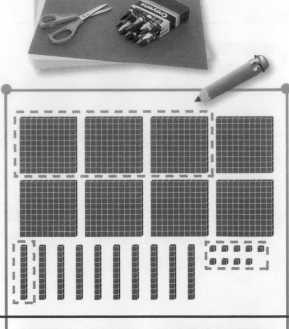

2. Alvin has 4 tens, 0 hundreds,
   and 3 ones. What number is
   Alvin showing?

   _____

   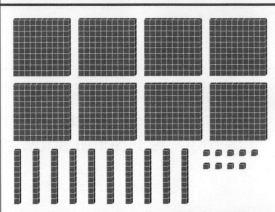

3. Carmen has 7 hundreds,
   5 ones, and 1 ten. What
   number is Carmen showing?

   _____

   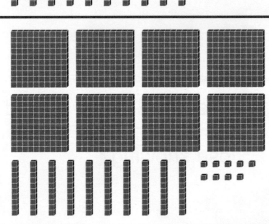

4. Yasmin has 8 ones, 3 tens,
   and 8 hundreds. What number
   is Yasmin showing?

   _____

   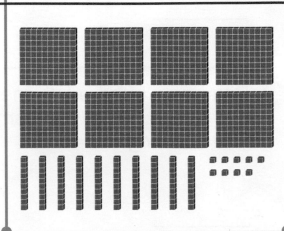

Home Note Your child modeled three-digit numbers.
ACTIVITY Have your child explain how he or she solved one of the problems.

388 three hundred eighty-eight

Chapter 24

Harcourt Brace School Publishers

You can show $1.00 with pennies.

$1.00 = 100 pennies
$1.00 = 100¢

Use coins.
Show $1.00 with the coins named.
Draw the coins. Write how many.

①

___2___ half-dollars

② _____ quarters

③ _____ dimes

④ _____ nickels

Talk About It • Critical Thinking

How many pennies equal $2.00?

Use coins.
Show other ways to make $1.00.
Write how many of each coin.

1	1	1	2	1	0
2					
3					
4					
5					

Problem Solving • **Reasoning**

Use coins.
Solve.

6 Dan has 11 coins. Together the coins equal $1.00. What coins could Dan have?

_____

 Home Note Your child used coins to show the value of $1.00.
ACTIVITY Have your child use coins to show $1.00 in as many ways as possible.

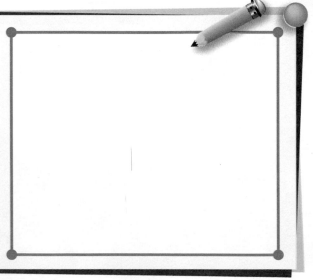

Name _____

Concepts and Skills

Review/Test

Write the number the model shows.

1  _____

2 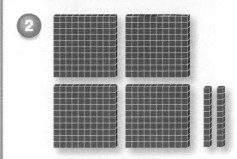 _____

Write the number.

3 9 ones   3 hundreds   4 tens = _____

4 6 tens   9 hundreds   5 ones = _____

Circle the models that show the number.
Write the number.

5 Ann has 4 hundreds, 9 ones,
and 6 tens. What number is
Ann showing?

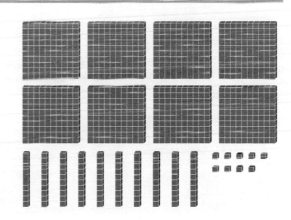

_____

Use coins to show $1.00 two ways. Draw and label the coins.

6

7

Name _____

Test Prep

Mark the best answer.

1 Which is the total amount?

○ 95¢   ○ 90¢

○ 85¢   ○ 80¢

2 Which shows 432?

3 What part is green?

○ $\frac{1}{6}$ ○ $\frac{4}{5}$

○ $\frac{2}{3}$ ○ $\frac{5}{6}$

4 Which is the number?

○ 678

○ 768

○ 786

○ 867

5 How many sides and corners?

○ 3 sides, 3 corners

○ 4 sides, 4 corners

○ 5 sides, 6 corners

○ 6 sides, 6 corners

6 How many like swimming the best?

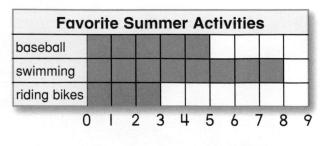

Favorite Summer Activities									
baseball									
swimming									
riding bikes									

    0   1   2   3   4   5   6   7   8   9

○ 6   ○ 8

○ 5   ○ 3

Standardized Test Prep • Chapters 1–24

Comparing and Ordering Large Numbers

Is the number of ladybugs greater than or less than the number of frogs? How do you know?

Home Note In this chapter, your child will learn how to compare and order large numbers. **ACTIVITY** Show a large group of objects and a small group. Ask your child which group has the greater number of objects.

SCHOOL-HOME CONNECTION

Dear Family,
    Today we started Chapter 25. We will compare large numbers. Here is the vocabulary and an activity for us to do together at home.

Love,

_____

Vocabulary

hundreds	tens	ones		hundreds	tens	ones
2	0	3		2	3	0

Compare 203 and 230 to find the **greater** number.

• Compare the digits in the hundreds place. Both numbers have 2 hundreds.

• Compare the digits in the tens place. The number 203 has 0 tens. The number 230 has 3 tens.

• Because the number 230 has more tens, it is the greater number.

ACTIVITY

Write the numerals from 0 to 9 on slips of paper, making two "cards" for each number. Shuffle the cards, and deal three each, face up, to yourself and your child. Each of you should make the greatest three-digit number possible. The player with the greater number keeps all six cards. Deal again. Play until all the cards have been used.

Visit our Web site for additional ideas and activities.
http://www.hbschool.com

Harcourt Brace School Publishers

Name _____

Greater Than

Compare the two models.
Write both numbers.
Circle the number that is greater.

First compare the
hundreds, then the tens,
and then the ones.

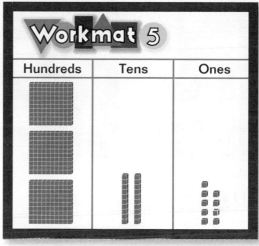
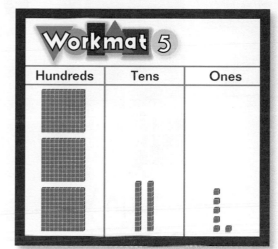

1. ◯329◯   326

2.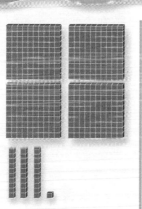

_____   _____

3.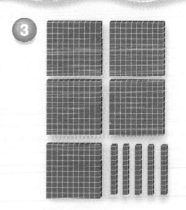

_____   _____

4.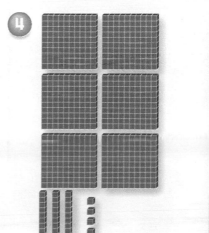

_____   _____

5.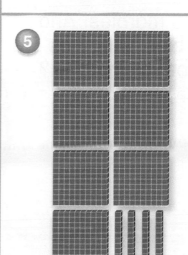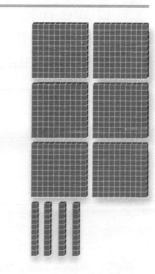

_____   _____

Chapter 25 • Comparing and Ordering Large Numbers

Harcourt Brace School Publishers

Practice

Compare the two numbers.
Circle the number that is greater.

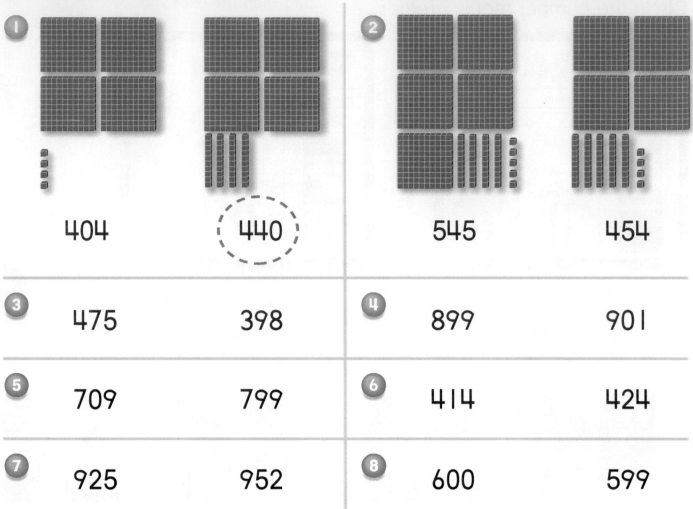

1   404   (440)

2   545   454

3 475 398	**4** 899 901
5 709 799	**6** 414 424
7 925 952	**8** 600 599

Problem Solving

Solve.

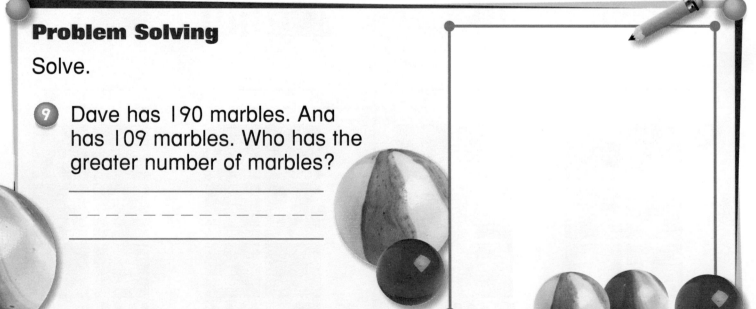

9   Dave has 190 marbles. Ana has 109 marbles. Who has the greater number of marbles?

_____

- - - - - - - - - - - - - - - - - -

_____

Home Note Your child determined which of two numbers is greater.
ACTIVITY Name some pairs of numbers, such as 450 and 405. Have your child tell you which number is greater and why.

Harcourt Brace School Publishers

Name _____

Compare the two models.
Write both numbers.
Circle the number that is less.

First compare the hundreds, then the tens, and then the ones.

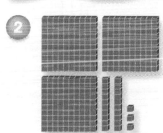 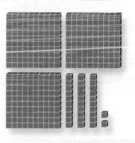 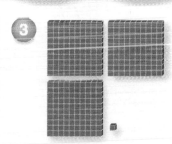 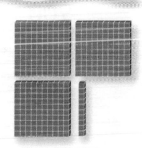

1 (405)   450

_____

2 _____   _____   **3** _____   _____

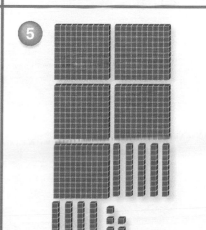

4 _____   _____   **5** _____   _____

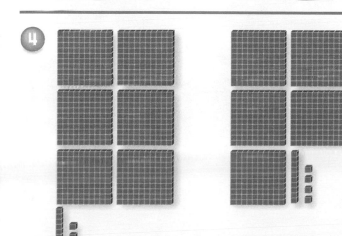 

Harcourt Brace School Publishers

Practice

Compare the two numbers.
Circle the number that is less.

1
299   (289)

2
128   182

3   479   480

4   989   979

5   800   822

6   313   323

7   900   899

8   610   601

9   690   780

10   511   510

Mixed Review

Write the total amount.

11   _____ ¢

12   _____ ¢

Home Note **Your child determined which of two numbers is less.**
ACTIVITY **Have your child tell you how he or she knew which number of each pair on this page is less.**

Harcourt Brace School Publishers

Name _____

102 is less than 120.

102 < 120

120 is greater than 102.

120 > 102

Write greater or less.
Then write > or < in the circle.

1

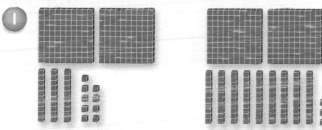

239 is ___less___ than 293.

239 ⟨<⟩ 293

2

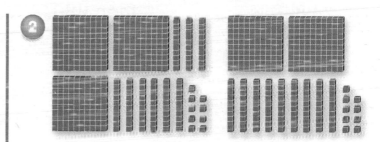

399 is _____ than 299.

399 ◯ 299

3

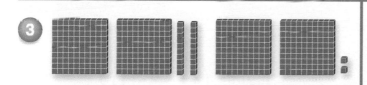

220 is _____ than 202.

220 ◯ 202

4

119 is _____ than 120.

119 ◯ 120

Talk About It • Critical Thinking

How is comparing three-digit numbers different from comparing two-digit numbers? How is it the same?

Practice

Write greater or less.
Then write > or < in the circle.

1 570 is _greater_ than 57.

570 (>) 57

2 256 is _____ than 265.

256 ( ) 265

3 606 is _____ than 660.

606 ( ) 660

4 100 is _____ than 10.

100 ( ) 10

5 840 is _____ than 480.

840 ( ) 480

6 799 is _____ than 800.

799 ( ) 800

7 36 is _____ than 360.

36 ( ) 360

8 699 is _____ than 599.

699 ( ) 599

9 909 is _____ than 899.

909 ( ) 899

10 120 is _____ than 102.

120 ( ) 102

11 96 is _____ than 296.

96 ( ) 296

12 434 is _____ than 424.

434 ( ) 424

 Home Note Your child used symbols to compare numbers.
ACTIVITY Show your child 2 three-digit numbers, and have him or her tell you which is less.

400 four hundred

Name _____

The number just after 540 is 541.

The number just before 540 is 539.

The number between 539 and 541 is 540.

Write the number that is just after,
just before, or between.

after	before	between
1 234, _235_	_299_, 300	299, _300_, 301
2 100, _____	_____, 825	519, _____, 521
3 969, _____	_____, 601	333, _____, 335
4 609, _____	_____, 150	698, _____, 700
5 499, _____	_____, 777	997, _____, 999

Write the number that is just after, just before, or between.

1. **788** , 789

2. 449, _____ , 451

3. 299, _____

4. _____ , 501

5. 99, _____ , 101

6. 698, _____

7. 89, _____

8. _____ , 350

9. _____ , 400

10. 209, _____ , 211

11. 767, _____

12. _____ , 888

Problem Solving • Mental Math

Write the number.

13. Emery Raccoon counts 139 cups for his picnic. He has 1 more cup to count. How many cups does he have in all?

_____ cups

14. At the picnic, 300 of Emery Raccoon's friends sing. 1 friend leaves to go home. How many of Emery Raccoon's friends are still singing?

_____ friends

Home Note Your child identified the number that is just after, just before, or between. **ACTIVITY** Say any three-digit number and have your child tell you which number comes before and after.

Harcourt Brace School Publishers

Write 168, 148, and 163 in order from least to greatest.

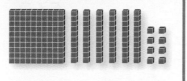 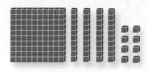 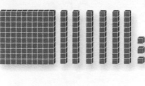

168   148   163

148 , 163 , 168

Write the number for each model.
Compare the three numbers.
Then write them in order from least to greatest.

  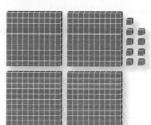 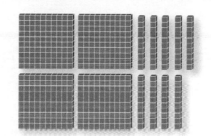 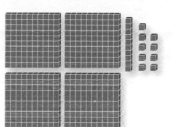

_____   _____   _____

_____ , _____ , _____

  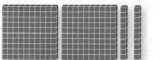  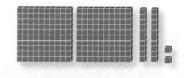

_____   _____   _____

_____ , _____ , _____

Talk About It ● Critical Thinking

How would you order the numbers from greatest to least?

Write the numbers in order from least to greatest.

1.   356   536   353   563

          353 ,   356 ,   536 ,   563

2.   818   880   808   800

          _____ , _____ , _____ , _____

3.   635   625   655   695

          _____ , _____ , _____ , _____

4.   105   510   150   151

          _____ , _____ , _____ , _____

5.   620   430   360   750

          _____ , _____ , _____ , _____

Write About It

6. Write a story that has 3 numbers in it. Each number should be greater than 100 and less than 200. Write the numbers in order from least to greatest.

Math Journal

Home Note Your child ordered numbers from least to greatest.
ACTIVITY Show your child some three-digit numbers, such as 387, 425, and 199. Have him or her write them in order from least to greatest.

Concepts and Skills

Compare the two numbers.
Circle the number that is greater.

1 796   798 | **2** 401   399

Compare the two numbers.
Circle the number that is less.

3 139   140 | **4** 601   610

Write greater or less.
Then write > or < in the circle.

5 303 is _____ than 330. | **6** 700 is _____ than 70.

303 330 | 700 70

Write the number that is just after,
just before, or between.

7 _____, 900 | **8** 199, _____ | **9** 289, _____, 291

Write the numbers in order from least to greatest.

10 909   900   919   999

_____, _____, _____, _____

Name _____

Test Prep

Mark the best answer.

1 Which is the number?

- ⬭ 372
- ⬭ 470
- ⬭ 427
- ⬭ 742

2 What number comes between?

943, _____, 945

- ⬭ 942
- ⬭ 944
- ⬭ 946
- ⬭ 950

3 Which one is $\frac{3}{4}$ yellow?

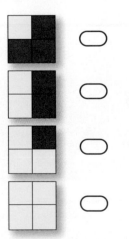

4 Which is the total amount?

- ⬭ 50¢
- ⬭ 55¢
- ⬭ 80¢
- ⬭ 85¢

5 A squirrel found 38 nuts. Then it found 56 more nuts. How many nuts did the squirrel find?

- ⬭ 18
- ⬭ 82
- ⬭ 94
- ⬭ 98

6 Which takes about a minute?

- ⬭ to take a nap
- ⬭ to wash your hands
- ⬭ to do your homework
- ⬭ to watch a TV show

Harcourt Brace School Publishers

Adding and Subtracting Large Numbers

MeNU

Chicken Soup	$1.25
Turkey Burger	$4.50
Fish Sandwich	$3.75
Mixed Salad	$2.60
Hot Cocoa	$1.85

**What two items would you buy?
How much would you spend?**

Home Note In this chapter, your child will learn to add and subtract large numbers.
ACTIVITY Have your child tell you which items he or she chose. Have him or her tell you the total amount.

SCHOOL-HOME CONNECTION

Dear Family,
   Today we started Chapter 26. We will look at ways to add and subtract large numbers. Here are some activities for us to do together at home.
   Love,

_____

Vocabulary

Have your child tell you the steps for solving this addition problem.

hundreds	tens	ones
	1	
2	3	4
+ 6	5	8
8	9	2

Add the ones first. 4 + 8 = 12.

The 12 ones are regrouped as 1 ten and 2 ones. The two is written in the ones column, and the 1 above the tens column.

Add the tens. Add the hundreds.

ACTIVITY

Together, look through newspaper ads to find two items priced between $1.00 and $4.99. Have your child use real money, if possible, to find the cost of buying both items. Then help your child check his or her answer with a calculator.

Visit our Web site for additional ideas and activities.
http://www.hbschool.com

Harcourt Brace School Publishers

Modeling Addition of Three-Digit Numbers

$135 + 146 =$ ___

Step 1

Add the ones.
Regroup 11 ones to
make 1 ten and 1 one.
Write 1 to show the
new ten.

hundreds	tens	ones
	3	5
+ 1	4	6

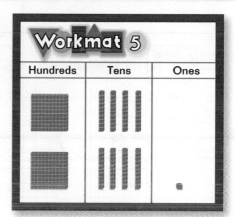

Step 2

Add the tens.
Write the number
of tens.

hundreds	tens	ones
1	3	5
+ 1	4	6
	8	1

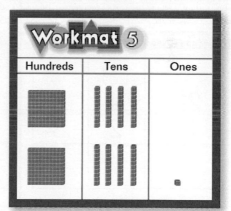

Step 3

Add the hundreds.
Write the number
of hundreds.

hundreds	tens	ones
1	3	5
+ 1	4	6
2	8	1

Use Workmat 5 and   .
Add.

1

hundreds	tens	ones
6	4	5
+ 1	3	5

2

hundreds	tens	ones
3	3	6
+ 2	2	7

3

hundreds	tens	ones
4	6	7
+ 5	1	8

Practice

Use Workmat 5 and  .
Add.

1

hundreds	tens	ones
2	☐ 1	9
+ 2	5	4
4	7	3

2

hundreds	tens	ones
3	☐ 5	8
+ 1	1	2

3

hundreds	tens	ones
1	☐ 6	5
+ 4	2	9

4

hundreds	tens	ones
2	☐ 8	4
+ 5	0	7

5

hundreds	tens	ones
7	☐ 0	5
+ 1	3	5

6

hundreds	tens	ones
3	☐ 6	8
+	1	6

7

hundreds	tens	ones
2	☐ 4	9
+ 1	2	3

8

hundreds	tens	ones
6	☐ 3	9
+ 1	5	6

9

hundreds	tens	ones
4	☐ 4	7
+ 3	4	3

10

hundreds	tens	ones
9	☐ 0	9
+	4	3

11

hundreds	tens	ones
8	☐ 2	7
+ 1	0	7

12

hundreds	tens	ones
2	☐ 2	4
+ 5	3	6

 Home Note Your child modeled and added three-digit numbers.
ACTIVITY Ask your child to tell you how he or she knows when to regroup. Use one of the problems on this page.

Harcourt Brace School Publishers

Adding Three-Digit Numbers

142 + 185 = ____

Step 1
Add the ones.
Write the number
of ones.

hundreds	tens	ones
☐	☐	
1	4	2
+ 1	8	5
		7

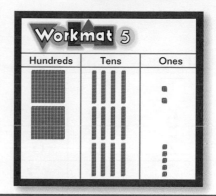

Step 2
Add the tens.
Regroup 12 tens as
1 hundred and 2 tens.
Write the number
of tens.

hundreds	tens	ones
☐	☐	
1	4	2
+ 1	8	5
	2	7

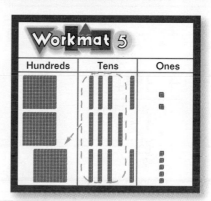

Step 3
Add the hundreds.
Write the number
of hundreds.

hundreds	tens	ones
1	☐	
1	4	2
+ 1	8	5
3	2	7

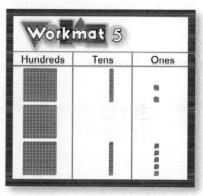

Add.

1

hundreds	tens	ones
☐	☐	
5	6	8
+ 2	5	0

2

hundreds	tens	ones
☐	☐	
6	7	7
+ 2	0	3

3

hundreds	tens	ones
☐	☐	
4	7	7
+ 1	4	2

Talk About It • Critical Thinking

How is adding three-digit numbers like adding
two-digit numbers?

Practice

Add.

1

hundreds	tens	ones
□	□	
5	9	3
+ 2	8	6
8	7	9

2

hundreds	tens	ones
□	□	
3	2	9
+ 3	4	2

3

hundreds	tens	ones
□		
6	7	3
+ 2	3	4

4
153
+354
507

5
132
+622

6
408
+356

7
710
+197

8
238
+559

9
463
+374

10
953
+ 27

11
690
+309

12
418
+479

13
184
+713

14
537
+248

15
835
+ 94

Problem Solving

Solve.

16 There are 365 days in one year. How many days are in two years?

_____ days

 Home Note Your child added 3-digit numbers.
ACTIVITY Make up some three-digit story problems for your child to solve.

Harcourt Brace School Publishers

Modeling Subtraction of Three-Digit Numbers

$236 - 129 = $ _____

Step 1
Show 236.
Look at the ones.
Can you subtract 9?

Yes (No)

hundreds	tens	ones
	☐	☐
2	3	6
− 1	2	9

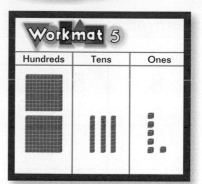

Step 2
Regroup 1 ten as
10 ones.
Write the number of tens
and ones.
Subtract 9 from 16.
Write how many ones are
left.

hundreds	tens	ones
	2	16
2	3̸	6̸
− 1	2	9
		7

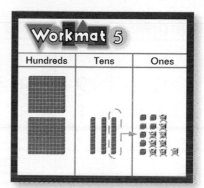

Step 3
Subtract the tens.
Subtract the hundreds.
Write how many tens and
hundreds are left.

hundreds	tens	ones
	2	16
2	3̸	6̸
− 1	2	9
1	0	7

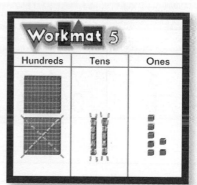

Use Workmat 5 and  .
Subtract.

1

hundreds	tens	ones
	☐	☐
9	6	3
− 7	5	7

2

hundreds	tens	ones
	☐	☐
7	8	5
− 2	4	7

3

hundreds	tens	ones
	☐	☐
6	4	1
− 3	2	5

Use Workmat 5 and .
Subtract.

1

hundreds	tens	ones
8	⁴5̸	¹⁰0̸
− 6	1	3
2	3	7

2

hundreds	tens	ones
	□	□
9	8	2
− 9	1	9

3

hundreds	tens	ones
	□	□
5	9	0
− 2	3	8

4

hundreds	tens	ones
	□	□
4	2	3
− 1	1	8

5

hundreds	tens	ones
	□	□
7	9	4
− 2	5	7

6

hundreds	tens	ones
	□	□
6	4	8
−	3	9

7

hundreds	tens	ones
	□	□
3	9	1
− 1	0	6

8

hundreds	tens	ones
	□	□
8	6	5
−	3	8

9

hundreds	tens	ones
	□	□
7	7	5
− 6	0	7

Mixed Review

Write the numbers in order from least to greatest.

10 990   999   919   909

_____ , _____ , _____ , _____

Home Note Your child modeled subtraction of three-digit numbers.
ACTIVITY Have your child choose a subtraction problem on this page and tell you the steps he or she followed to solve it.

Name _____

Subtract.

329 − 197 = _____

Step 1

Show 329.
Subtract the ones.
Write the number
of ones.

hundreds	tens	ones
☐	☐	
3	2	9
− 1	9	7
		2

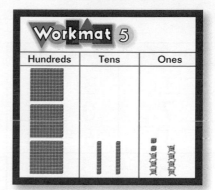

Step 2

Look at the tens.
Can you subtract 9 tens?
Regroup 1 hundred as
10 tens.
Subtract the tens.

hundreds	tens	ones
2	12	
3	2	9
− 1	9	7
	3	2

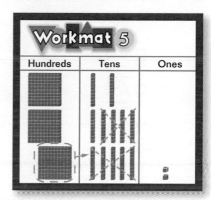

Step 3

Subtract the hundreds.

hundreds	tens	ones
2	12	
3	2	9
− 1	9	7
1	3	2

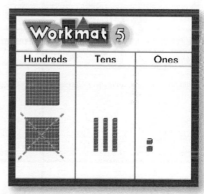

1

hundreds	tens	ones
☐	☐	
8	4	8
− 4	7	5

2

hundreds	tens	ones
☐	☐	
9	2	4
− 6	5	3

3

hundreds	tens	ones
☐	☐	
7	5	9
− 1	9	5

Talk About It • Critical Thinking

Why do you subtract the ones first when
subtracting three-digit numbers?

Subtract.

1

hundreds	tens	ones
[6] 7	[10] 0	7
− 1	6	3
5	4	4

2

hundreds	tens	ones
[ ] 9	[ ] 4	6
− 5	8	3

3

hundreds	tens	ones
3	[ ] 8	[ ] 1
−	4	4

4
```
  7 12
  828
− 674
  154
```

5
```
  527
− 245
```

6
```
  842
− 626
```

7
```
  804
− 310
```

8
```
  865
− 613
```

9
```
  987
− 169
```

10
```
  736
− 717
```

11
```
  926
−  45
```

12
```
  739
− 284
```

13
```
  409
− 206
```

14
```
  198
−  48
```

15
```
  542
− 226
```

Write About It

16 Write a subtraction story. Use 2 three-digit numbers in your story.

Math Journal

Home Note Your child subtracted 3-digit numbers.
ACTIVITY Give your child 2 three-digit numbers, and have him or her subtract.

Understand • Plan • Solve • Look Back

Problem Solving
Choose the Operation

Remember, 1 dollar is the same as 100 cents.

Add or subtract.

1 Rob bought a sandwich for $2.95.
Leslie bought a sandwich for $1.50.
How much money did they spend in all?

$4.45

$2.95
+ 1.50

$4.45

2 Lin bought a drink for $3.25.
Cecil bought a drink for $1.10.
How much more did Lin's drink cost?

_____

3 Charles had $4.11. He gave $2.71
to Carol. How much money does
Charles have now?

_____

4 Babs got $2.45 for washing the dishes.
Bob got $1.35 for drying the dishes.
How much money did they get in all?

_____

5 Renee had $1.09 in her piggy bank. Then
Jack put in $1.90. How much money does
Renee have in her piggy bank now?

_____

Add or subtract.

1. Candy had $2.92 in her purse. She spent $1.36 on a pack of crayons. How much money does Candy have left?

   $1.56

   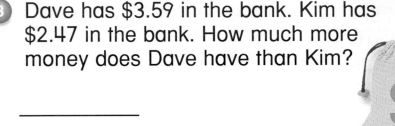

   8 12
   $2.92
   − 1.36

   $1.56

2. Ann Lee bought a goldfish for $2.29. She bought fish food for $1.46. How much money did Ann Lee spend?

   _____

3. Dave has $3.59 in the bank. Kim has $2.47 in the bank. How much more money does Dave have than Kim?

   _____

4. Bill bought a hamburger for $1.65. Joe bought a hot dog for $1.19. How much money did Bill and Joe spend in all?

   _____

5. Mary had $3.90. She gave $2.61 to Steve. How much money does Mary have now?

   _____

Harcourt Brace School Publishers

Home Note Your child chose the operation to solve problems.
ACTIVITY Have your child tell how he or she knew whether to add or subtract in the story problems.

Name _____

Concepts and Skills

Add or subtract.

1
$$341$$
$$+137$$

2
$$791$$
$$+133$$

3
$$675$$
$$+\ 19$$

4
$$547$$
$$+127$$

5
$$946$$
$$-875$$

6
$$991$$
$$-327$$

7
$$798$$
$$-509$$

8
$$765$$
$$-123$$

9
$$409$$
$$-135$$

10
$$845$$
$$+\ 135$$

11
$$515$$
$$-\ 309$$

12
$$411$$
$$+289$$

Problem Solving

Add or subtract.

13 George had $4.25. He spent $2.80 on a toy. How much money does he have left?

$ _____

14 Gina earned $2.95 on Tuesday and $1.10 on Thursday. How much money did she earn altogether?

$ _____

Name _____

Test Prep

Mark the best answer.

1 Which number is shown by the model?

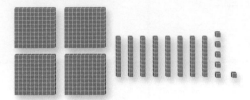

- ○ 864
- ○ 648
- ○ 468
- ○ 486

2 Which numbers are in order from least to greatest?

- ○ 782, 418, 843
- ○ 418, 843, 782
- ○ 418, 782, 843
- ○ 843, 418, 782

3 Which is the total amount?

- ○ 73¢
- ○ 55¢
- ○ 88¢
- ○ 98¢

4 What is the temperature?

- ○ 60°F
- ○ 85°F
- ○ 80°F
- ○ 90°F

5 The Lees drove 58 miles on Saturday and 39 miles on Sunday. How many miles did they drive?

- ○ 21
- ○ 87
- ○ 19
- ○ 97

6 Linda lives 25 miles away from the mall. Greg lives 19 miles away. How many miles farther away from the mall does Linda live?

- ○ 6
- ○ 44
- ○ 16
- ○ 34

Harcourt Brace School Publishers

Name _____

Antique Elevator

You will need:

1. Start with 998.

2. Spin 3 times to make a 3-digit number.

3. Write the number in the space marked 1. Subtract it from 998.

4. Make another 3-digit number. Write it in the space marked 2.

5. Subtract the number from the number just above it.

6. The player closest to 0 after 4 turns wins.

998

1

2

3

4

Home Note Your child learned to subtract three-digit numbers.
ACTIVITY Make up a 3-digit subtraction problem. Have your child solve it.

Harcourt Brace School Publishers

Name _____

Calculator   Computer

Use a .

➤ Find the sum or difference.
➤ Turn your calculator upside down.
➤ Write the word you see.

1 | ON/C | 4 | 9 | 6 | + | 4 | 4 | 2 | = | 9 3 8 | BEG

2 | ON/C | 2 | 7 | 1 | + | 5 | 3 | 7 | =

3 | ON/C | 7 | 1 | 5 | + | 1 | 9 | 2 | =

4 | ON/C | 6 | 0 | 0 | − | 2 | 8 | 3 | =

5 | ON/C | 5 | 5 | 2 | + | 3 | 6 | 6 | =

6 | ON/C | 9 | 2 | 0 | − | 1 | 0 | 2 | =

7 | ON/C | 9 | 4 | 0 | − | 2 | 3 | 0 | =

Harcourt Brace School Publishers

A Tunnel for Pepper

written by Linda Cave

illustrated by Manuel King

This book will help me review adding and subtracting larger numbers.

This book belongs to _____ .

Harcourt Brace School Publishers

A

Mrs. Davis's class decided to collect pennies to buy a new tunnel for Pepper, the classroom pet.

"Wow, we sure have a lot of pennies," said Brian as he looked at the jar of pennies. "Can we buy Pepper his new tunnel?"

"Not yet—we have only 646 pennies," said Kevin. "We need 999 pennies to buy Pepper's new tunnel."

"I guess Pepper will just have to wait," said Brian disappointedly. He turned to Pepper and said, "Don't worry, Pepper. Soon we'll have enough pennies for a tunnel."

"We still need less than 400 pennies," said Kevin. "It will not take too long for us to get that many more pennies.

How many pennies do the children need?

_____ pennies

Shana and Cassie came into the classroom and went straight to Pepper's table. "I have some pennies for the tunnel," said Shana as she opened her bag of pennies. "Here are 137 pennies."

"I have more pennies than you," said Cassie to Shana. "I have 129 pennies."

Does Cassie have more pennies? _____

Write the numbers to show who has more pennies.

_____ > _____

Harcourt Brace School Publishers

"Oh no!" said Brian when he saw that the girls had poured their pennies into the jar. "Don't dump the pennies! Now we have to count them all again."

"No we don't," said Kevin. "We can add the pennies. We know how many pennies Shana brought and how many Cassie brought."

"Yes," said Shana. "I had 137 pennies, and Cassie had 129 pennies."

How many pennies did Shana and Cassie bring in?

_____ pennies

"Wow! 266 more pennies!" said Kevin when he had added the girls' pennies. "We are getting close. Pepper is going to get his tunnel soon."

"Yes, Pepper, you are going to have a tunnel very soon," said Shana. Then Shana turned to Brian and asked, "How many pennies do we have now?"

How many pennies do the children have in all?

_____ pennies

"Look, here comes Nick. He has a bag. Maybe he has more pennies," said Cassie.

"I wonder how many he has," said Brian. "I hope we can get Pepper's tunnel soon."

"I think we need less than 100 pennies now!" said Cassie excitedly.

How many pennies do the children need?

_____ pennies

G

"I brought some pennies for the tunnel," said Nick. "Here are 93 pennies. Do we still need a lot more?"

"We needed 87 pennies," said Cassie. "93 is more than 87. We have more than 999 pennies."

"Great!" said Brian. "Pepper, you will have a new tunnel."

Harcourt Brace School Publishers

Concepts and Skills

Write the number the model shows.

 1
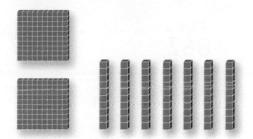

_____

2

_____

3

_____

4

_____

Use coins to show $1.00 two ways. Draw and label the coins.

 5

6

Compare the two numbers.

Circle the number that is greater.	Circle the number that is less.
7 499 502	**8** 867 869

Write the number that is just after, just before, or between.

9

896, _____

10

_____ ,190

11

299, _____ , 301

Write the numbers in order from least to greatest.

12   770   709   707   790

_____   _____   _____   _____

Add or subtract.

13   319
    +421

14   650
    +257

15   892
    −478

16   730
    −125

Problem Solving

Add or subtract.

17 Adam earned $1.75. His sister Kari earned $1.50. How much money did they earn in all?

$ _____

Performance Assessment

Use Workmat 5 and 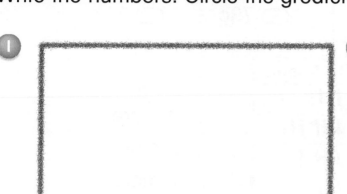 .
Build two numbers between 100 and 499.
Draw a picture of each model.
Write the numbers. Circle the greater number.

1
_____

2
_____

3 Write an addition problem with the numbers.
Add. Regroup if you need to.

4 Write a subtraction problem with the numbers.
Subtract the number that is less from the number that is greater.
Regroup if you need to.

Write About It

5 Write an addition story.
Use 2 three-digit numbers in your story.

Math Journal

Name _____

Fill in the ⬭ for the correct answer.

1 Does this show an even or odd number?

○ even   ○ odd

2 Todd has 2 quarters, 2 dimes, and 3 pennies. How much money does he have?

○ 47¢   ○ 63¢
○ 73¢   ○ 82¢

3 How many more votes did the triangle get than the circle?

Our Favorite Shapes	
circle	IIII
square	⊞⊞ III
triangle	⊞⊞ I
rectangle	III

○ 1 more
○ 4 more
○ 2 more
○ 6 more

4
```
  7    ○ 11
+6     ○ 13
       ○ 14
       ○ 15
```

5
```
 15    ○ 4
- 9    ○ 5
       ○ 6
       ○ 7
```

6
```
 146    ○ 462
+326    ○ 472
        ○ 562
        ○ 572
```

7 How can you move the first letter to make it look like the second letter?

○ flip it   ○ turn it   ○ slide it

8 How long is the worm?

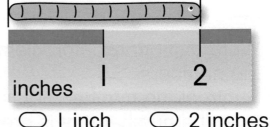

inches

○ 1 inch   ○ 2 inches
○ 3 inches   ○ 4 inches

9 Which number is shown?

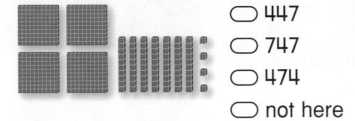

○ 447
○ 747
○ 474
○ not here

10 Which number is just before 381?

_____, 381

○ 370   ○ 379
○ 380   ○ 382

Multiplication

What multiplication stories can you tell about the picture?

Home Note In this chapter, your child will learn how to multiply.
ACTIVITY Have your child tell you a multiplication story about the picture.

SCHOOL-HOME CONNECTION

Dear Family,
    Today we started Chapter 27. We will learn how to multiply. Here are the new vocabulary words and an activity for us to do together at home.

Love,

_____

Vocabulary

You can add 2 + 2 + 2 = 6

These are 3 **equal groups**.

You can also **multiply**.

$$3 \times 2 = 6$$

This is a **multiplication sentence**. The answer is called the **product**.

ACTIVITY

Together, look for equal groups of 2, 3, 4, and 5. Groups of 2 might be the ears on 4 neighborhood animals. Groups of 3, 4, and 5 might be flowers in a garden. Have your child draw pictures of the groups and write multiplication sentences to tell about the pictures.

Visit our Web site for additional ideas and activities.
http://www.hbschool.com

Name _____

Make 3 equal groups.
Put 2 in each group.

You can add equal groups
to find how many in all.

<u>2</u> + <u>2</u> + <u>2</u> = <u>6</u>

Use Workmat 6 and .
Make equal groups.
Draw a picture. Write how many in all.

1 Make 2 equal groups.
Put 4 ▪ in each group.

2 Make 2 equal groups.
Put 5 ▪ in each group.

____ + ____ = ____

____ + ____ = ____

3 Make 3 equal groups.
Put 4 ▪ in each group.

4 Make 3 equal groups.
Put 3 ▪ in each group.

____ + ____ + ____ = ____

____ + ____ + ____ = ____

Talk About It ● **Critical Thinking**

Why are all the addends the same?

Practice

Use Workmat 6 and 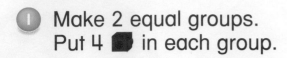.
Make equal groups.
Draw a picture. Write how many in all.

1 Make 2 equal groups.
Put 4 ⬛ in each group.

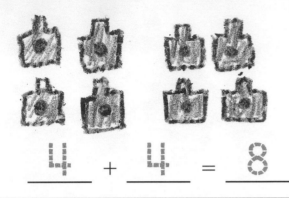

4 + 4 = 8

2 Make 3 equal groups.
Put 6 ⬛ in each group.

____ + ____ + ____ = ____

3 Make 4 equal groups.
Put 4 ⬛ in each group.

____ + ____ + ____ + ____ = ____

4 Make 4 equal groups.
Put 5 ⬛ in each group.

____ + ____ + ____ + ____ = ____

 Home Note Your child learned to add equal groups to find how many in all.
ACTIVITY Ask your child to show you equal groups such as pairs of shoes and legs of tables and chairs.

Harcourt Brace School Publishers

Chapter 27

Name _____

3 groups of 2

Add.
2 + 2 + 2 = 6
The answer is called the sum.

Multiply.
3 × 2 = 6
The answer is called the product.

2 + 2 + 2 = __6__   3 × 2 = __6__

Write the sum.
Then write the product.

   2 groups of 2

1   2 + 2 = _____   2 × 2 = _____ in all

4 groups of 2

2   2 + 2 + 2 + 2 = _____   4 × 2 = _____ in all

3   2 + 2 + 2 + 2 + 2 = _____   5 × 2 = _____ in all

Talk About It ● **Critical Thinking**

How is 5 × 2 the same as 2 + 2 + 2 + 2 + 2?

Write the sum.
Then write the product.

1 $5 + 5 =$ __10__ $2 \times 5 =$ __10__ in all

2 $5 + 5 + 5 =$ ____ $3 \times 5 =$ ____ in all

3 $5 + 5 + 5 + 5 =$ ____ $4 \times 5 =$ ____ in all

4 $5 + 5 + 5 + 5 + 5 =$ ____ $5 \times 5 =$ ____ in all

Mixed Review

Add or subtract.

5 Mr. Farley's class sold 256 circus tickets. Ms. Li's class sold 349 circus tickets. How many tickets did the two classes sell in all?

_____ tickets

 Home Note Your child learned to use repeated addition and multiplication to find how many in all. **ACTIVITY** Have your child set out pennies in 5 groups of 5, count by fives to find the total amount, and say the multiplication sentence.

Name _____

There are 3 wheels on 1 tricycle.
How many wheels are on 2 tricycles?

2 × 3 = 6 is a multiplication sentence.

2 groups of 3

3 + 3 = __6__   __2__ × __3__ = __6__ wheels

Look for a pattern.
Complete the table.

Groups	Write the sum.	Write the multiplication sentence.
3 groups of 3	3 + 3 + 3 = ____	____ × ____ = ____
4 groups of 3	3 + 3 + 3 + 3 = ____	____ × ____ = ____
5 groups of 3	3 + 3 + 3 + 3 + 3 = ____	____ × ____ = ____
6 groups of 3	3 + 3 + 3 + 3 + 3 + 3 = ____	____ × ____ = ____

Talk About It ● Critical Thinking

What pattern do you see when you multiply by 3?

Practice

There are 4 legs on 1 dog.
How many legs are on 2 dogs?

2 groups of 4

$4 + 4 = \underline{8}$ $\underline{2} \times \underline{4} = \underline{8}$ legs

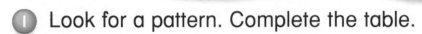

1 Look for a pattern. Complete the table.

Groups	Write the sum.	Write the multiplication sentence.
3 groups of 4	$4 + 4 + 4 = \underline{\quad}$	$\underline{\quad} \times \underline{\quad} = \underline{\quad}$
4 groups of 4	$4 + 4 + 4 + 4 = \underline{\quad}$	$\underline{\quad} \times \underline{\quad} = \underline{\quad}$
5 groups of 4	$4 + 4 + 4 + 4 + 4 = \underline{\quad}$	$\underline{\quad} \times \underline{\quad} = \underline{\quad}$
6 groups of 4	$4 + 4 + 4 + 4 + 4 + 4 = \underline{\quad}$	$\underline{\quad} \times \underline{\quad} = \underline{\quad}$

Write About It

2 Write about the pattern you see when you multiply by 4.

Home Note Your child learned to multiply by 3 and 4.
ACTIVITY Have your child set out small objects in 6 groups of 4 and tell you the multiplication sentence.

Name _____

Understand • Plan • Solve • Look Back

Draw a picture to solve the problem.
Write the multiplication sentence.

1. There are 4 butterflies in the garden.
Each butterfly has 2 wings. How many
wings in all do the 4 butterflies have?

___4___ × ___2___ = ___8___ wings

2. There are 3 dogs in the park.
Each dog has 4 legs. How many
legs in all do the 3 dogs have?

_____ × _____ = _____ legs

3. There are 3 squirrels in the tree.
Each squirrel has 2 eyes. How many
eyes in all do the 3 squirrels have?

_____ × _____ = _____ eyes

4. There are 2 rabbits in the woods.
Each rabbit has 2 ears. How many
ears in all do the 2 rabbits have?

_____ × _____ = _____ ears

Draw a picture to solve the problem.
Write the multiplication sentence.

1 There are 5 bumper cars at the fair. Each car has 2 lights. How many lights altogether do the 5 cars have?

$$\underline{5} \times \underline{2} = \underline{10}$$ lights

2 There are 3 funny cars in the show. Each car has 3 clowns in it. How many clowns in all are in the cars?

$$\underline{} \times \underline{} = \underline{}$$ clowns

3 There are 2 people buying tickets. They each buy 4. How many tickets altogether are they buying?

ADMIT ONE

$$\underline{} \times \underline{} = \underline{}$$ tickets

4 There are 3 booths at the fair. Each booth has 5 people working in it. How many people in all are working in the booths?

$$\underline{} \times \underline{} = \underline{}$$ people

Home Note Your child used the strategy draw a picture to solve problems.
ACTIVITY Make up a simple multiplication problem. Have your child draw a picture to solve the problem.

Name _____

Concepts and Skills

Review/Test

Write the sum.
Then write the product.

① $2 + 2 + 2 + 2 + 2 =$ _____ $5 \times 2 =$ _____

② How many wheels are on
5 tricycles?

____ × ____ = ____ wheels

③ How many legs are on
3 dogs?

____ × ____ = ____ legs

Problem Solving

Draw a picture to solve the problem.
Write the multiplication sentence.

④ There are 4 race cars at the fair.
Each car has 5 stripes on it. How
many stripes in all are on the cars?

____ × ____ = ____ stripes

Name _____

Test Prep

Mark the best answer.

1 Kim has 36 stamps. Is 36 closer to 30 or 40? About how many stamps does Kim have?

30 31 32 33 34 35 36 37 38 39 40

- ◯ 30
- ◯ 40

2 What multiplication sentence matches the picture?

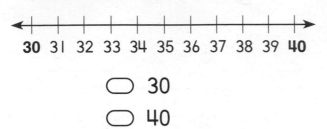

- ◯ $5 \times 2 = 10$
- ◯ $4 \times 4 = 16$
- ◯ $5 \times 3 = 15$
- ◯ $5 \times 4 = 20$

3 Joan and Michelle ate some pizza. How many parts are left? Mark the fraction.

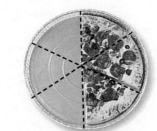

- ◯ $\frac{4}{3}$ ◯ $\frac{2}{3}$
- ◯ $\frac{3}{6}$ ◯ $\frac{3}{2}$

4 Roger has 48 shells. Jacinda has 39 shells. How many shells do they have in all?

- ◯ 77
- ◯ 78
- ◯ 87
- ◯ 79

5 There are 10 green crayons, 5 yellow crayons, and 2 orange crayons in a box. Is it more likely to pull an orange crayon or a green crayon from the box?

- ◯ orange
- ◯ green

6 What solid figure is this? It has six faces. It can slide. It can be stacked.

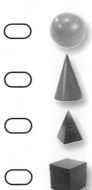

- ◯
- ◯
- ◯
- ◯

438 four hundred thirty-eight

Division

Which things are divided into 3 equal groups? How many are in each group?

Harcourt Brace School Publishers

Home Note In this chapter, your child will learn about division.
ACTIVITY Ask your child to tell you how the objects in the picture are divided into equal groups.

SCHOOL-HOME CONNECTION

Dear Family,
    Today we started Chapter 28. We will begin to learn about division. Here are the new vocabulary words and an activity for us to do together at home.

Love,

_____

Vocabulary

Have your child look at the spoons and describe how to make **equal groups**.

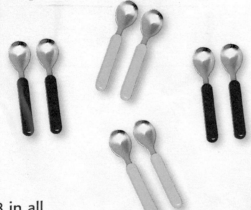

8 in all

4 **equal groups**

2 in each group

ACTIVITY

Give your child dried beans to divide into equal groups. Cut egg cartons into 3-cup, 4-cup, and 5-cup sections. Have your child count out 15 beans into the 3-cup section, forming 3 equal groups. Ask how many beans are in each cup. Repeat, using different numbers of beans and cups.

Visit our Web site for additional ideas and activities.
http://www.hbschool.com

Harcourt Brace School Publishers

Name _____

1 Use 9 ■. Make 3 equal groups.
How many are in each group?

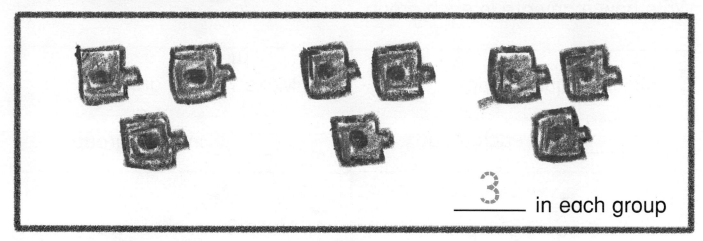

_____ in each group

2 Use 8 ■. Make 4 equal groups.
How many are in each group?

_____ in each group

3 Use 10 ■. Make 2 equal groups.
How many are in each group?

_____ in each group

Talk About It ● Critical Thinking

How did you know how many cubes to put into
each group?

Harcourt Brace School Publishers

Practice

Use Workmat 1 and ▪.
Make equal groups.
Write how many are in each group.

1 Use 8 ▪.
Make 2 equal groups.

__4__ in each group

2 Use 14 ▪.
Make 7 equal groups.

_____ in each group

3 Use 16 ▪.
Make 8 equal groups.

_____ in each group

4 Use 18 ▪.
Make 2 equal groups.

_____ in each group

5 Use 12 ▪.
Make 6 equal groups.

_____ in each group

6 Use 12 ▪.
Make 4 equal groups.

_____ in each group

7 Use 21 ▪.
Make 3 equal groups.

_____ in each group

8 Use 20 ▪.
Make 4 equal groups.

_____ in each group

Mixed Review

Add or subtract.

9

tens	ones
□	□
9	4
−3	7

10

tens	ones
□	□
3	2
+3	8

11

tens	ones
□	□
1	6
+3	7

12

tens	ones
□	□
4	1
−1	6

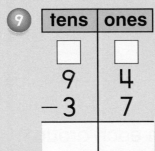 **Home Note** Your child learned to divide a group of objects into smaller equal groups.
ACTIVITY Have your child divide a group of 10 small objects into 2 equal groups and 5 equal groups.

Chapter 28

1 Use 12 . Put 4 in each group.
How many groups are there?

_____ groups

2 Use 15 ▪. Put 5 in each group.
How many groups are there?

_____ groups

3 Use 10 ▪. Put 2 in each group.
How many groups are there?

_____ groups

Talk About It • Critical Thinking

What do you do to find the
number of equal groups?

Practice

Use Workmat 1 and .
Put an equal number in each group.
Write how many groups.

1. Use 12 ■.
   Put 2 in each group.

   _____6_____ groups

2. Use 14 ■.
   Put 7 in each group.

   _____ groups

3. Use 16 ■.
   Put 2 in each group.

   _____ groups

4. Use 24 ■.
   Put 3 in each group.

   _____ groups

5. Use 25 ■.
   Put 5 in each group.

   _____ groups

6. Use 27 ■.
   Put 9 in each group.

   _____ groups

7. Use 28 ■.
   Put 4 in each group.

   _____ groups

8. Use 30 ■.
   Put 10 in each group.

   _____ groups

Write About It

9. Write a story about making sandwiches.
   Tell how many pieces of bread were used.
   Tell how many sandwiches were made.

Math Journal

Home Note Your child learned to divide a group of objects into equal groups of a given number.
ACTIVITY Have your child find how many groups of 4 there are in one dozen eggs.

Name _____

Problem Solving
Draw a Picture

Understand • Plan • Solve • Look Back

First draw the total amount.
Then make equal groups.

Draw a picture to solve.

1. There are 12 sugar cookies. There are 4 children. Each child gets the same number of cookies. How many sugar cookies does each child get?

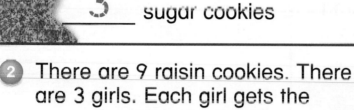

____3____ sugar cookies

2. There are 9 raisin cookies. There are 3 girls. Each girl gets the same number of cookies. How many raisin cookies does each girl get?

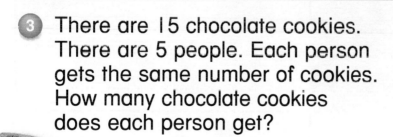

_____ raisin cookies

3. There are 15 chocolate cookies. There are 5 people. Each person gets the same number of cookies. How many chocolate cookies does each person get?

_____ chocolate cookies

4. There are 10 gingerbread cookies. There are 5 boys. Each boy gets the same number of cookies. How many gingerbread cookies does each boy get?

_____ gingerbread cookies

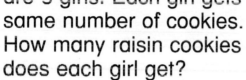

Harcourt Brace School Publishers

Draw a picture to solve.

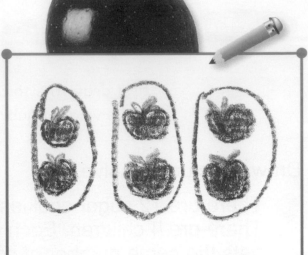

1. Peggy had 6 apples. She gave an equal number of apples to 3 friends. How many apples did each friend get?

    __2__ apples

2. Mr. Polt cut an orange into 8 pieces. He gave an equal number of pieces to each of his 4 children. How many pieces of orange did each child get?

    _____ pieces of orange

3. Sam picked 12 peaches. He gave an equal number of peaches to his mother and his grandmother. How many peaches did each one get?

    _____ peaches

4. There are 14 grapes. There are 2 children. Each child will get the same number. How many grapes will each child get?

    _____ grapes

 Home Note Your child used the strategy Draw a Picture to solve problems.
ACTIVITY Make up a problem for your child to solve. For example: "If you made 12 pancakes and 4 people wanted equal shares, how many could each one have?"

Name _____

Understand • Plan • Solve • Look Back

Draw a picture or make a
model to solve.

1. Juan's mom made 12 peanut
butter cookies. She gave 2 to each
of her children. There are none
left. How many children are in
Juan's family?

_____6_____ children

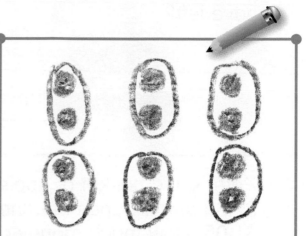

2. Carla had 35 boxes of animal
crackers to sell. She sold 27
of them. How many boxes
does she have left?

_____ boxes

3. One cookie costs 2¢. George
has 20¢. How many cookies
can he buy?

_____ cookies

4. There are 6 girls. Each girl has
2 cookies. How many cookies
in all do the girls have?

_____ cookies

Harcourt Brace School Publishers

Draw a picture or make a model to solve.

1 Linda had 25 grapes. She ate 9 of them. How many grapes does she have left?

_16_ grapes

2 Peter got a basket of apples for $2.85 and a bunch of bananas for $1.05. How much money did he spend in all?

$ _____

3 Denise, Monika, and Nathan went to the store. They each spent $3.00. How much money did they spend in all?

$ _____

4 Lorna had 16 plums. She gave an equal number of plums to 4 friends. How many plums did each friend get?

_____ plums

Home Note Your child learned to choose a strategy to solve problems.
ACTIVITY Make up addition, subtraction, multiplication, and division problems for your child to solve.

Name _____

Concepts and Skills

Make equal groups.
Write how many are in each group.

1 Use 16 ▪.
Make 2 equal groups.

_____ in each group

2 Use 12 ▪.
Make 3 equal groups.

_____ in each group

Put an equal number in each group.
Write how many groups.

3 Use 15 ▪.
Put 3 in each group.

_____ groups

4 Use 12 ▪.
Put 4 in each group.

_____ groups

Problem Solving

Draw a picture or make a model to solve.

5 There are 15 stickers and 3 children. Each child gets the same number of stickers. How many does each child get?

_____ stickers

6 The fair costs $2.00. Greg and 3 friends buy tickets. How much money do they pay in all?

$ _____

Harcourt Brace School Publishers

Name _____

Test Prep

Mark the best answer.

1. There are 8 red tiles, 2 blue tiles, and 1 yellow tile in a bag. Which color are you most likely to pull from the bag?

   ○ red
   ○ blue
   ○ yellow

2. Chris has 29¢. Joan has 38¢. How much money do they have in all?

   ○ 57¢
   ○ 58¢
   ○ 67¢
   ○ 68¢

3. Look at the clock. What time does it show?

   ○ 3:15
   ○ 4:20
   ○ 3:20
   ○ 4:15

4. Jill picked 12 apples. She gave an equal number of apples to 4 friends. How many apples did each friend get?

   ○ 2
   ○ 4
   ○ 6
   ○ 3

5. Look at the number line. Is 73 closer to 70 or 80?

   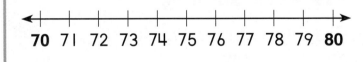

   70 71 72 73 74 75 76 77 78 79 80

   ○ 70
   ○ 80

6. Which multiplication sentence matches the picture?

   ○ $2 \times 2 = 4$
   ○ $3 \times 3 = 9$
   ○ $2 \times 3 = 6$
   ○ $3 \times 4 = 12$

Harcourt Brace School Publishers

Name _____

Cooking Up Equal Groups

① Pick a number card. Then spin.

② If the number on the ⊕ matches your card, make that many equal groups of ●. Write the number in each group in the table below.

③ If the number you spin does not match your card, it is your partner's turn.

④ Take turns until you have finished the table.

Number of Groups	2	3	4	6	8
Number in Each Group	12				

Harcourt Brace School Publishers

Home Note Your child has been learning about division.
ACTIVITY Play this game with your child to help him or her practice division.

Name _____

| Calculator | Computer |

What two numbers would make this multiplication sentence true?

_____ × _____ = 16

Try 2 and 7.
Press

    14.

Try 2 and 8.
Press

    16.

Write the numbers.

2 × 8 = 16

Use a .
Write two numbers that make each multiplication sentence true.

1 _____ × _____ = 12   2 _____ × _____ = 15

3 _____ × _____ = 18   4 _____ × _____ = 20

5 _____ × _____ = 21   6 _____ × _____ = 24

7 _____ × _____ = 27   8 _____ × _____ = 30

FARMER BROWN'S SURPRISE

written by F. R. Robinson

illustrated by Keith Baker

 This book will help me review multiplication.

This book belongs to _____

Rooster called all the animals together. "Farmer Brown is sick today," said Rooster. "We must help him get well."

The animals were very sad to hear that Farmer Brown was sick. They all went to get something to help Farmer Brown get well.

Harcourt Brace School Publishers

The five horses came galloping back with three apples each. "We always feel better after we have eaten an apple," they said. "He will like eating these delicious, red apples. Apples will be good for him."

How many apples are there in all?

_____ apples

The two goats came walking back with two carrots each. "We eat carrots when we are feeling bad," they said. "He will like eating these crispy carrots. Carrots will help him feel much better."

How many carrots are there in all?

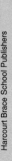

_____ carrots

D

The three dogs came running back with one bone each. "We chew on our best bone when we feel bad," they said. "He will like chewing on these delicious bones. These are our best bones."

How many bones are there in all?

_____ bones

The four hens came strutting back with four ears of corn each. "Corn tastes really good," they said. "If he eats this juicy corn, he will feel much better. He will be up and around in no time at all."

How many ears of corn are there in all?

_____ ears of corn

Harcourt Brace School Publishers

The three cows came strolling back with
two bales of hay each. "Hay is our favorite
food," they said. "We always feel much better
after we have eaten a bale of hay. Farmer
Brown is certain to feel better if he eats some
fine hay."

How many bales of hay are there in all?

_____ bales of hay

"Farmer Brown, come to the door!"
crowed Rooster.

"Surprise!" called the animals from
the yard.

"My! My! What a surprise!" said Farmer
Brown. "Thank you for all your delicious
food! I think I am feeling better already!"

Concepts and Skills

Write the sum.
Then write the product.

1 $2 + 2 + 2 + 2 + 2 + 2 =$ _____ $6 \times 2 =$ _____

2 $3 + 3 + 3 + 3 + 3 =$ _____ $5 \times 3 =$ _____

Look for a pattern.
Complete the table.

	Groups	Write the sum.	Write the multiplication sentence.
3	3 groups of 3	$3 + 3 + 3 =$ __	__ $\times$ __ $=$ __
4	4 groups of 3	$3 + 3 + 3 + 3 =$ __	__ $\times$ __ $=$ __
5	5 groups of 3	$3 + 3 + 3 + 3 + 3 =$ __	__ $\times$ __ $=$ __
6	6 groups of 3	$3 + 3 + 3 + 3 + 3 + 3 =$ __	__ $\times$ __ $=$ __

Make equal groups.
Write how many are in each group.

7 Use 18 ■.
Make 2 equal groups.

_____ in each group

8 Use 6 ■.
Make 3 equal groups.

_____ in each group

Put an equal number in each group.
Write how many groups.

9 Use 12 ■.
Put 3 in each group.

_____ groups

10 Use 12 ■.
Put 2 in each group.

_____ groups

Problem Solving

Solve.

11 Laurie, Jill, and Nancy went to the circus. Each girl paid $4.00 for a ticket. How much money did they pay in all?

$ _____

12 There are 8 apples. There are 4 children. Each child gets an equal number of apples. How many apples does each child get?

_____ apples

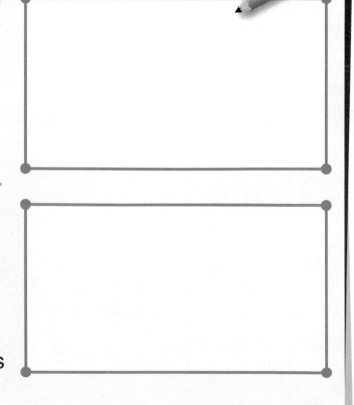

Name _____

Performance Assessment

Use Workmat 1 and 24 .
Make equal groups of .
Draw a picture of the equal groups.
Write how many in each group
and how many groups.
Write the multiplication sentence.

①

_____ in each group

_____ groups

_____ × _____ = _____

②

_____ in each group

_____ groups

_____ × _____ = _____

Write About It

③ Write a story about some friends
sharing a bag of carrots. Each
friend gets the same number
of carrots. Draw a picture
to show the equal groups.

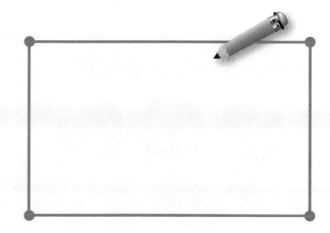

Name _____

Fill in the ⬭ for the correct answer.

1 You have

How much money do you have?

⬭ 55¢   ⬭ 65¢
⬭ 45¢   ⬭ 59¢

2 The game starts at  .

Bill gets there at  .

Is Bill early or late?

⬭ early   ⬭ late

3
38
+49

⬭ 77
⬭ 79
⬭ 87
⬭ 89

4
61
−18

⬭ 43
⬭ 47
⬭ 53
⬭ 57

5 Choose > or < for the circle.

202 ◯ 220

⬭ >   ⬭ <

6 Which fraction is shown?

⬭ $\frac{1}{2}$ ⬭ $\frac{1}{3}$ ⬭ $\frac{1}{6}$

7 Which figure has 6 faces?

⬭   ⬭

⬭    ⬭

8 Which is the product?

$3 \times 2 =$ _____

⬭ 2   ⬭ 3   ⬭ 6   ⬭ 8

9 Circle 2 equal groups. How many are in each group?

⬭ 2   ⬭ 3   ⬭ 4   ⬭ 5

add (page 3)

$$2 + 4 = 6$$

addend (page 3)

$$\downarrow \quad \downarrow$$
$$5 + 2 = 7$$

after (page 93)

29, **30**

bar graph (page 255)

Favorite Peanut Butter								
smooth								
crunchy								
	0 1 2 3 4 5 6 7 8							

before (page 93)

39, 40

between (page 93)

19, **20, 21**

calendar (page 151)

November						
S	M	Tu	W	Th	F	S
		1	2	3	4	5
6	7	8	9	10	11	12
13	14	15	16	17	18	19
20	21	22	23	24	25	26
27	28	29	30			

centimeter (page 337)

1 centimeter

circle (page 293)

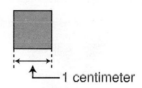

cone (page 281)

congruent figures (page 299)

Figures with the same size and shape are **congruent**.

corner (page 295)

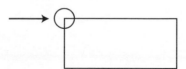

count back (page 19)

6, **5**

$7 - 2 = 5$

count on (page 9)

4, **5**

$3 + 2 = 5$

cube (page 281)

cup (page 349)

cylinder (page 281)

decimeter (page 339)

10 centimeters = 1 **decimeter**

difference (page 13)

$6 - 4 = \mathbf{2}$ ⟵ difference

dime (page 109)

10¢   10 cents

dollar (page 389)

$1.00   one dollar

doubles (page 27)

$3 + 3 = 6$

doubles minus one (page 29)

$3 + 2 = 5$

doubles plus one (page 29)

$3 + 4 = 7$

equal groups (page 429)

3 groups of 2

$2 + 2 + 2 = 6$

Harcourt Brace School Publishers

estimate (page 69)

about 10 cherries

even numbers (page 79)

0, 2, 4, 6, 8, 10 . . .

face (page 283)

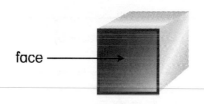

face ⟶

fact family (page 45)

$6 + 7 = 13$ $7 + 6 = 13$

$13 - 6 = 7$ $13 - 7 = 6$

flip (page 309)

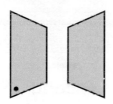

fractions (pages 361, 363)

one-half one-third one-fourth one-sixth

$\frac{1}{2}$ $\frac{1}{3}$ $\frac{1}{4}$ $\frac{1}{6}$

greater than > (page 91)

63 is **greater than** 29.

63 > 29

half-dollar (page 115)

50¢   50 cents

half-hour (page 137)

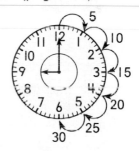

hour (page 139)

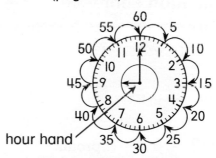

hour hand

hundreds (page 381)

2 **hundreds**

inch (page 325)

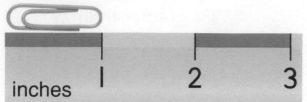

less than < (page 91)

29 is **less than** 63.

29 < 63

line of symmetry (page 305)

minute (page 139)

 — minute hand

multiplication sentence
(page 433)

$4 \times 3 = 12$

multiply (page 431)

$2 \times 3 = 6$ ⟵ **product**

nickel (page 109)

5¢   5 cents

number sentence (page 49)

$6 + 8 = 14$

odd numbers (page 79)

1, 3, 5, 7, 9, 11 . . .

ones (page 61)

2 **ones**

Order Property (page 5)

$6 + 3 = 9$

$3 + 6 = 9$

ordinal numbers (page 95)

first   second   third

pattern (page 83)

30, 40, 50, 60, 70 . . .

Count by tens.

penny (page 109)

I¢   I cent

perimeter (page 341)

2

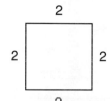

2   2

2

2 + 2 + 2 + 2 = 8

pictograph (page 253)

Favorite Peanut Butter	
smooth	
crunchy	

Each 🚶 stands for 2 children.

picture graph (page 251)

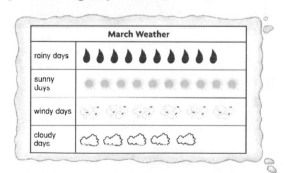

March Weather	
rainy days	
sunny days	
windy days	
cloudy days	

pint (page 349)

2 cups = I **pint**

quart (page 349)

4 cups = I **quart**

quarter (page 111)

25¢   25 cents

rectangle (page 293)

rectangular prism (page 281)

regroup (page 171)

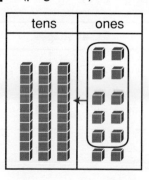

tens	ones

Harcourt Brace School Publishers

side (page 295)

← side

skip-count (page 75)

5, 10, 15, 20, 25 . . .

slide (page 311)

sphere (page 281)

square (page 293)

subtract (page 15)

6 − 2 = 4

sum (page 3)

6 + 9 = 15 ← **sum**

table (page 239)

Leaf Shapes		
broad leaf		卌 III
narrow leaf		IIII
needle leaf		II

tally marks (page 239)

temperature (page 353)

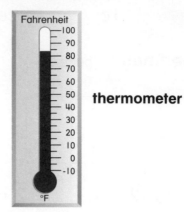

thermometer

The **temperature** is 84°F.

tens (page 61)

triangle (page 293)

turn (page 309)

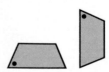

Zero Property (page 7)

5 + 0 = 5

Harcourt Brace School Publishers